DENNIS STOCK

DENNIS STOCK

TIME IS ON YOUR SIDE

Foreword by
ANTON CORBIJN

Essay by
CAROLE NAGGAR

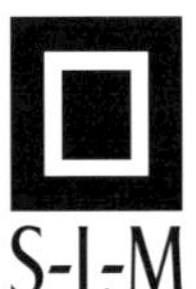

PRESTEL
MUNICH · LONDON · NEW YORK

CONTENTS

Foreword by Anton Corbijn

i regret never having met Dennis Stock, nor having been aware of his work the way i am now, in mid-edit on a film called LIFE that focuses on his work with James Dean. i have come into contact with his work through research for the film and then realized that i had seen his images without registering the name. peripheral vision i guess, but it felt like an inconceivable omission. even the famous image of THE PHOTOJOURNALIST by Andreas Feininger had not registered with me as being Dennis as i always thought it depicted a woman (sorry Dennis!), but if we'd have met it would have been a good starting point for a talk about what it is that we are seeing.

having looked in depth over the last year or so at his photographs, i find that his incredible eye for detail in life, humor, man, and surrounding made me want to explore more, go out into the world and discover how much there is to see. it is an unobtrusive and slight poetic language he is using to seduce us to observe and participate. the guy had a fantastic eye and he had great timing. timing can be the tool of a comedian. generally i find it very hard to make a "funny" picture, but Dennis seems to do this effortlessly. it is only a very sharp observer who manages to coordinate situations with timing, but a sharp observer he was. he was not really a portraitist—you'd be very hard-pressed to find more than five portraits amongst his work—but he set off people against their surroundings. backgrounds are an important and determined element in his work and i can very much relate to that. it colors the person with the added bonus later on that it tells you a lot about an era; although that obviously only starts playing a role as time passes, it is a fascinating characteristic of photography. probably one out of many differences in our work is the reason why one would work like that. in my case it came partly out of shyness, keeping a distance helped somehow, and a protestant upbringing that made me look at the situation people lived in, plus the absence of iconic images around our home made me somewhat unaware of portraits, iconic or otherwise. watching pieces about Dennis on film i would not put shyness as a factor in his way of operating in the world, but he obviously enjoyed context, which is what a background can give you. these days this is a very overlooked possibility in the photography of people who can be viewed as "well-known," or as "celebrities," that dreaded word. photographers want to sell their work, so it is all about portraits or about full body shots with an "idea." never mind that the idea is usually crap, it sells, which perplexes me. anyway, Dennis is very, very good at shooting people with and within a context. he calls his work "making essays," stories, and i can see why he looked at it that way.

preparing for the film i obviously had to delve into him as a private person, and found that his desire for adventure left his personal life with a lot to be desired, but i guess that is what it takes for some of us. he found beauty in his work and love with several wives over the course of his restless life, while his son Rodney, who visited the film set of LIFE for quite a few days, said he learned more about his father through the film than he had in real life. taking into account that we were kind to Dennis in the film (played by Rob Pattinson) compared to how he was in real life, that is a shocking reality but not one that makes his work any less interesting. for someone who couldn't share the love of life with his son, he miraculously certainly managed to share it with the rest of the world.

july 2014, new york

JAMES DEAN

James Dean in Times Square. New York City, 1955

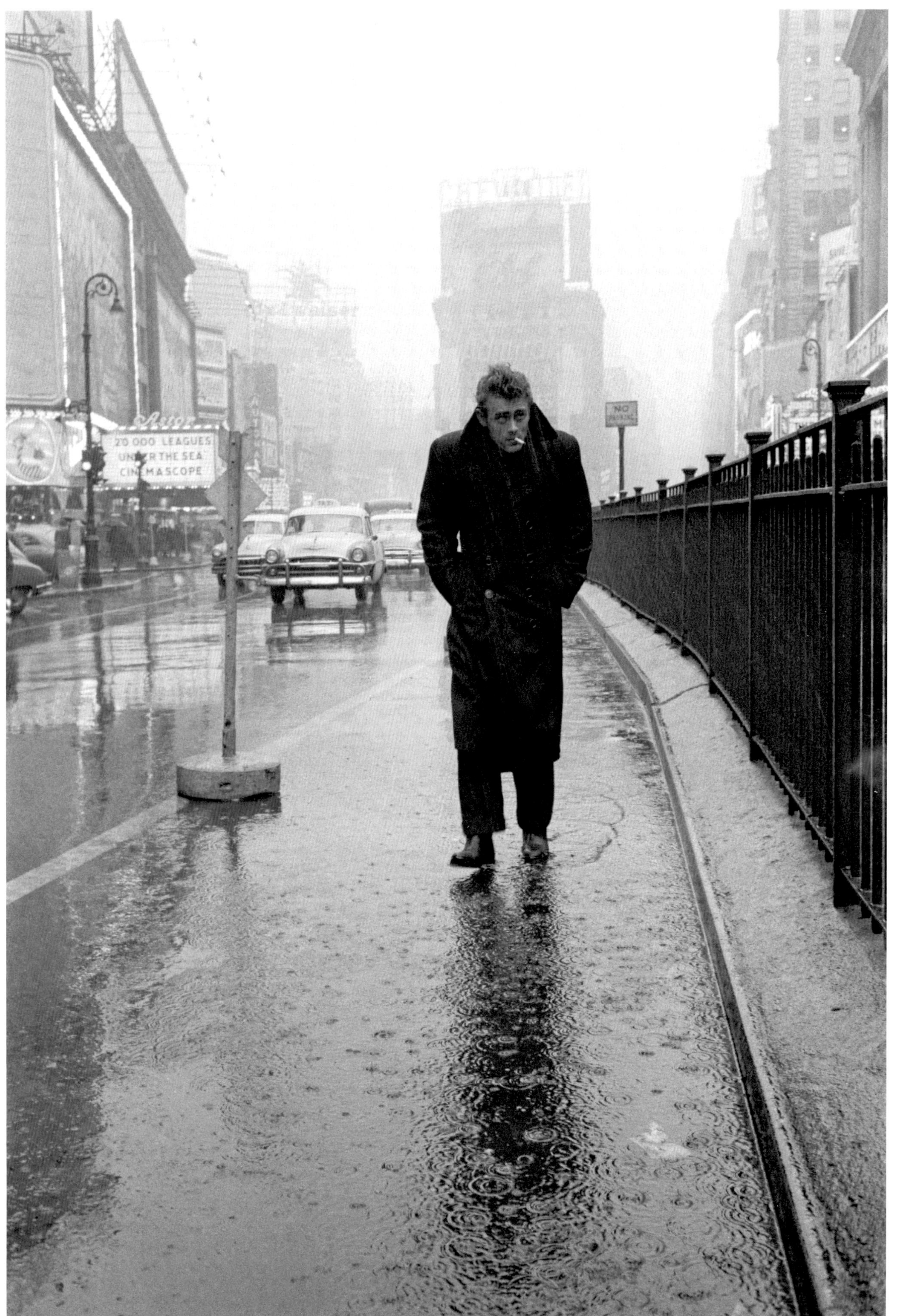

20 000 LEAGUES
UNDER THE SEA
CINEMASCOPE
NO PARKING
TAXI

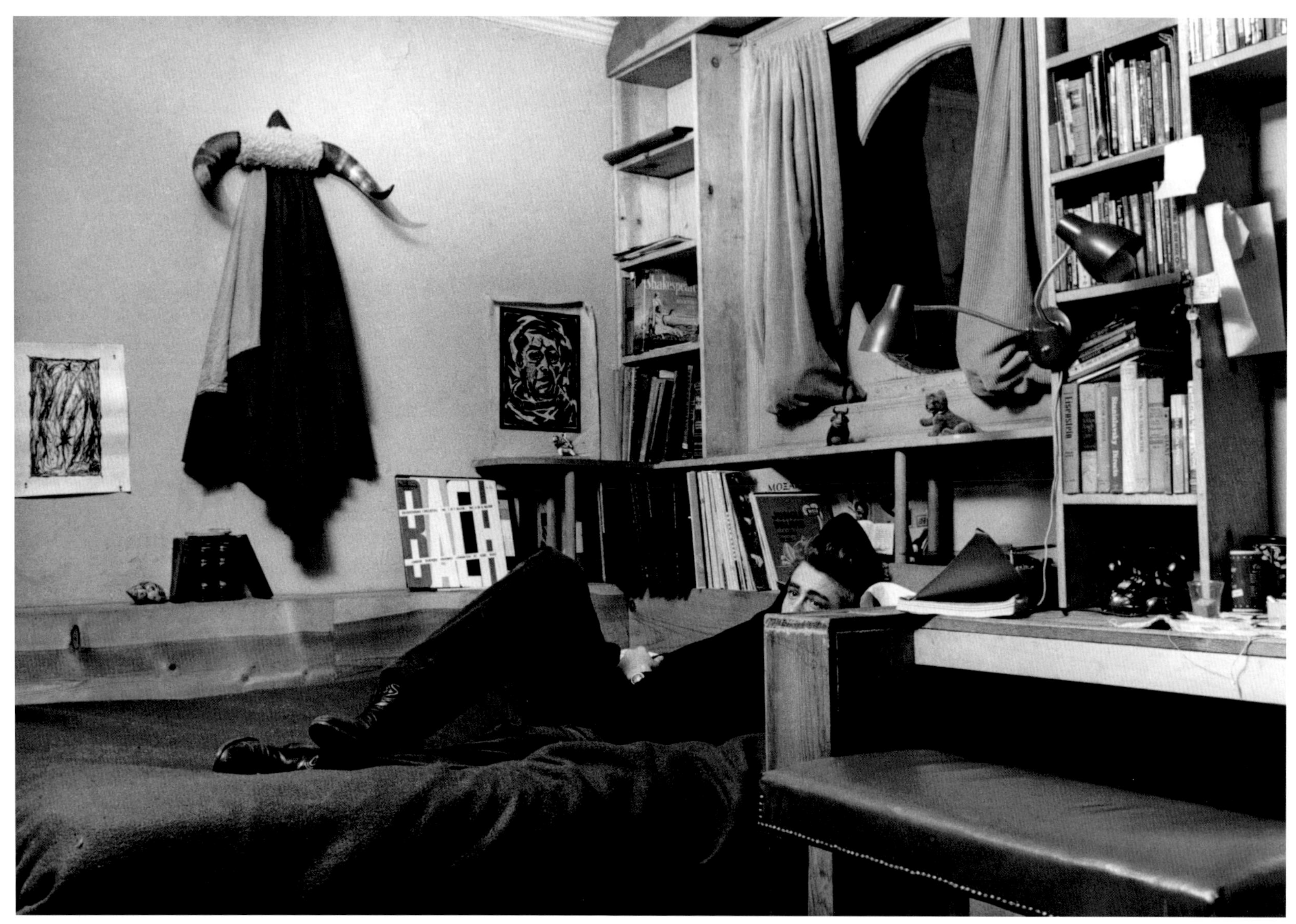

above

James Dean in his apartment on W. 68th Street, just off Central Park West. On the top floor,
it was small and stateroom-like—probably a maid's room in earlier days. It was crammed
with books and records. Jimmy had a need to be surrounded with books, but it's not sure if he
was a real reader. He collected all kinds of music: Schoenberg, Stravinsky, medieval music,
and even Frank Sinatra's SONGS FOR YOUNG LOVERS. New York City, 1955

right

James Dean. New York City, 1955

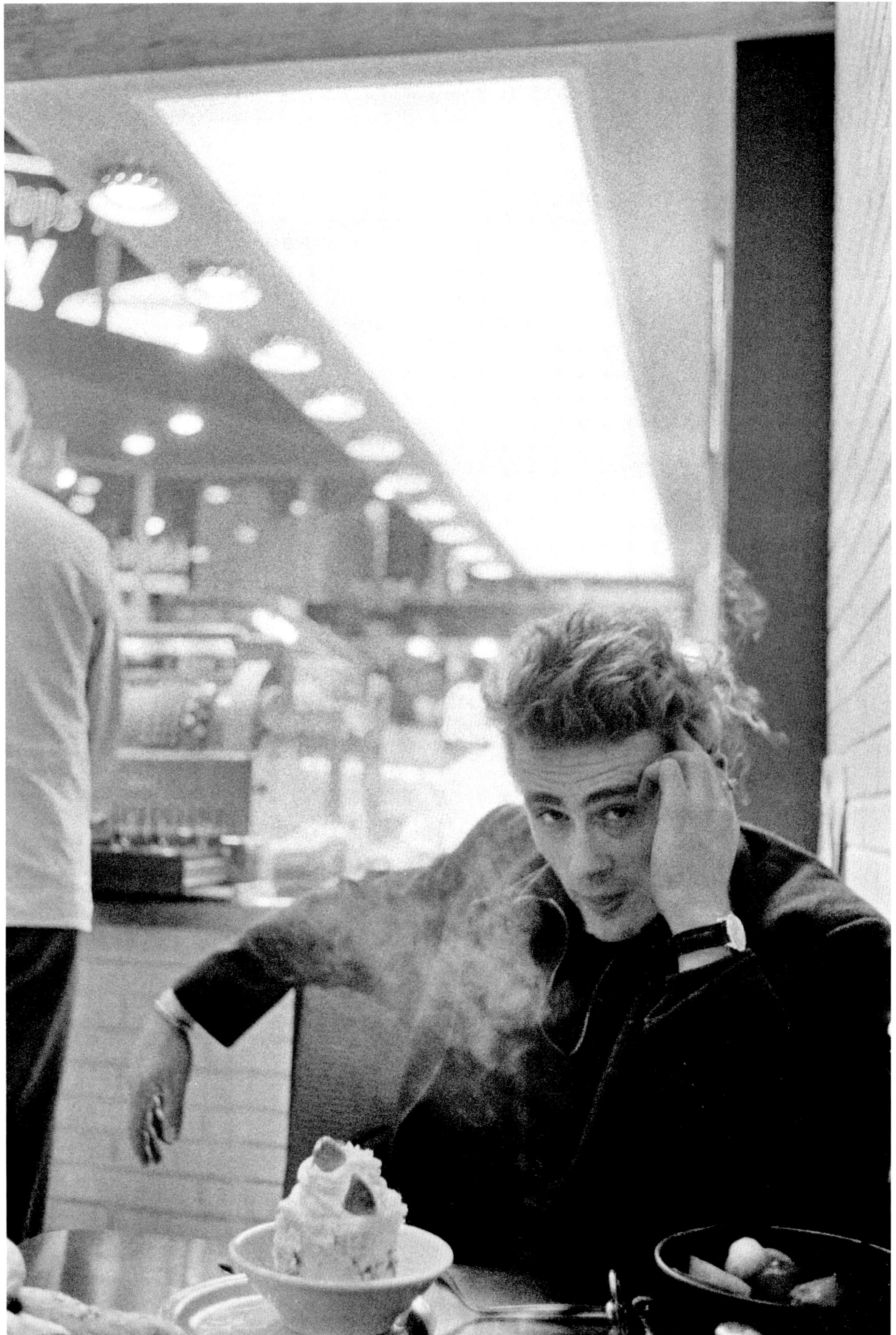

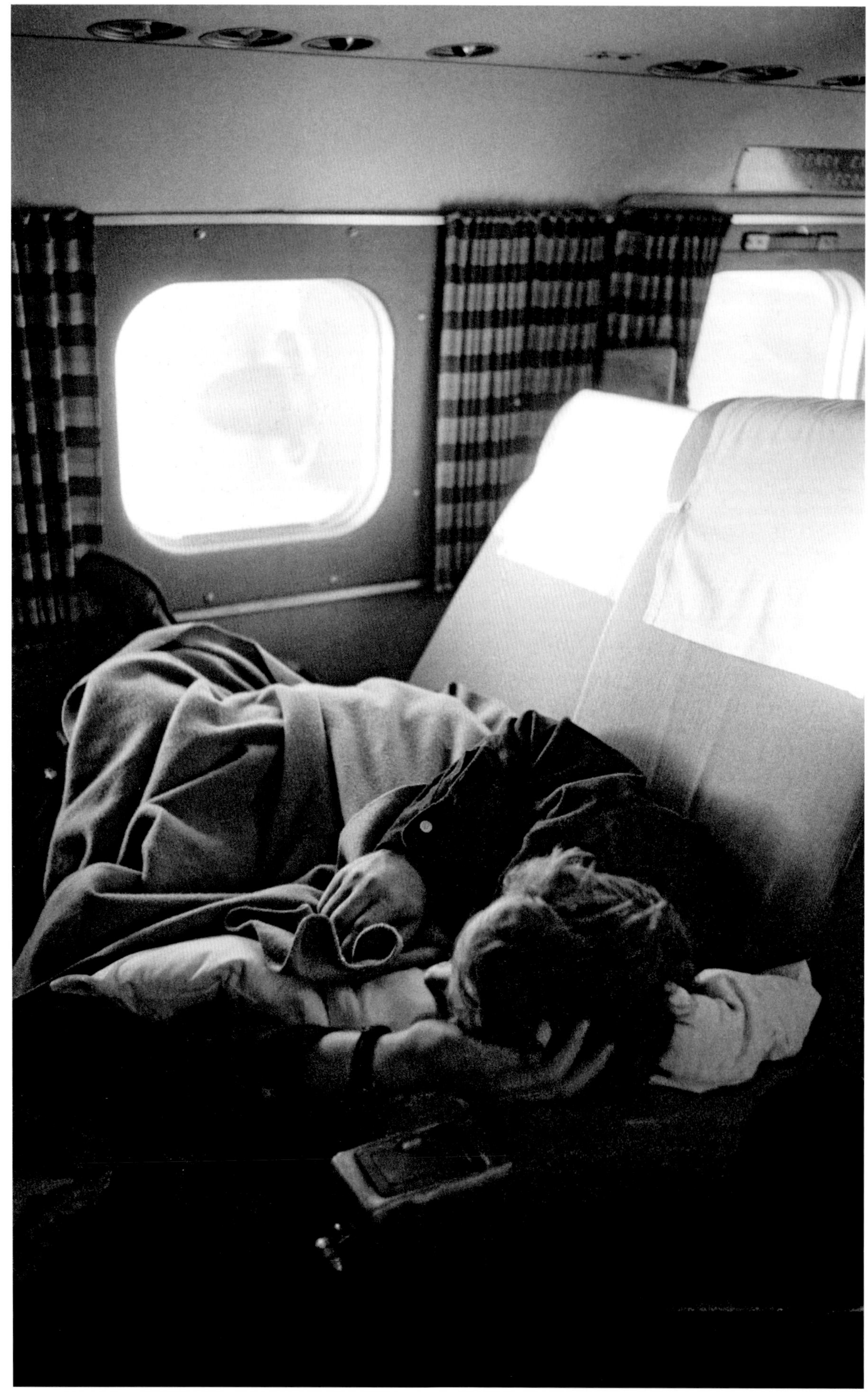

 James Dean flying back to California for the shooting of REBEL WITHOUT A CAUSE. 1955

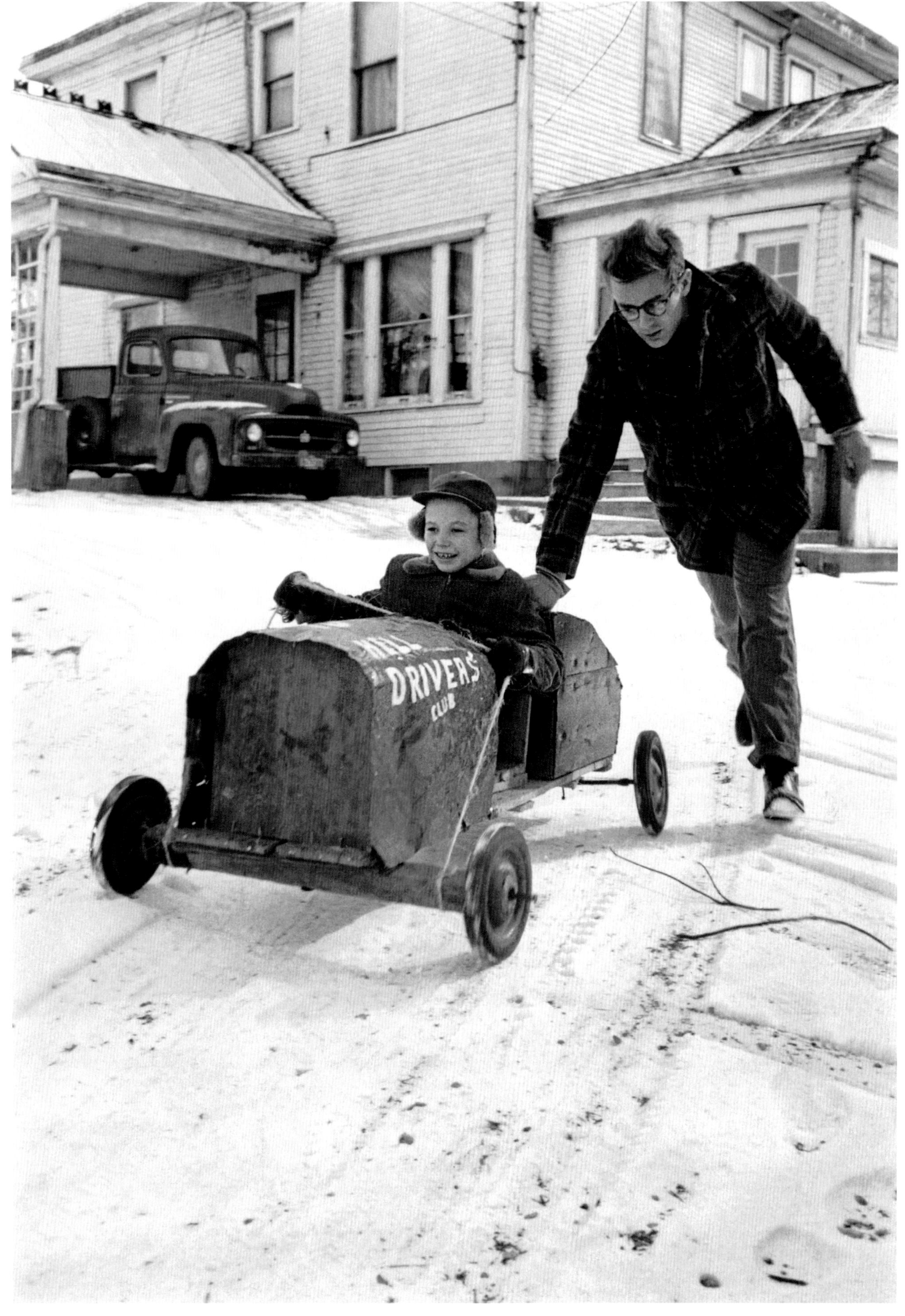

James Dean with his cousin Markie. Fairmount, Indiana, 1955

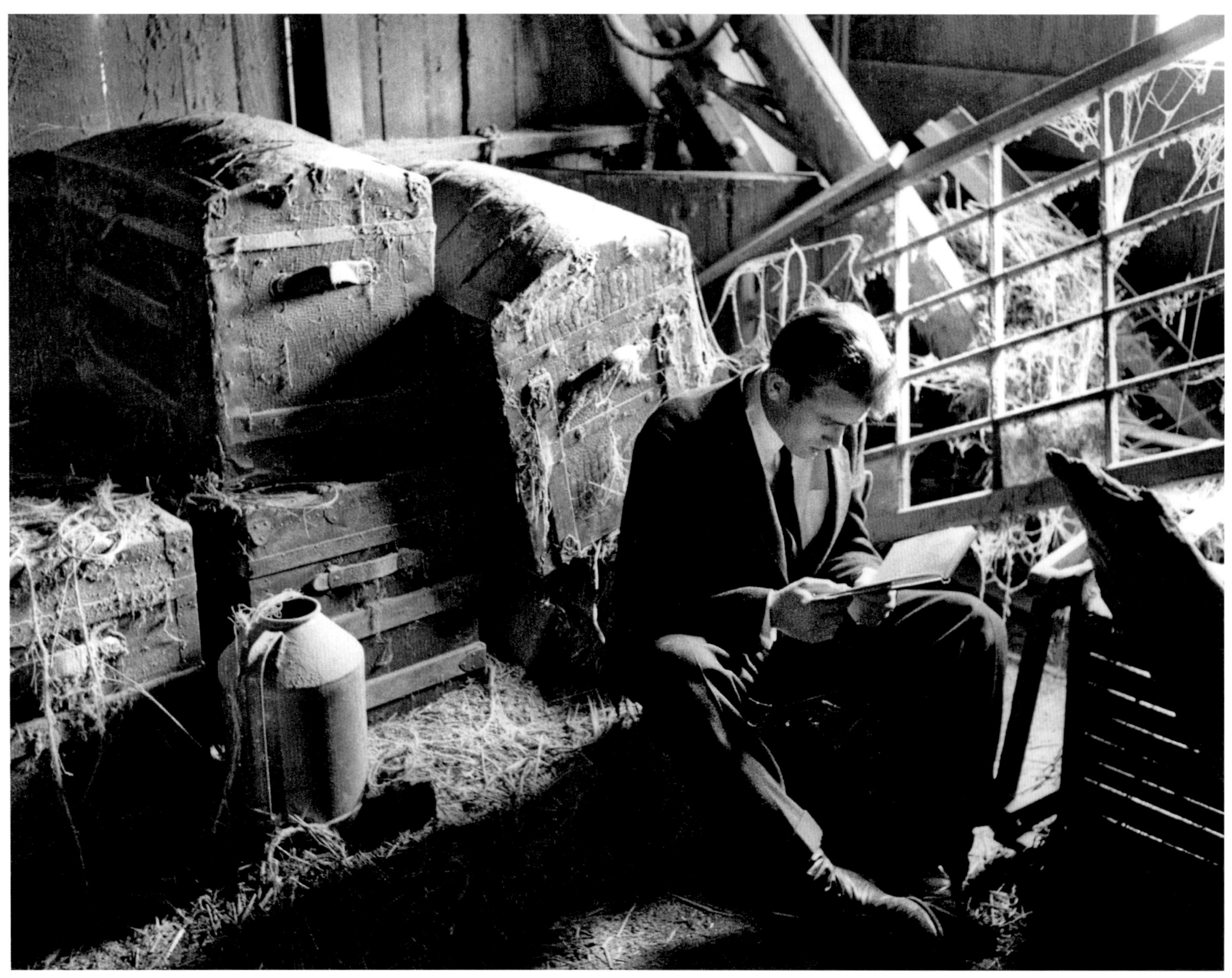

above
James Dean returned to the place he had spent his youth
and was educated; on the farm of his uncle Marcus Winslow he sorts
through some old books in the loft. Fairmount, Indiana, 1955

right
Dean on his uncle's farm. Fairmount, Indiana, 1955

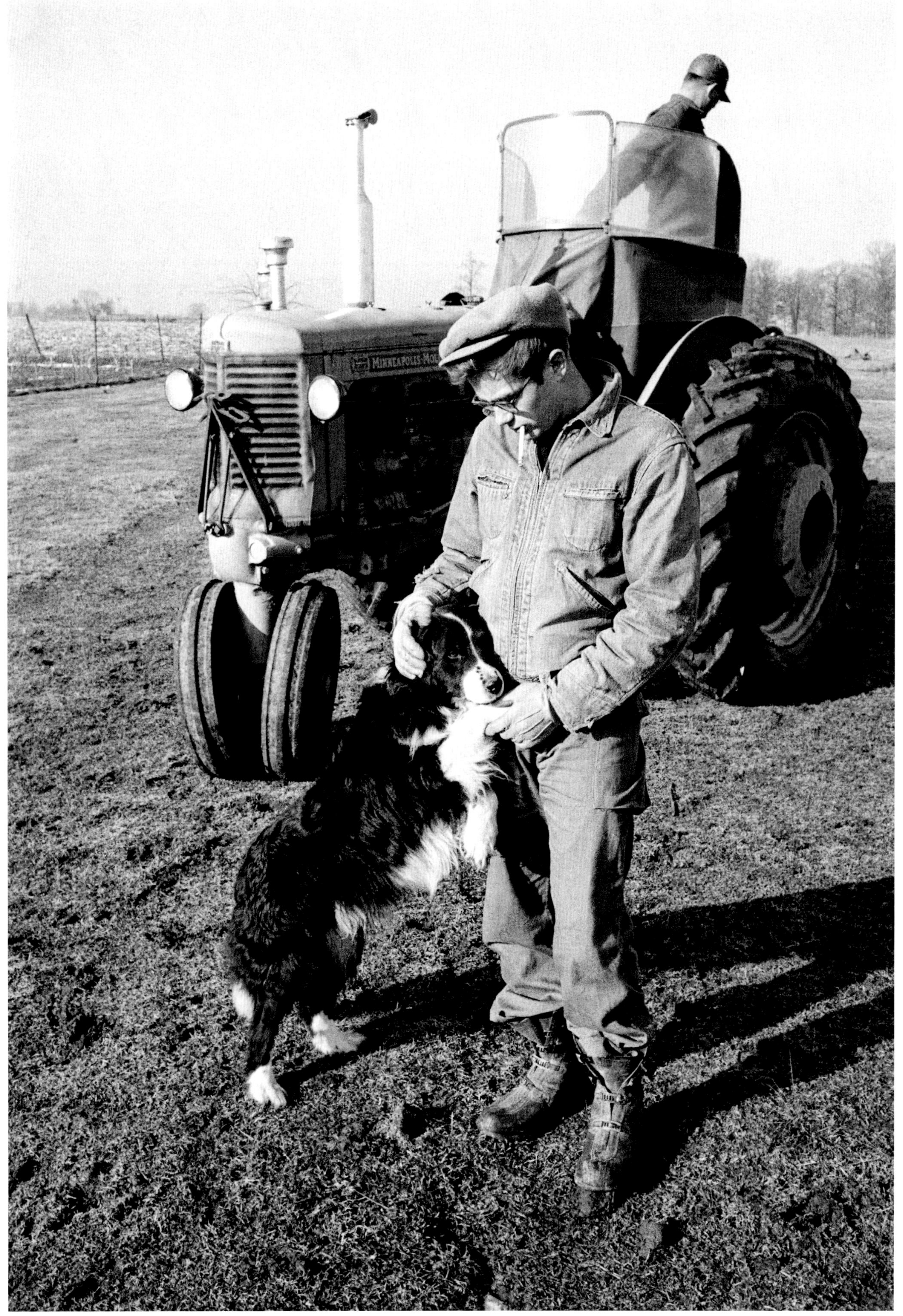

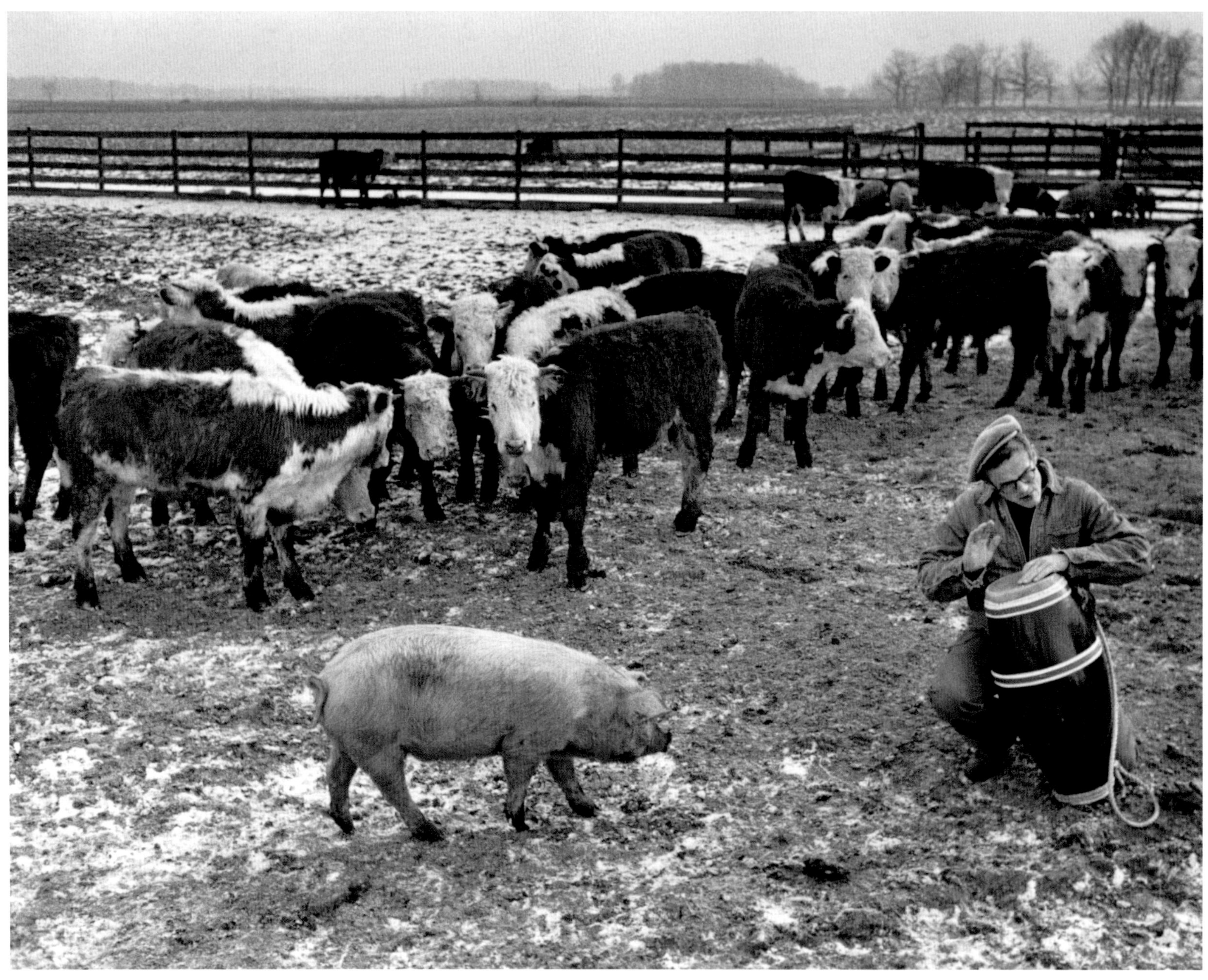

above
James Dean loved to mix with the animals in the barnyard, to explore and perform in the cattle pens and barns. He appreciated the surreal aspects of his own search for pleasure and responded to the pig's oinking to the accompaniment of the bongo drums. Fairmount, Indiana, 1955

right
Dean posing with a pig, asking himself, "Do I belong to the animals, to the pigs, the cattle, or the goats?" Fairmount, Indiana, 1955

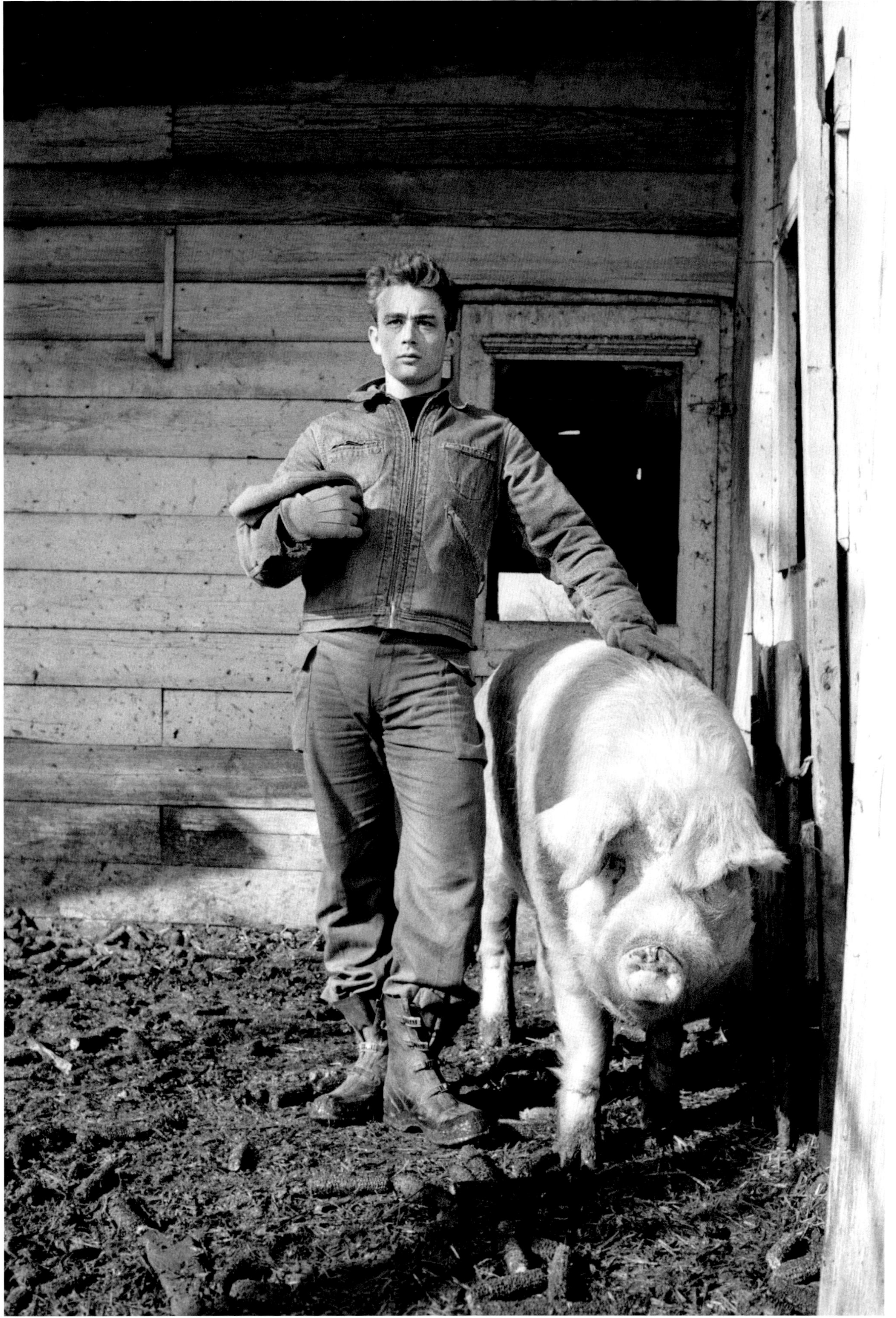

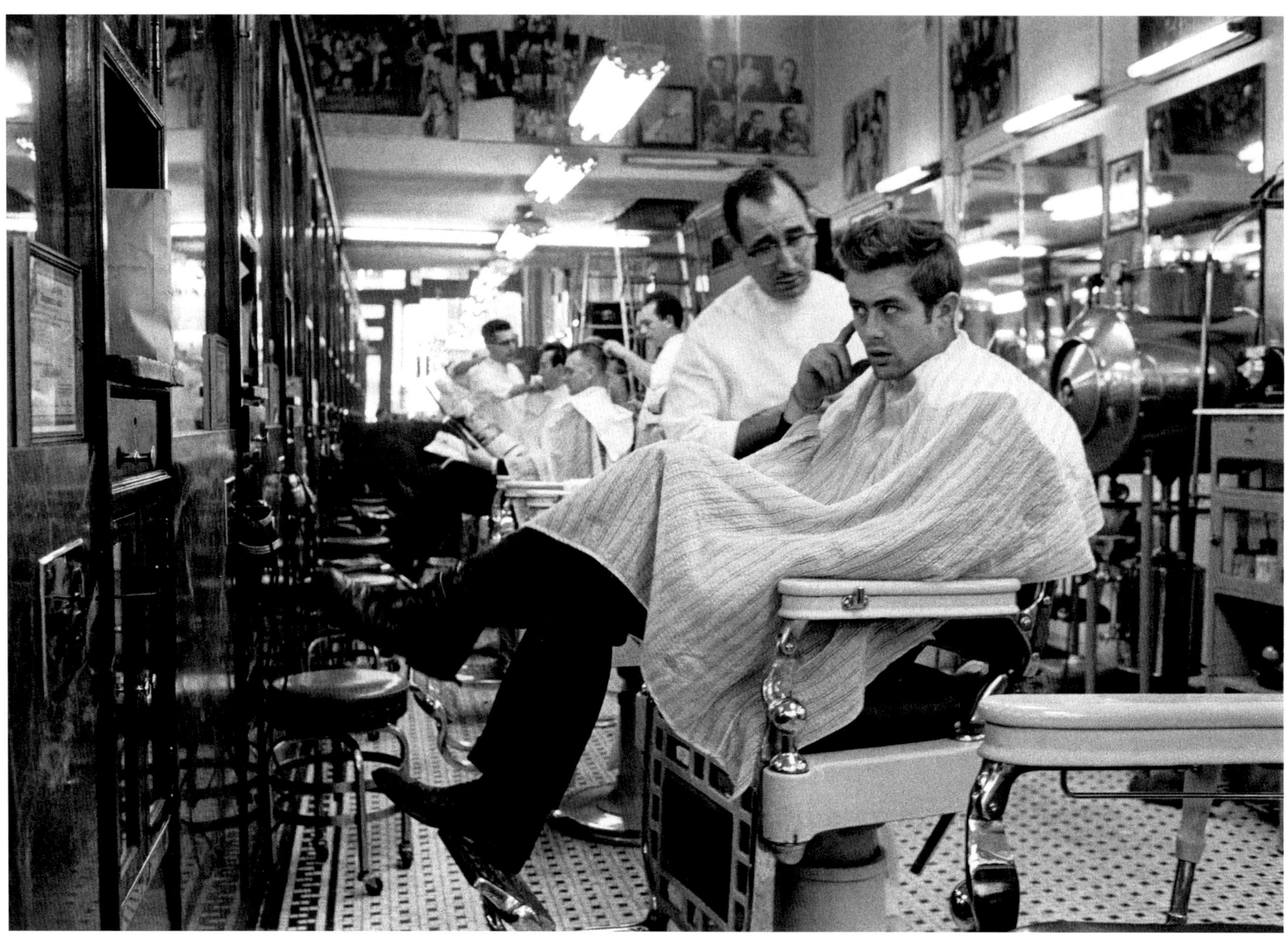

    James Dean in a barbershop. New York City, 1955

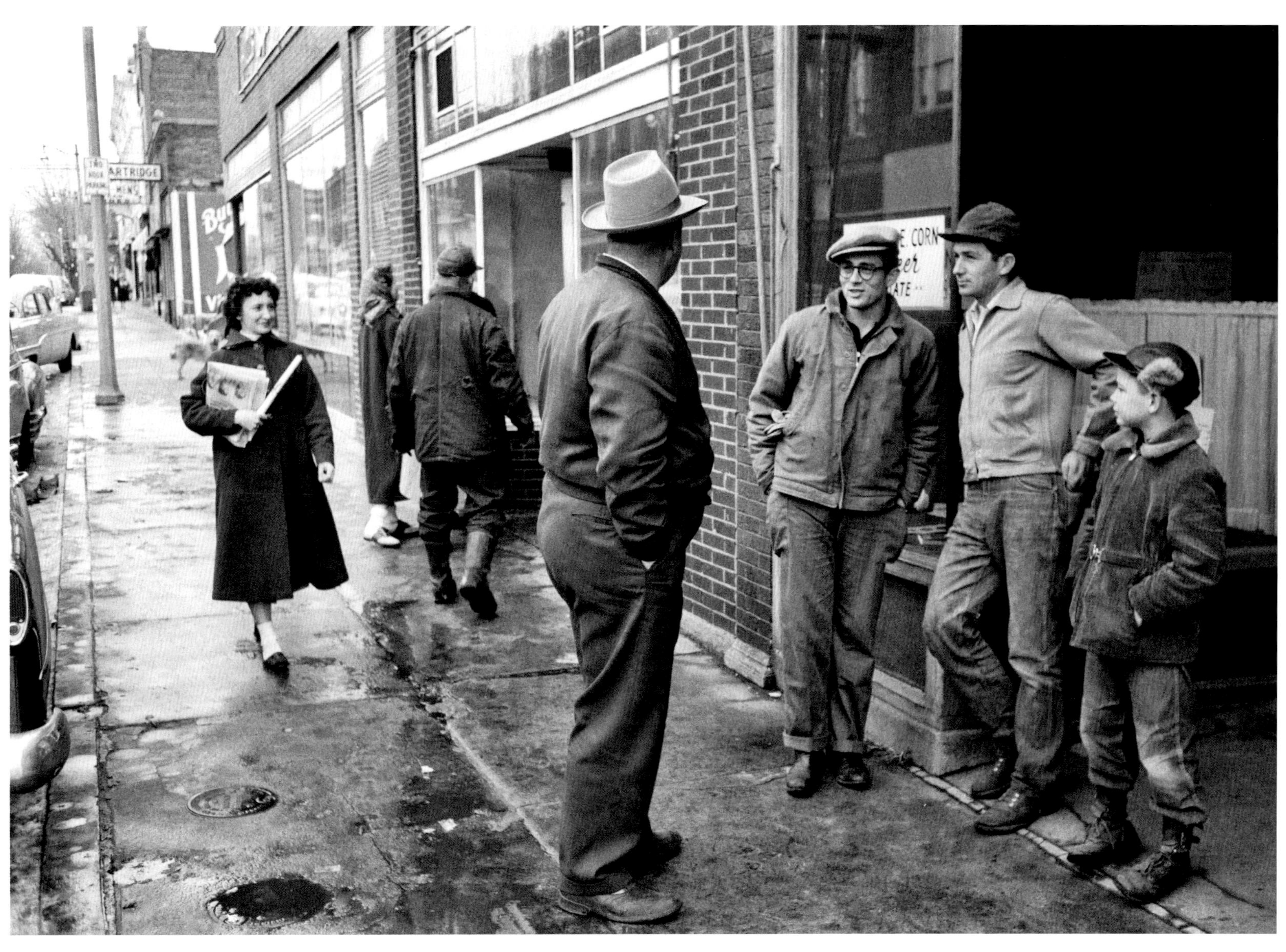

James Dean talking to locals. Fairmount, Indiana, 1955

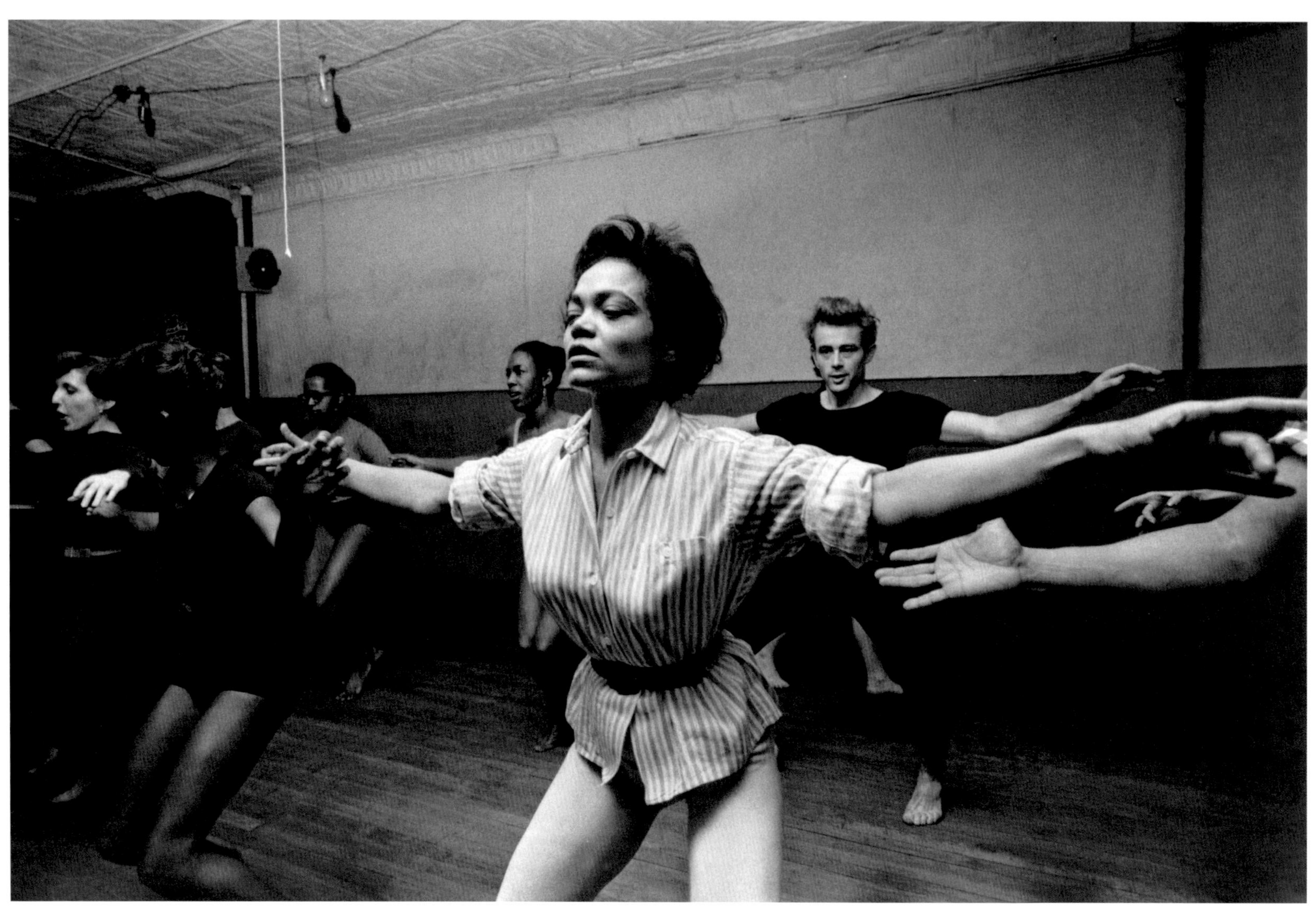

 James Dean attending Katherine Dunham dance classes, which included the singer Eartha Kitt. New York City, 1955

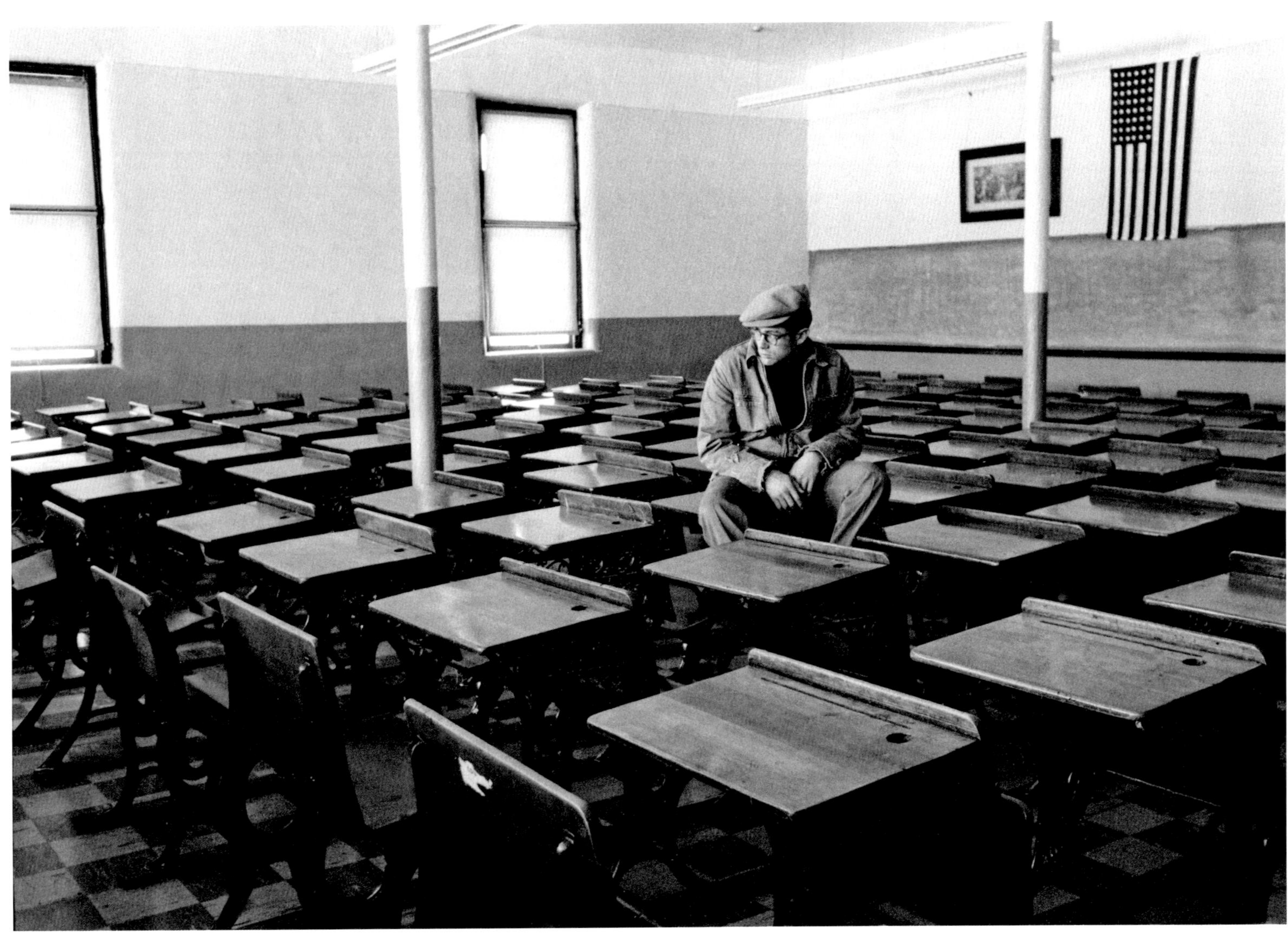

James Dean in his former schoolroom. Fairmount, Indiana, 1955   **023**

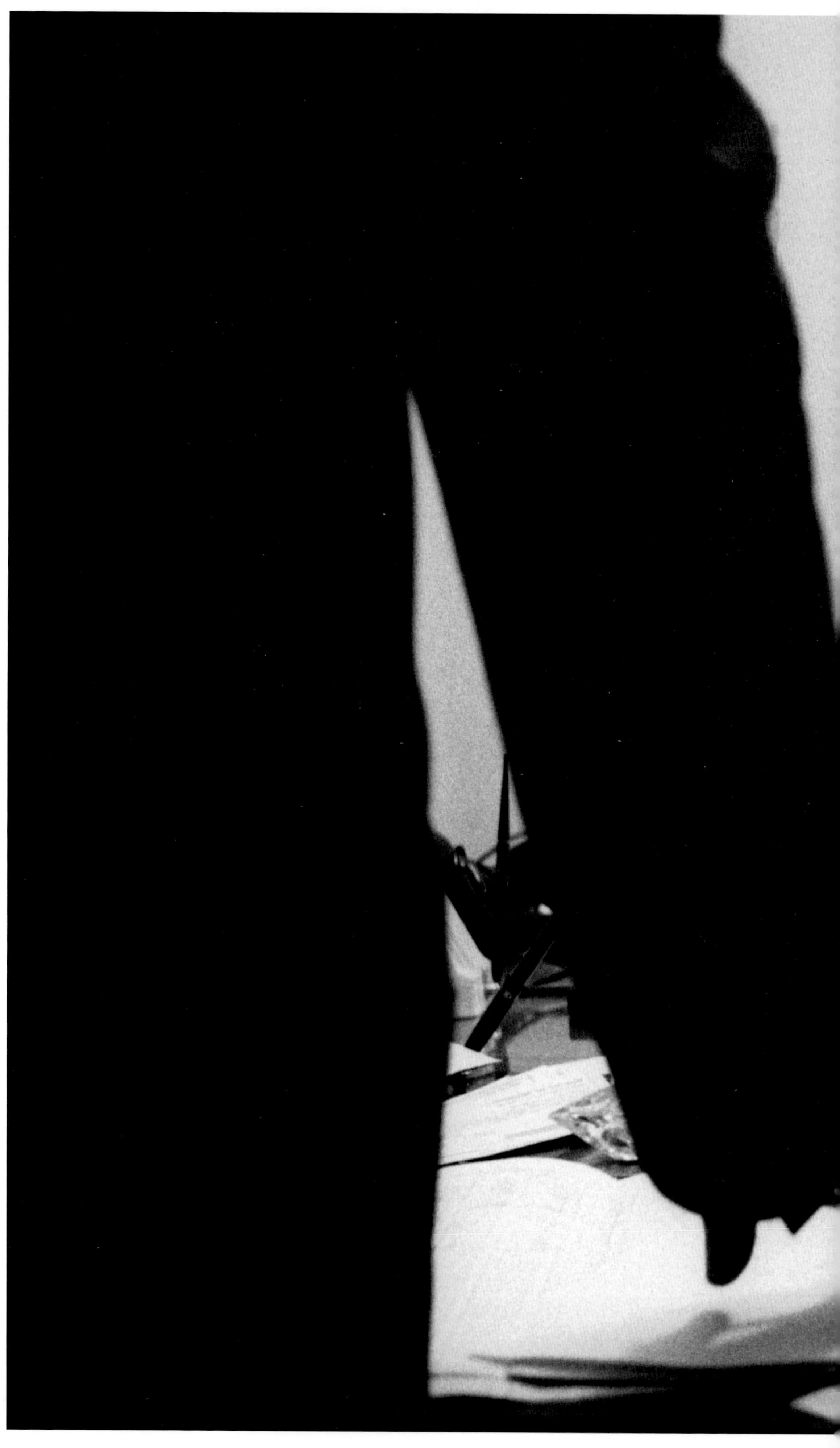

James Dean in the office of his agent,
Jane Deacy. New York City, 1955

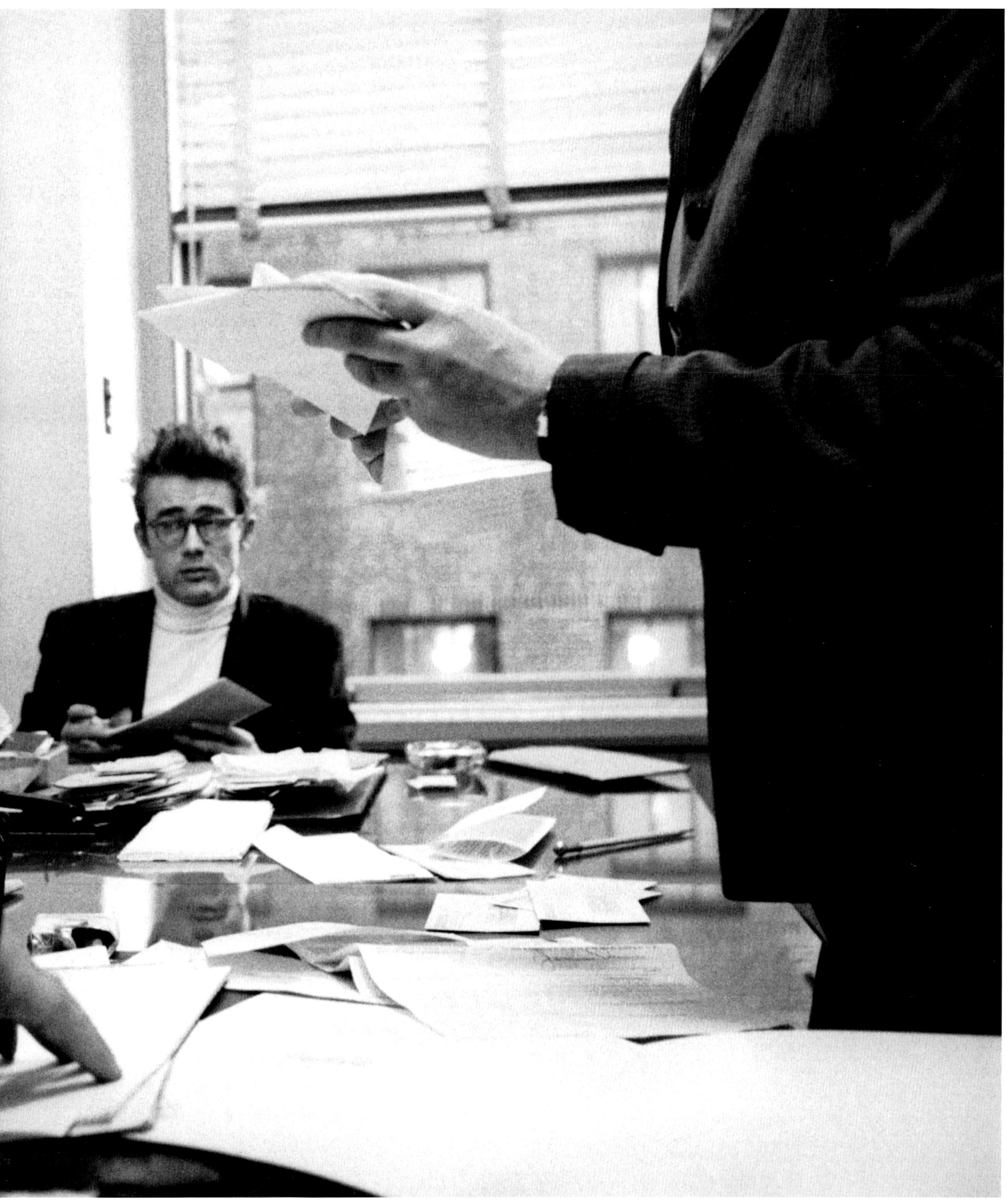

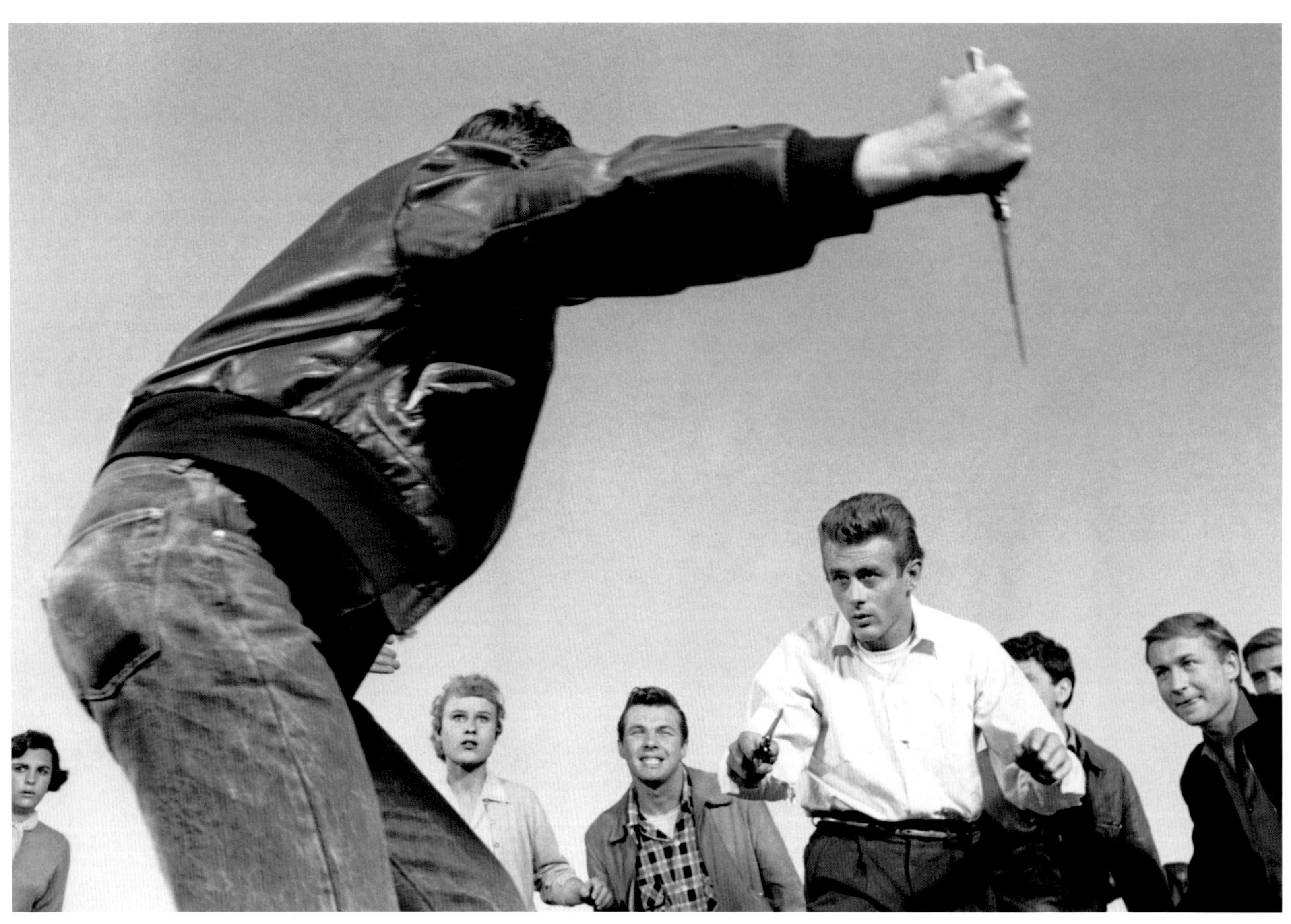

 James Dean's knife fight in REBEL WITHOUT A CAUSE, directed by Nicholas Ray. Hollywood, 1955

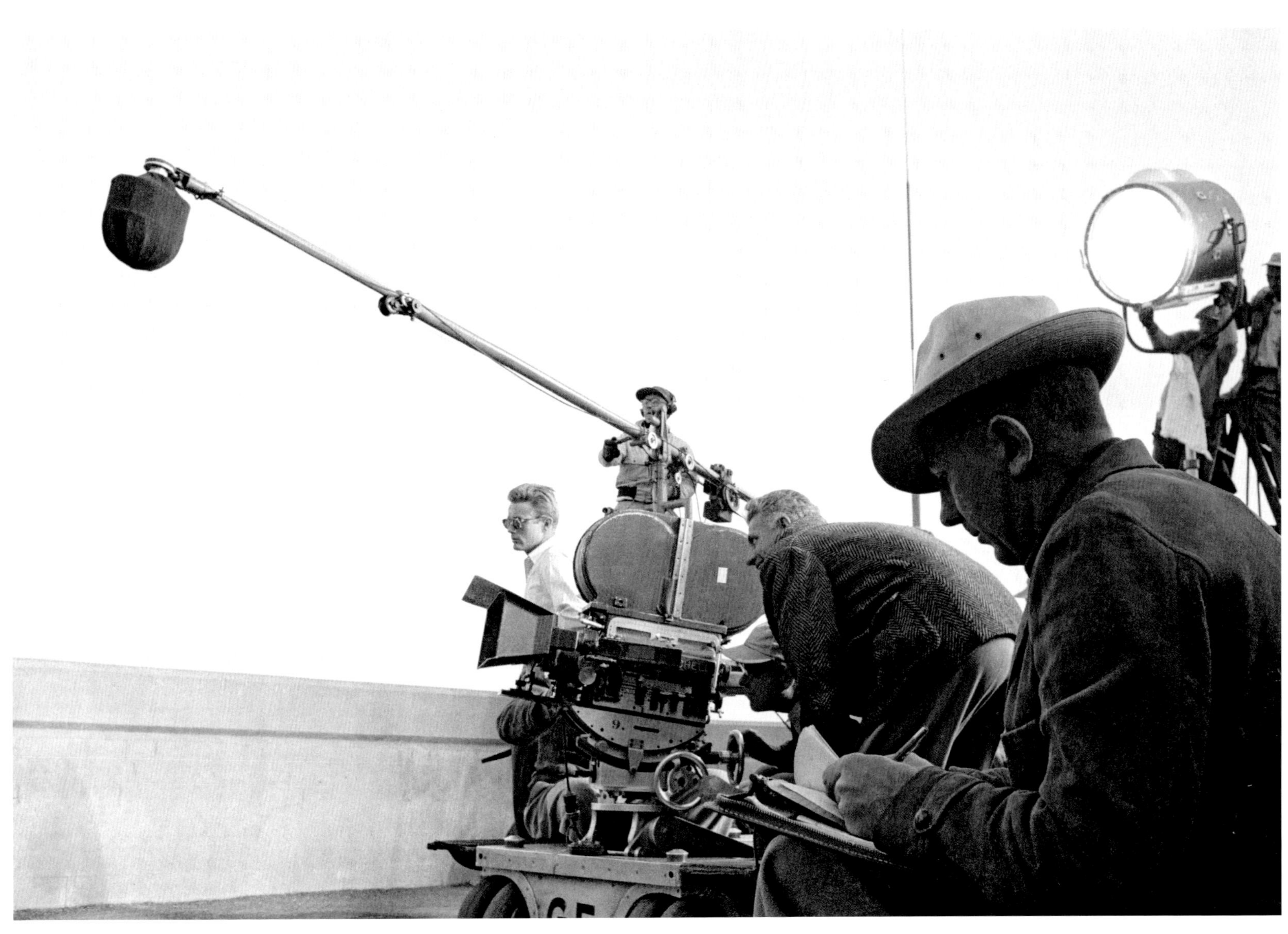

James Dean during the filming of REBEL WITHOUT A CAUSE. Hollywood, 1955

James Dean during a visit to his old school, Fairmount
High School. Fairmount, Indiana, 1955

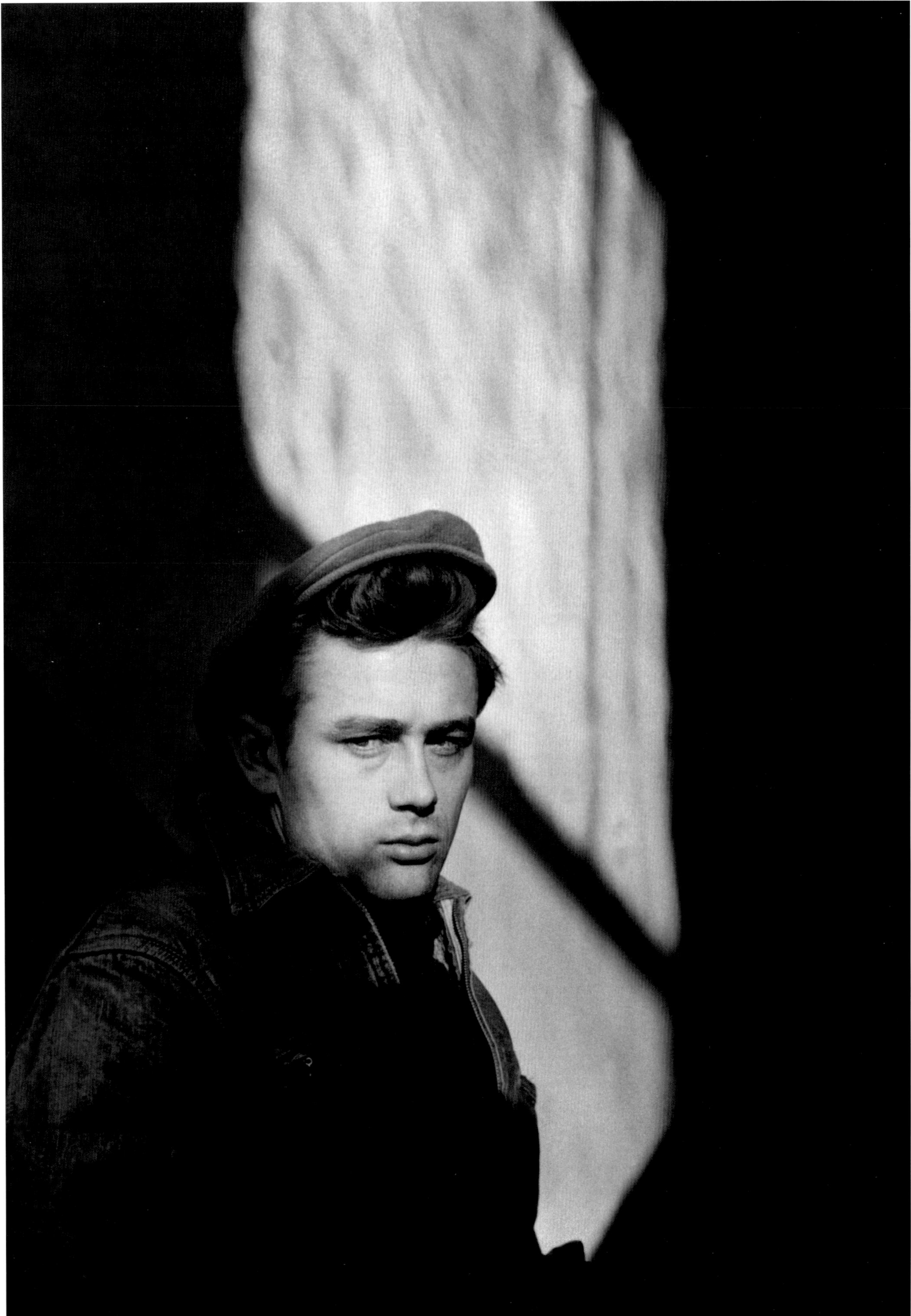

THE IMMIGRANTS

Refugee still aboard ship in New York Harbor. New York City, 1951

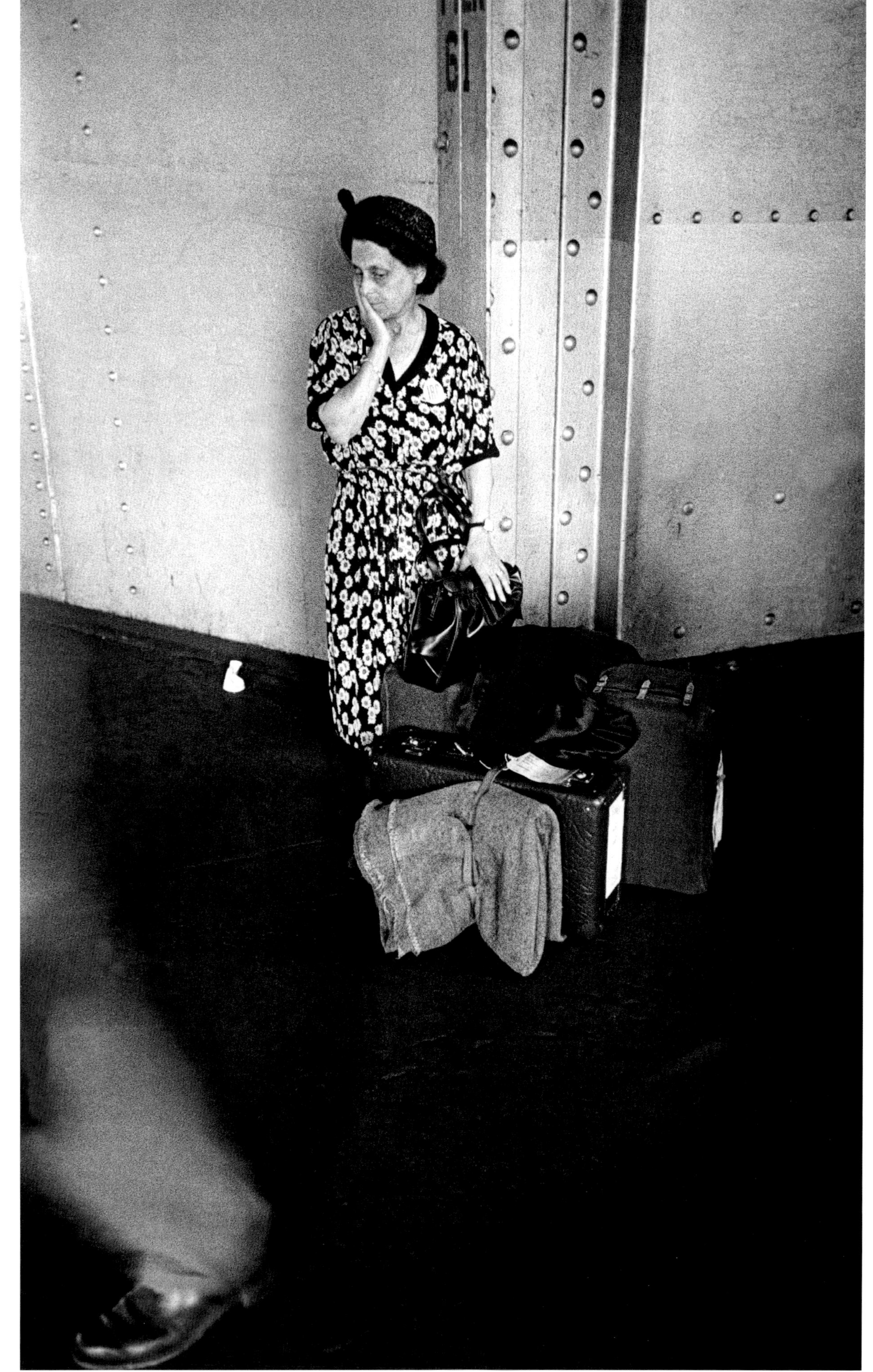

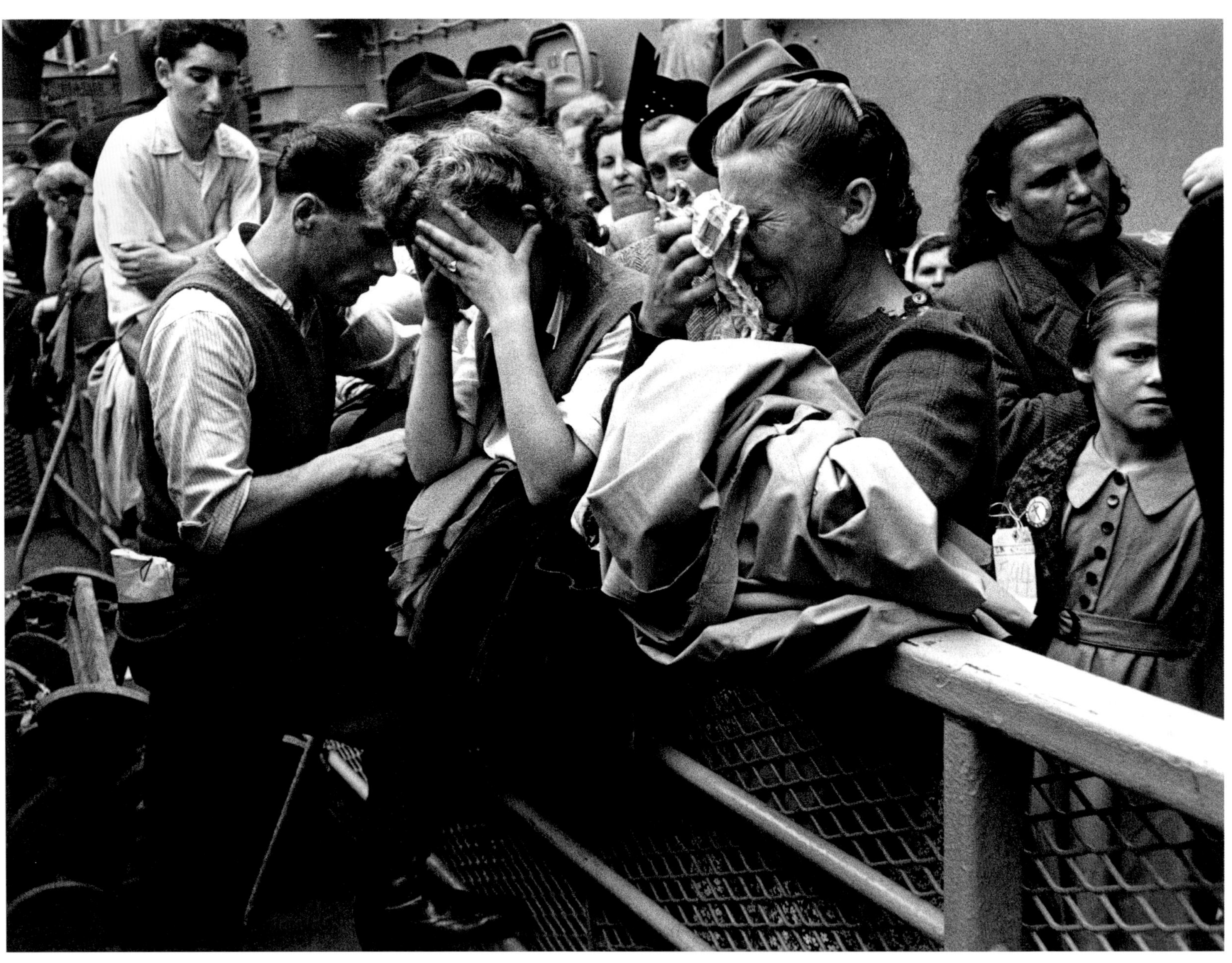

  Refugees still aboard ship in New York Harbor. New York City, 1951

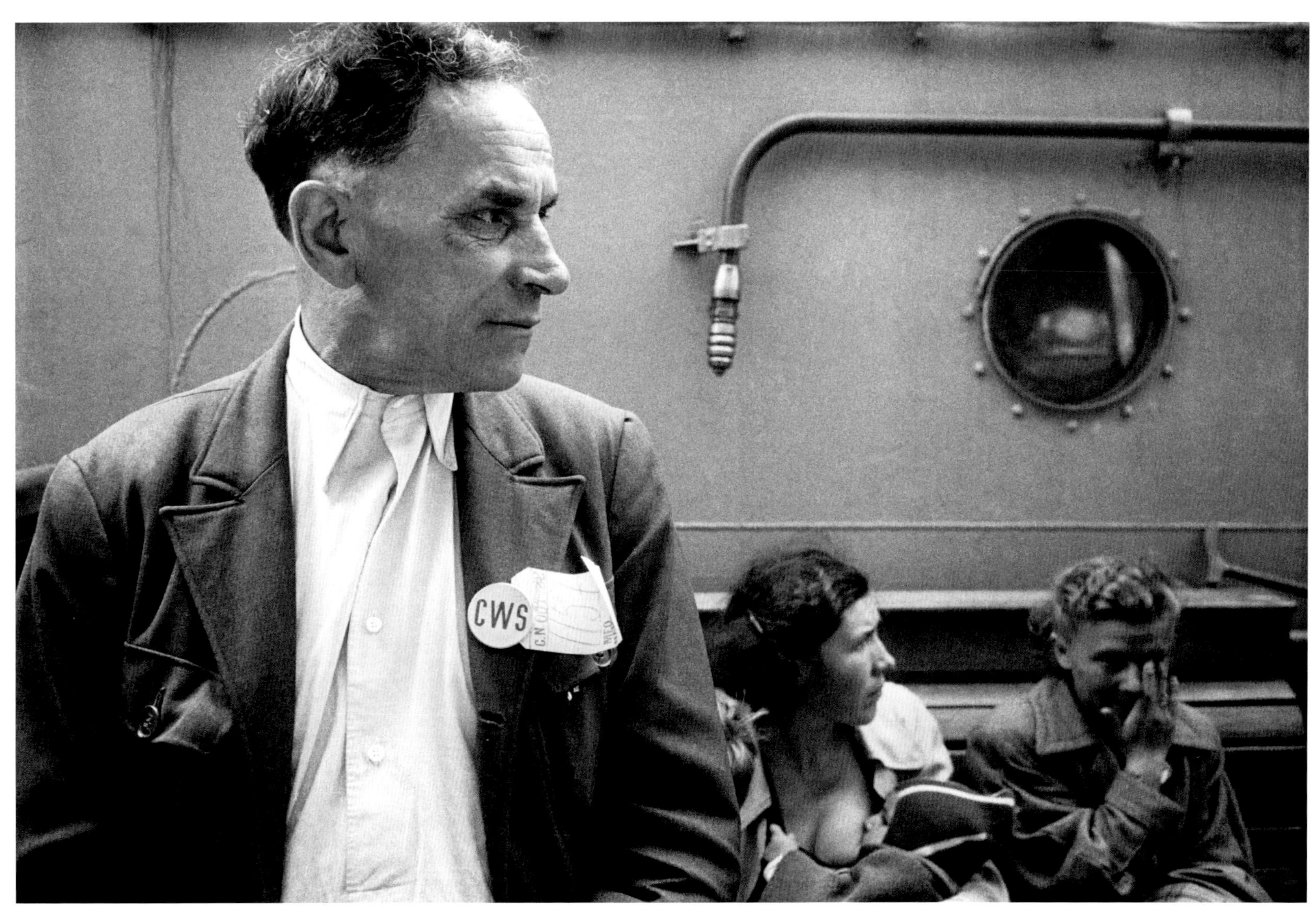

Immigrants. New York City, 1950　035

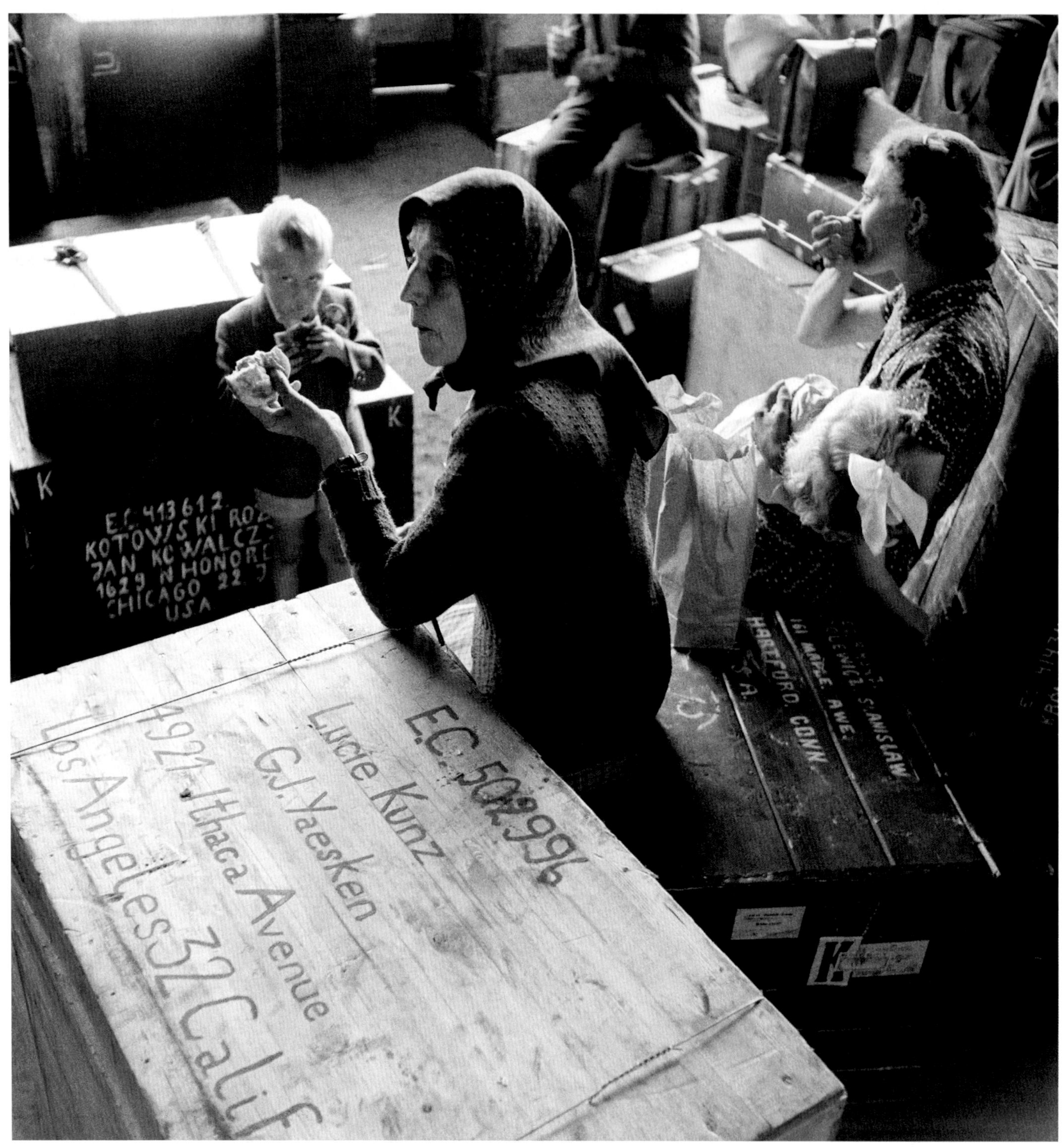

  Immigrants have their first meal on American soil. New York City, 1951

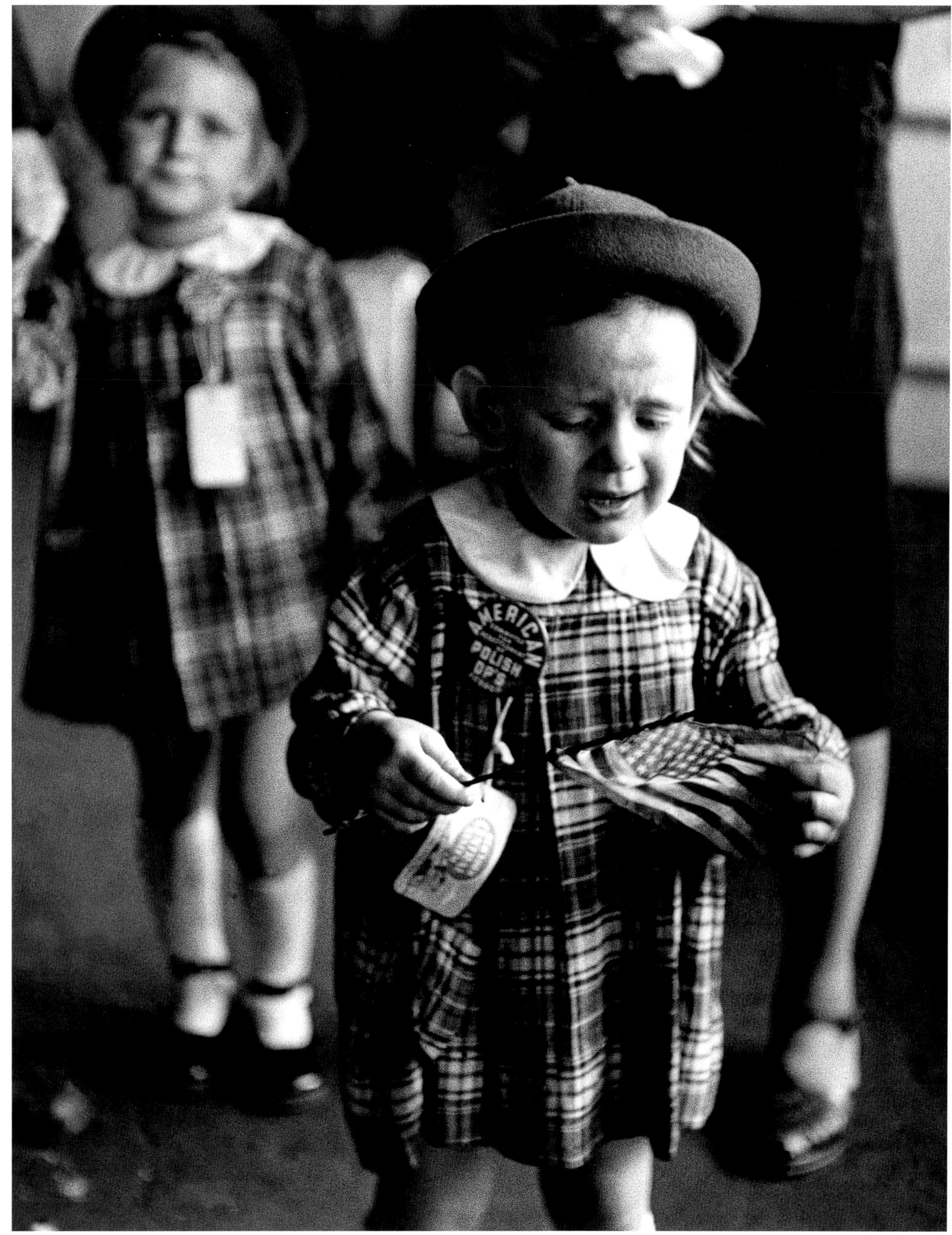

All ages showed fear. New York City, 1951   **037**

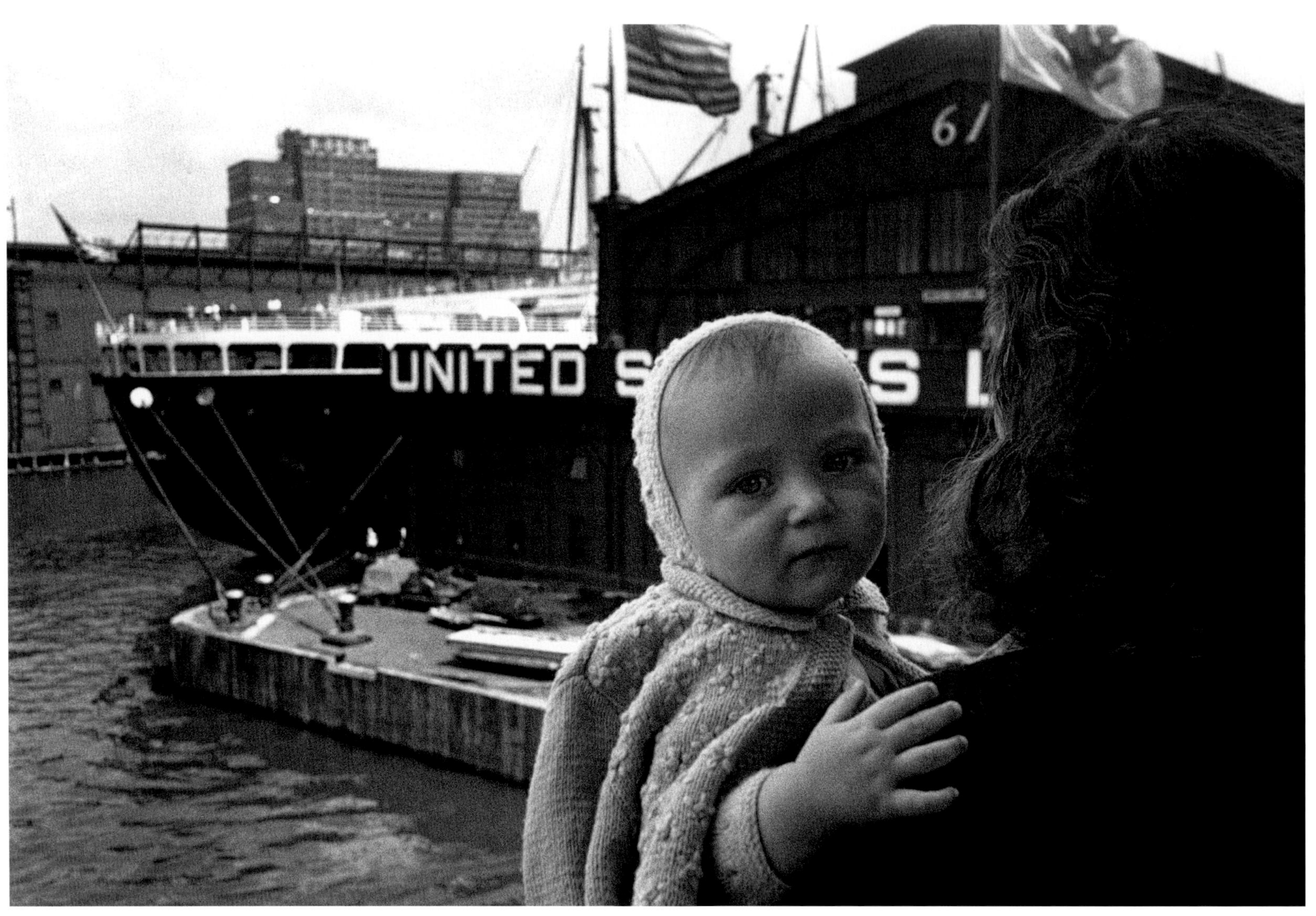

  A baby's arrival in the United States. New York City, 1951

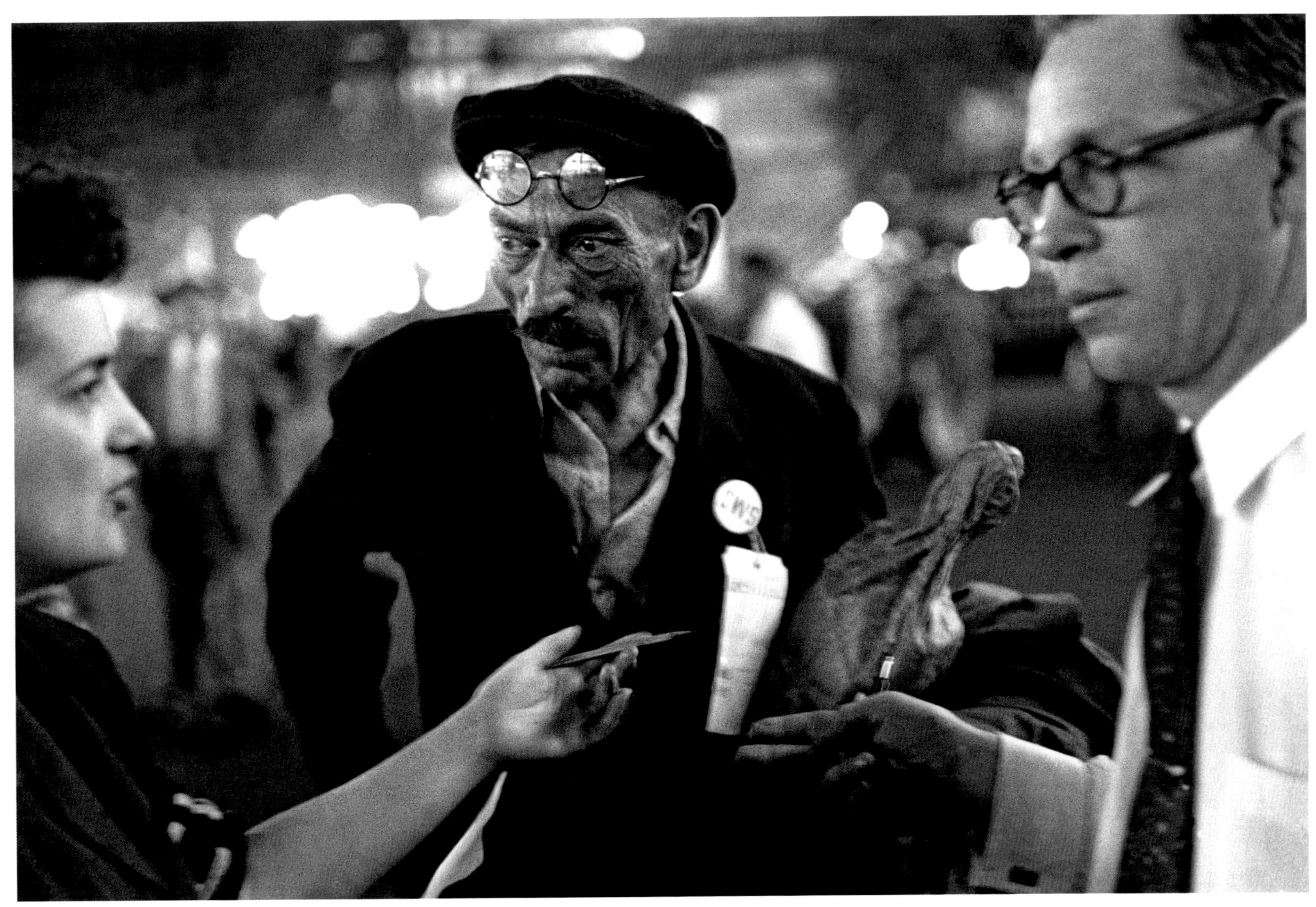

Refugee with immigration officers at New York dock. New York City, 1951

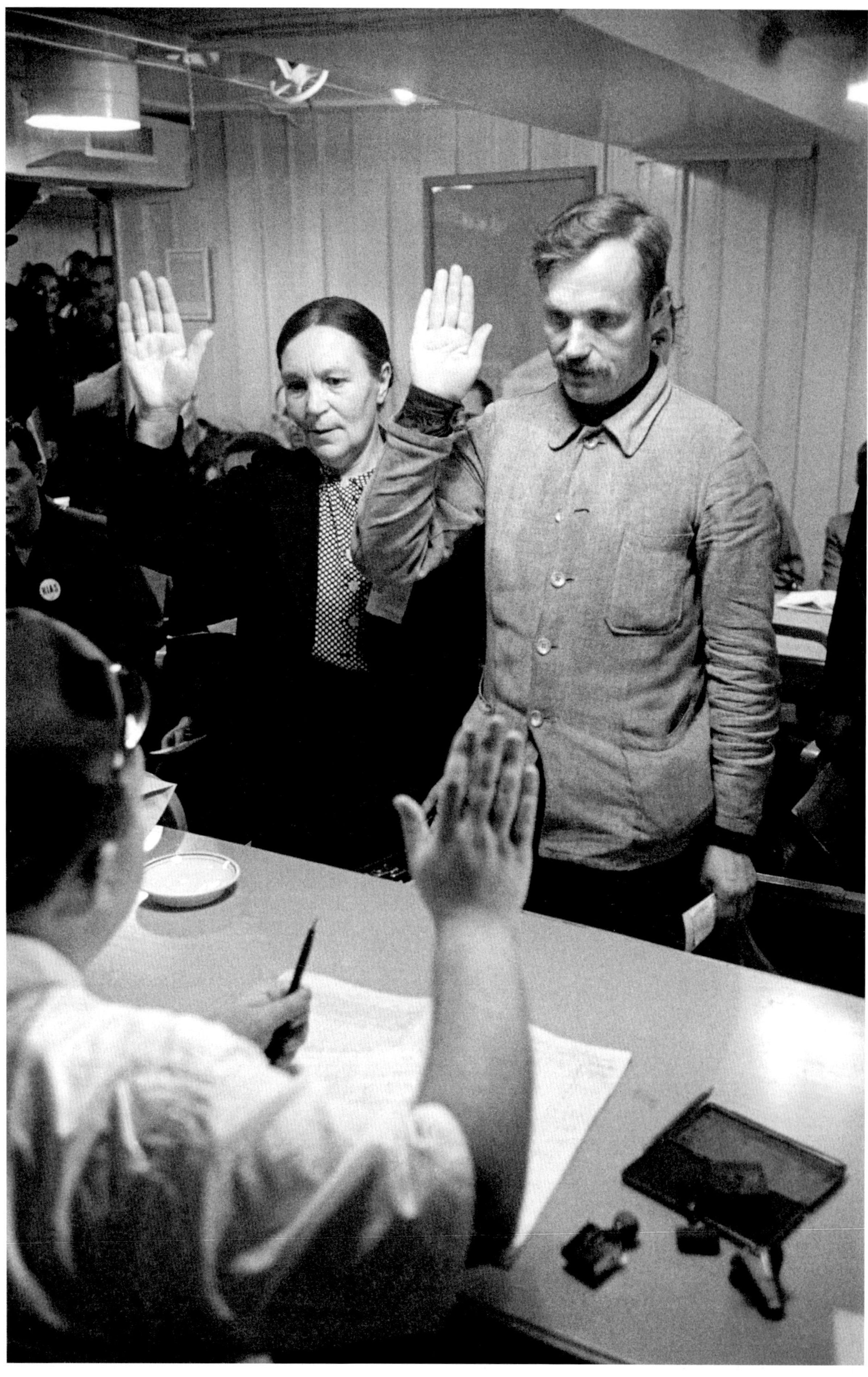

  Immigrants. New York City, 1950

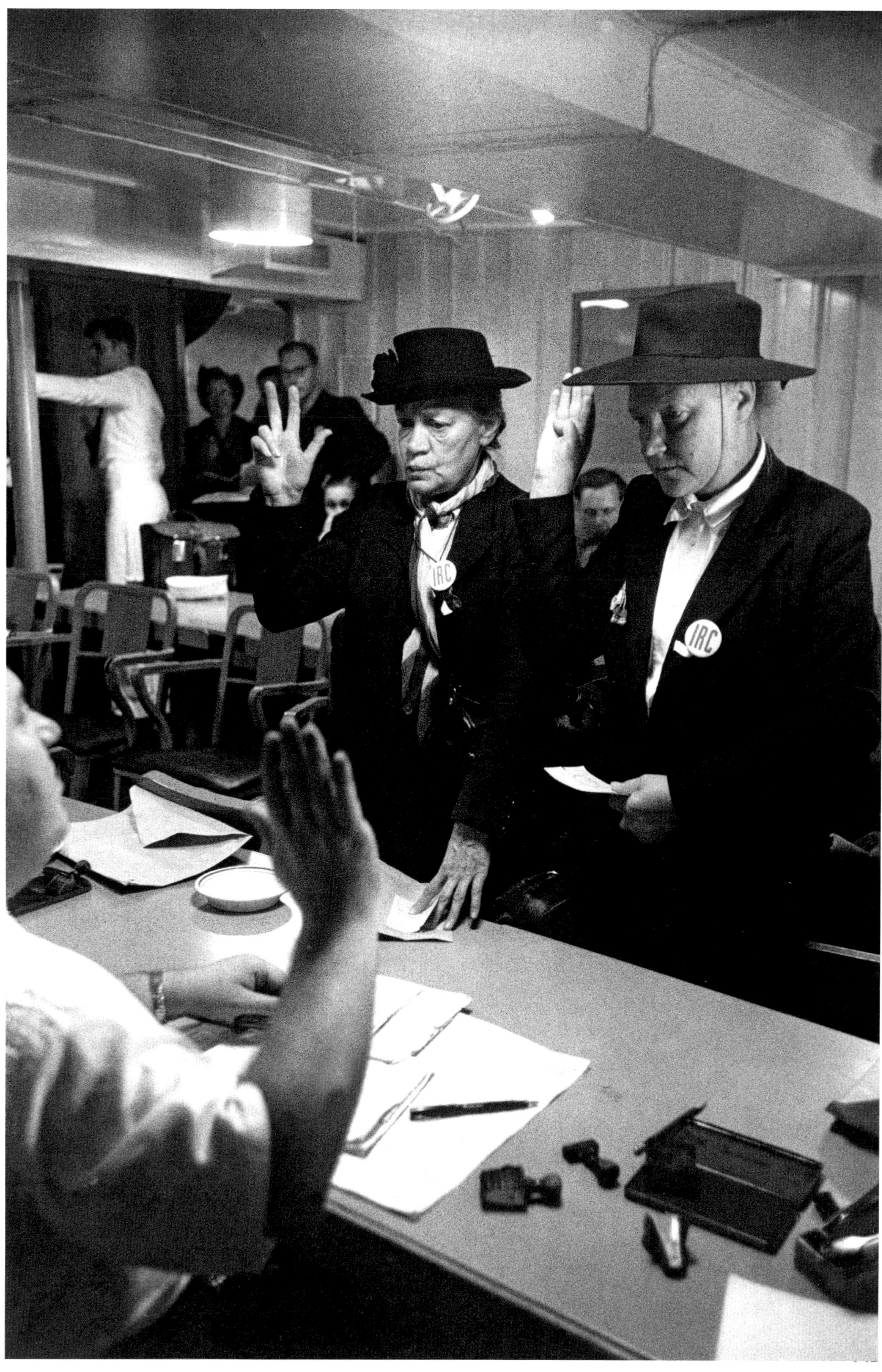

Bureaucratic absurdity: demanding an assurance of "No communist affiliation." New York City, 1951

MUSICIANS, ACTORS,JAZZ, & THEATER

Ernest "Kid Punch" Miller, trumpet player and singer,
returning home at 6 a.m. New Orleans, 1958

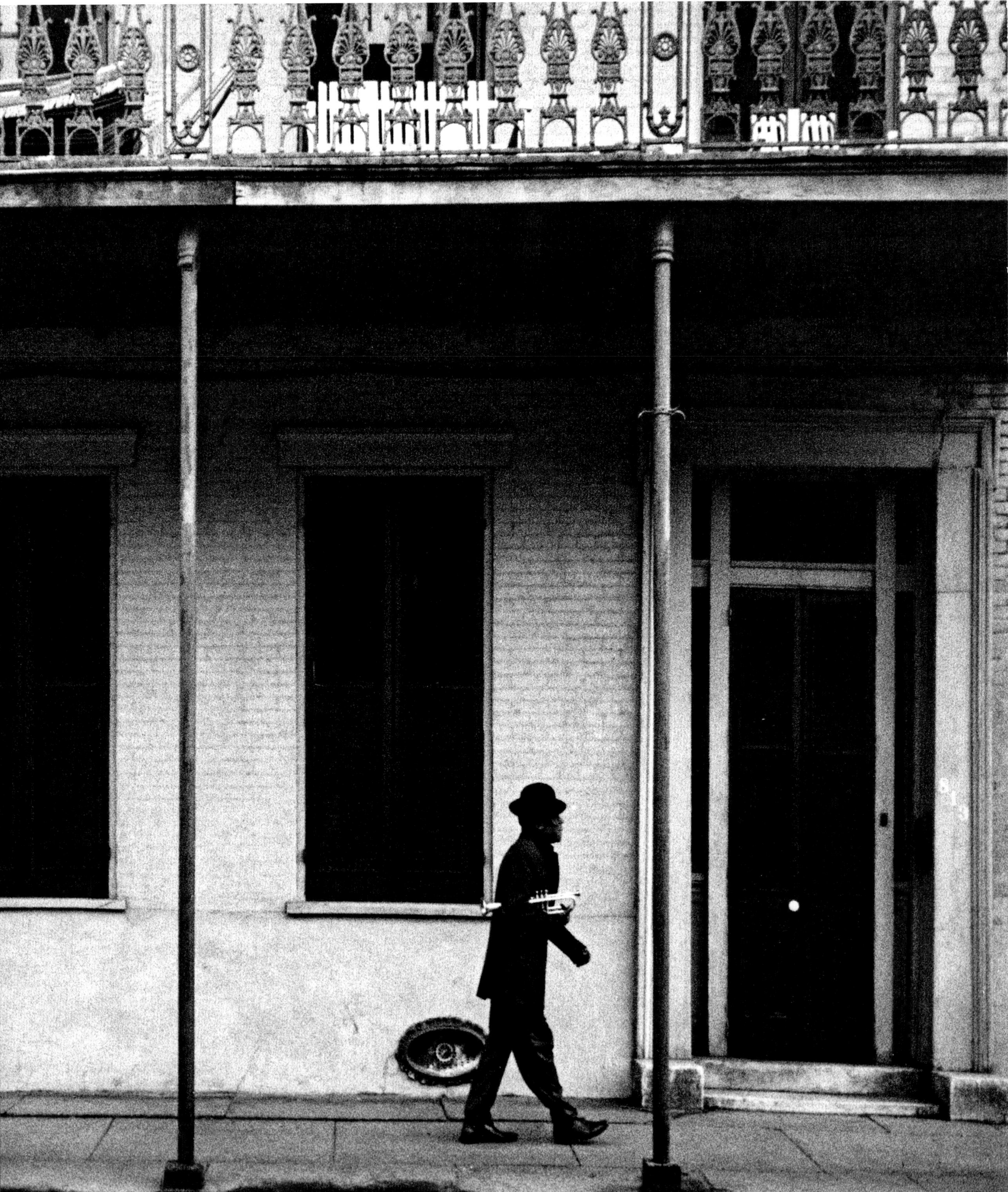

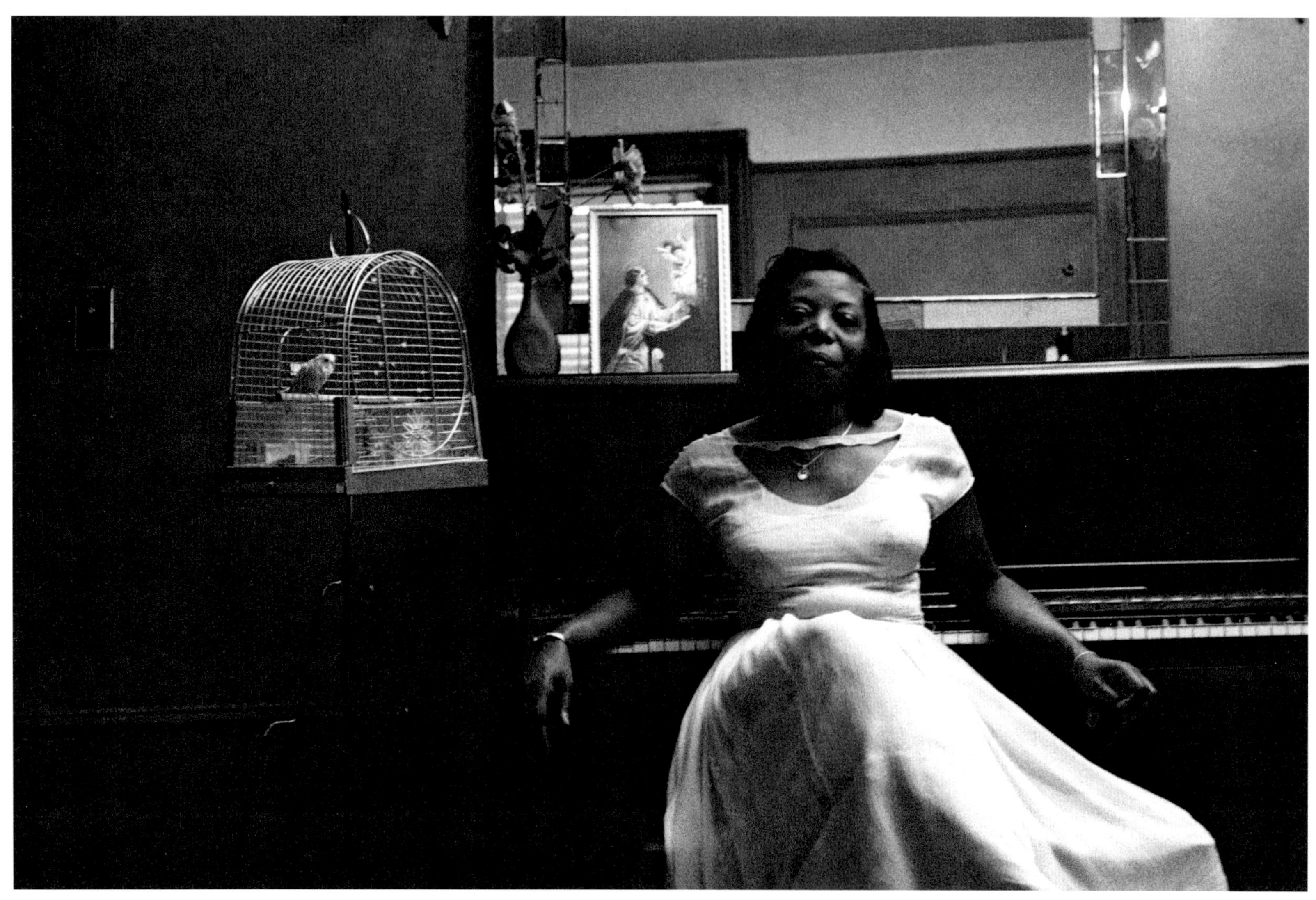

above
Mary Lou Williams (born Mary Elfrieda Scruggs), jazz pianist, composer, arranger,
educator, and humanitarian, in her apartment in Washington Heights. New York City, 1958

right
Robert "Bob" Brookmeyer, trombonist, composer, arranger, and pianist. 1958

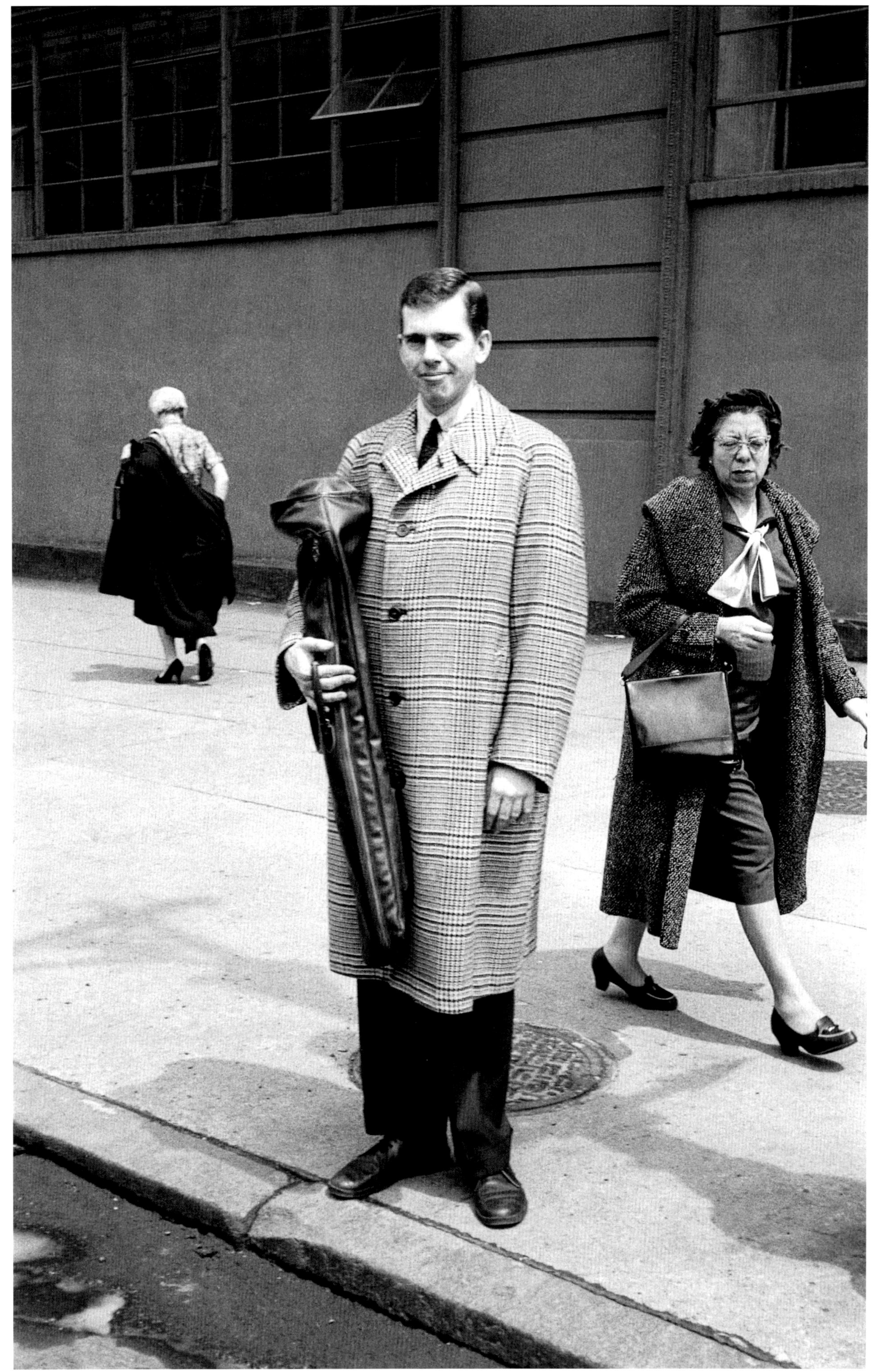

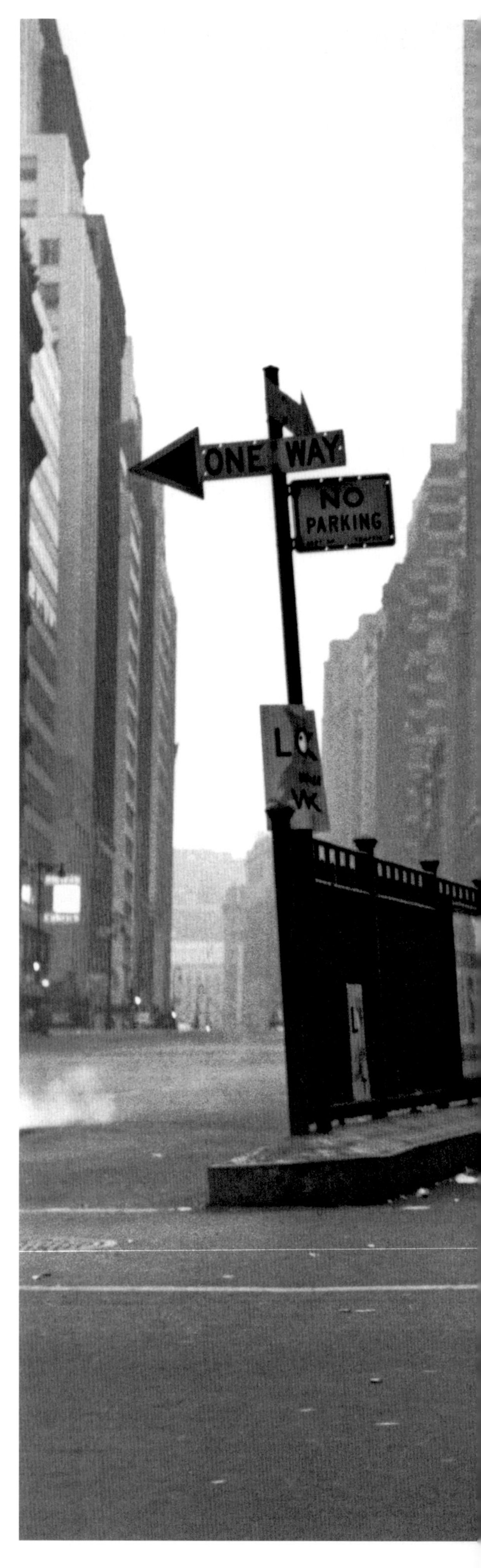
ONE WAY
NO
PARKING

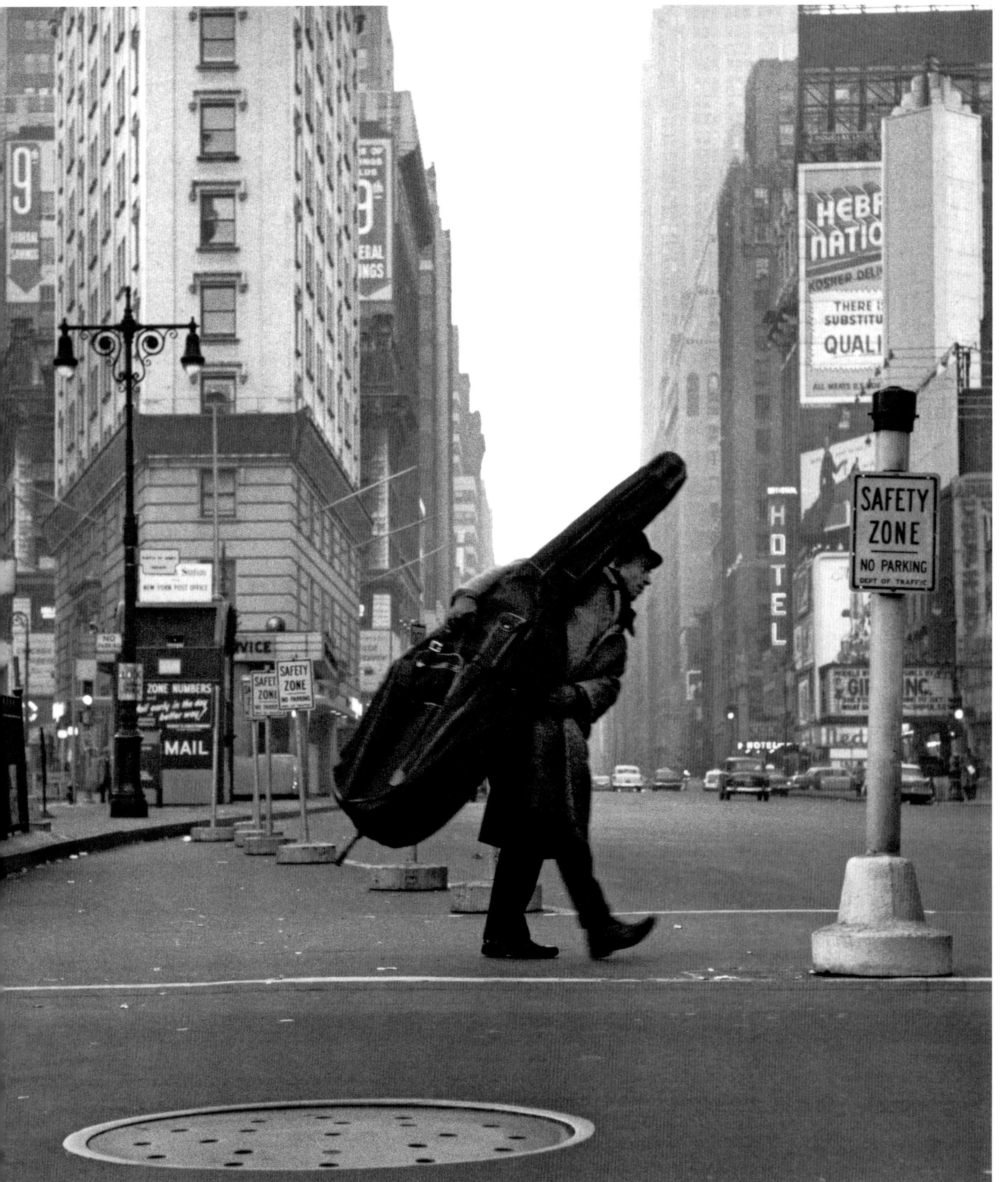
9¢
HEBR
NATIO
KOSHER DELI
THERE I
SUBSTITU
QUALI
SAFETY
ZONE
NO PARKING
DEPT OF TRAFFIC
HOTEL
MAIL
ZONE NUMBERS
NEW YORK POST OFFICE
SAFETY
ZONE
NO PARKING
SAFETY
ZONE
NO PARKING
NO
PARK

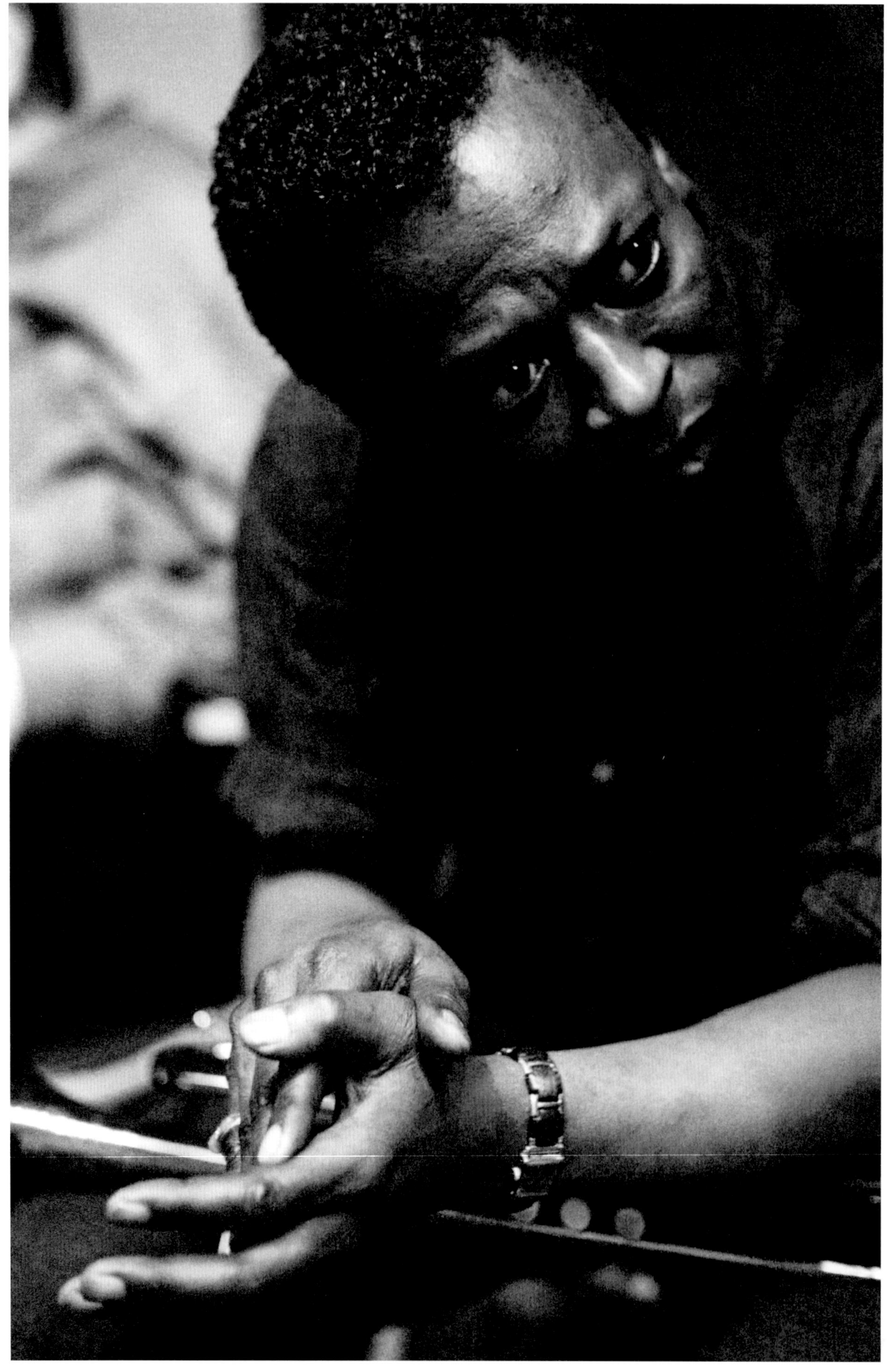

 Miles Davis. New York City, 1958

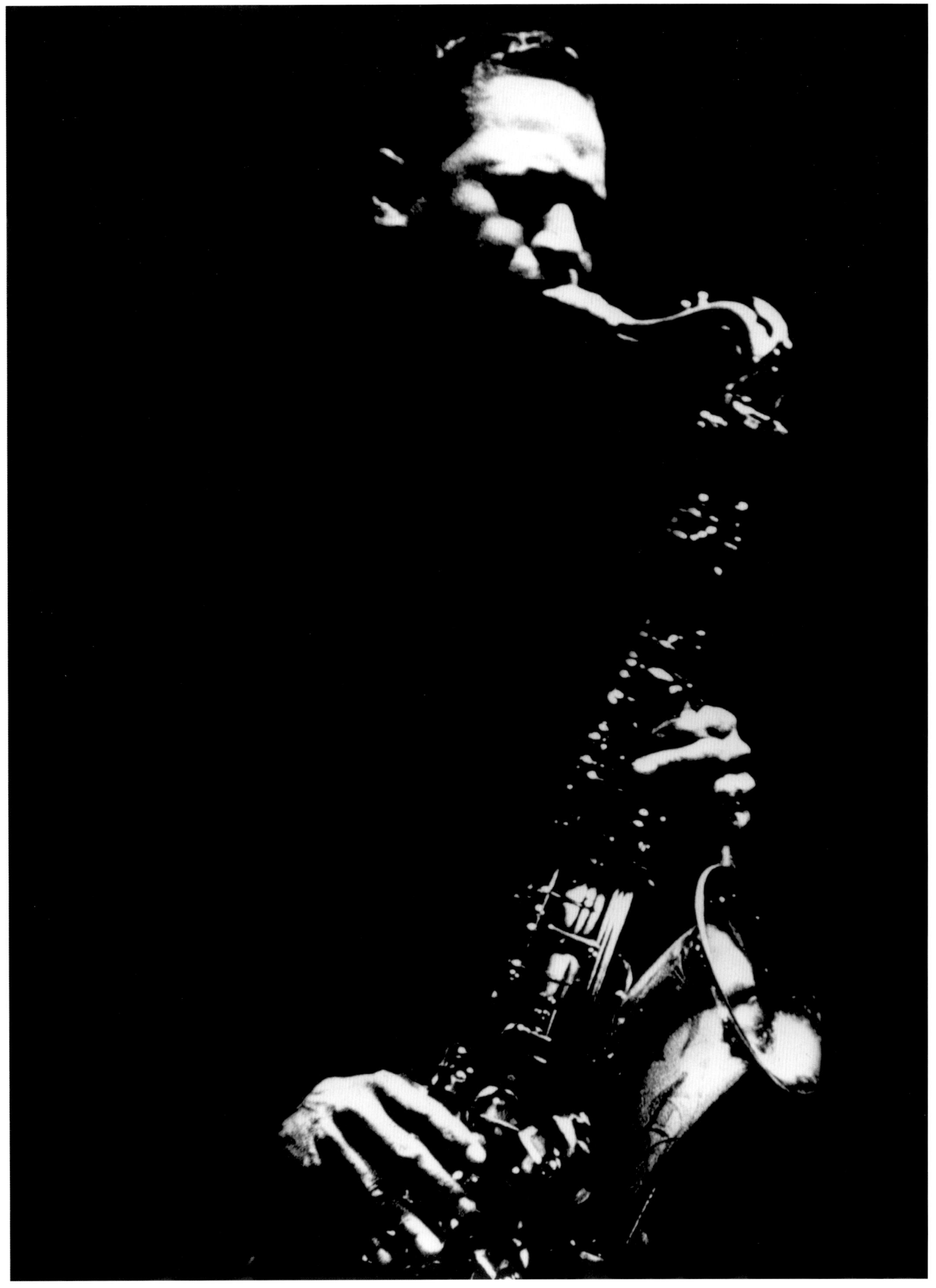

Tenor saxophonist Illinois Jacquet. New York City, 1958

Rufus Perryman, "Speckled Red," pianist, in local barbershop. New Orleans, 1958

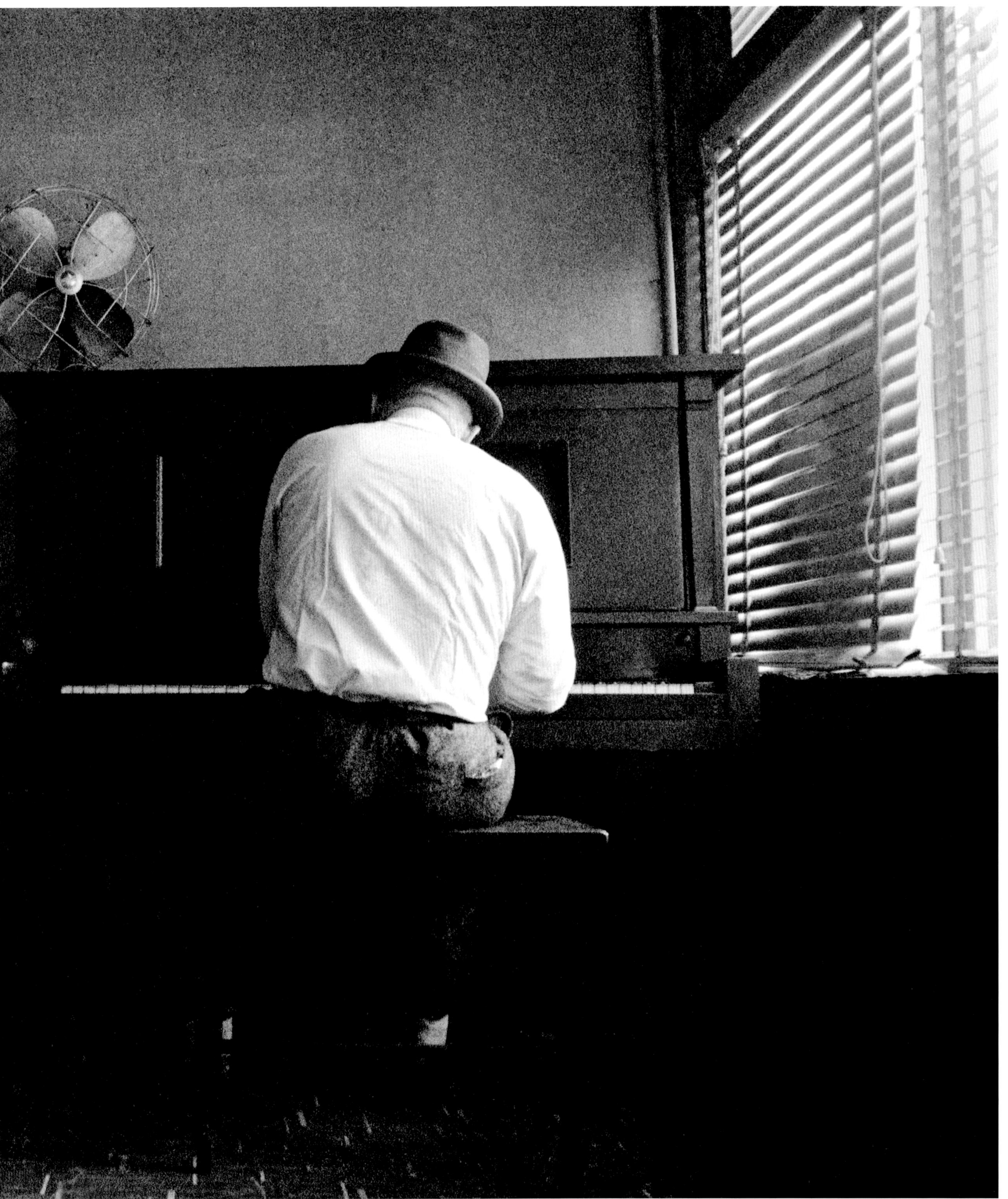

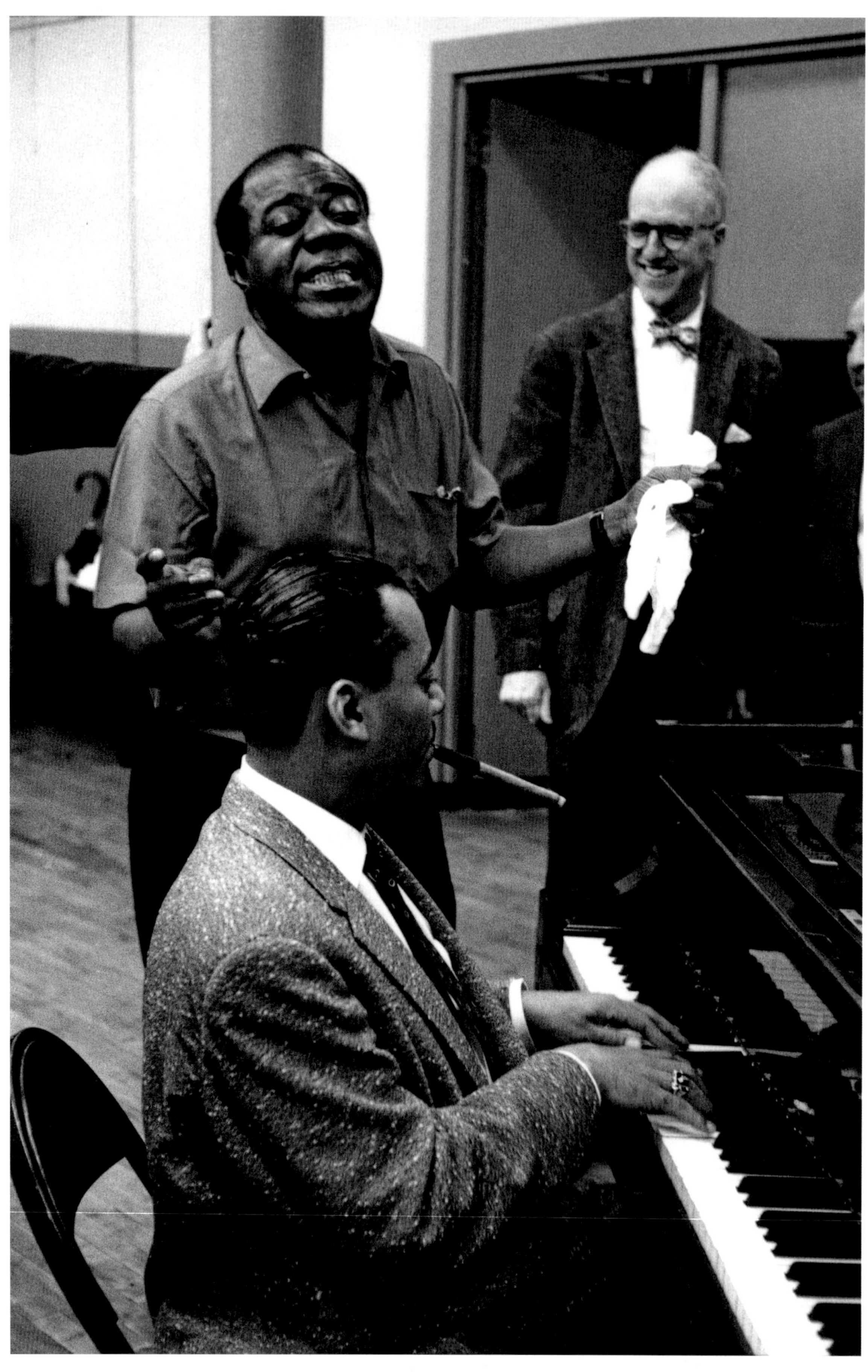

Louis Armstrong, trumpet player, singer, composer, and bandleader, during a rehearsal for one of his many TV appearances, accompanied by Billy Kyle, pianist and arranger. New York City, 1958

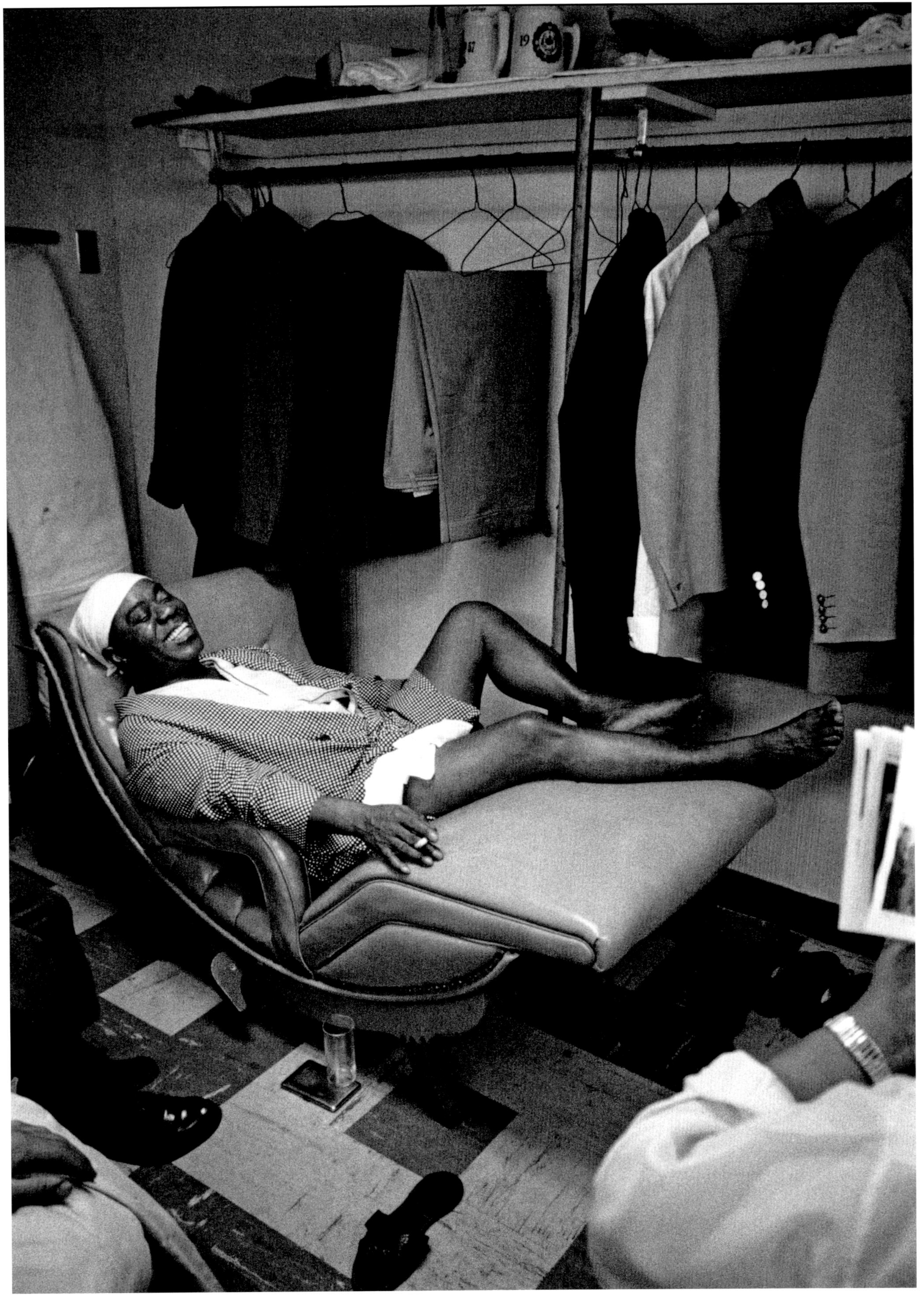

Louis Armstrong in his dressing room at the Latin Casino. Philadelphia, 1958

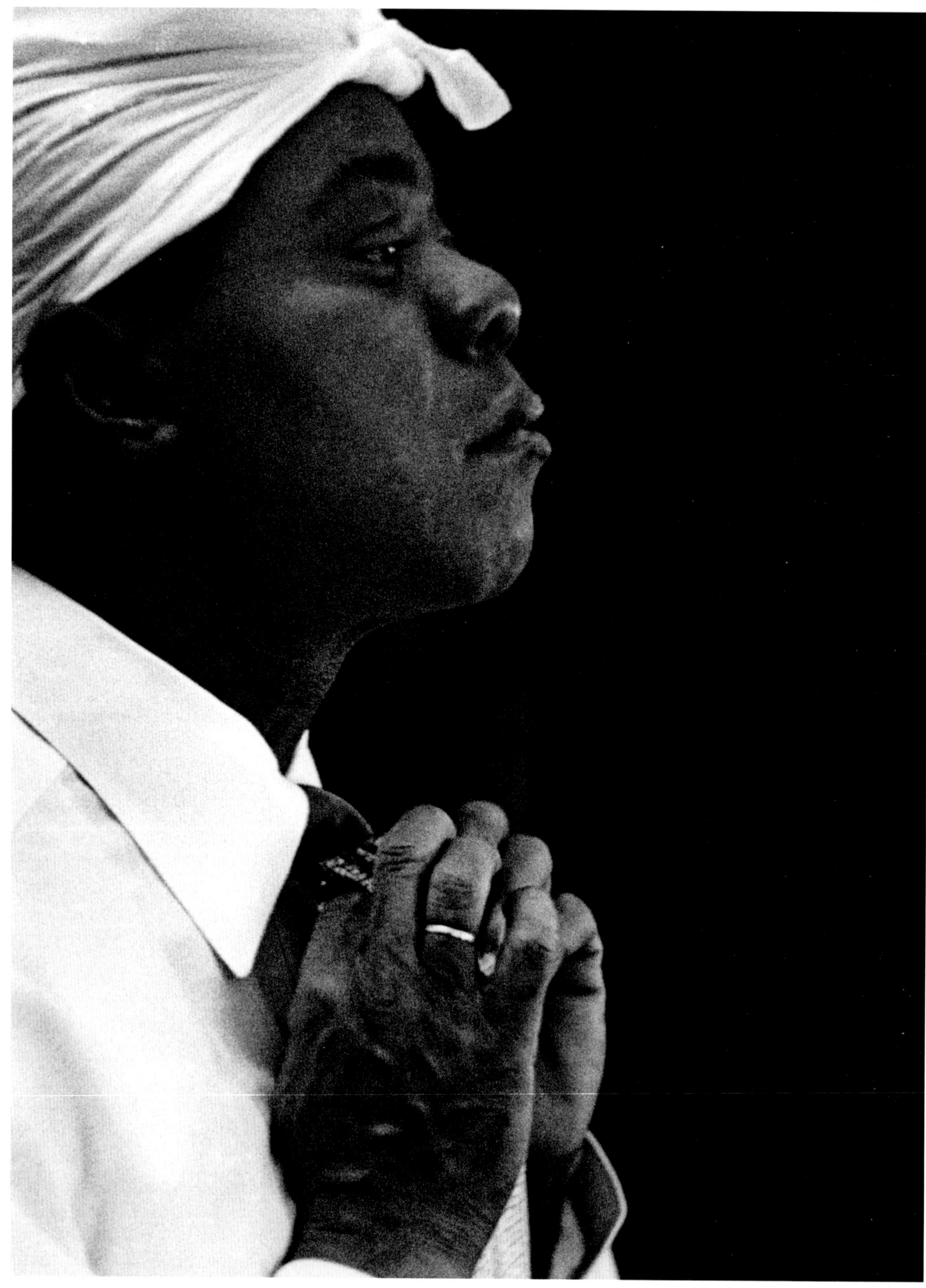

 Before every concert, Louis Armstrong gets dressed with great care. Philadelphia, 1958

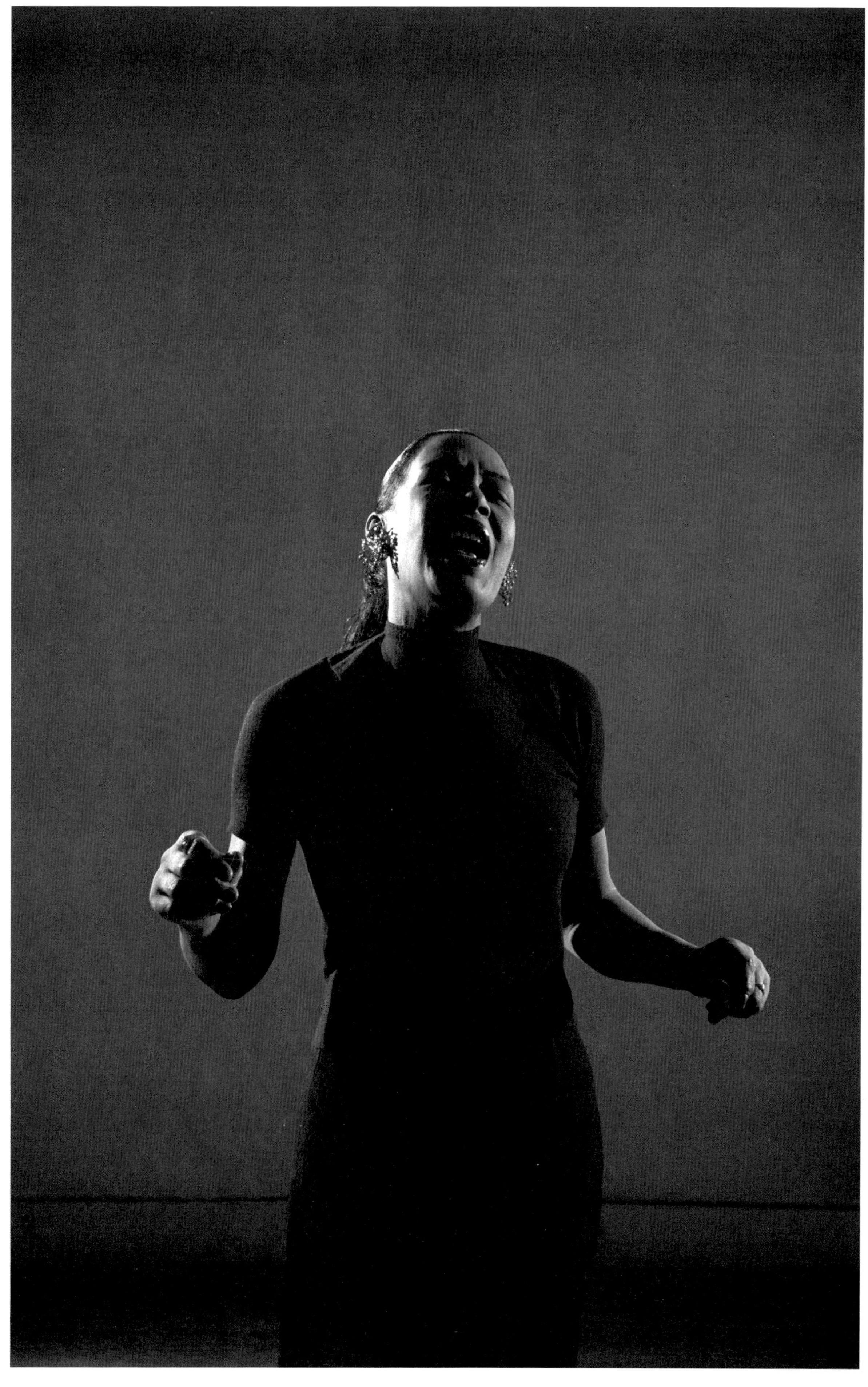

Singer Billie Holiday. 1958

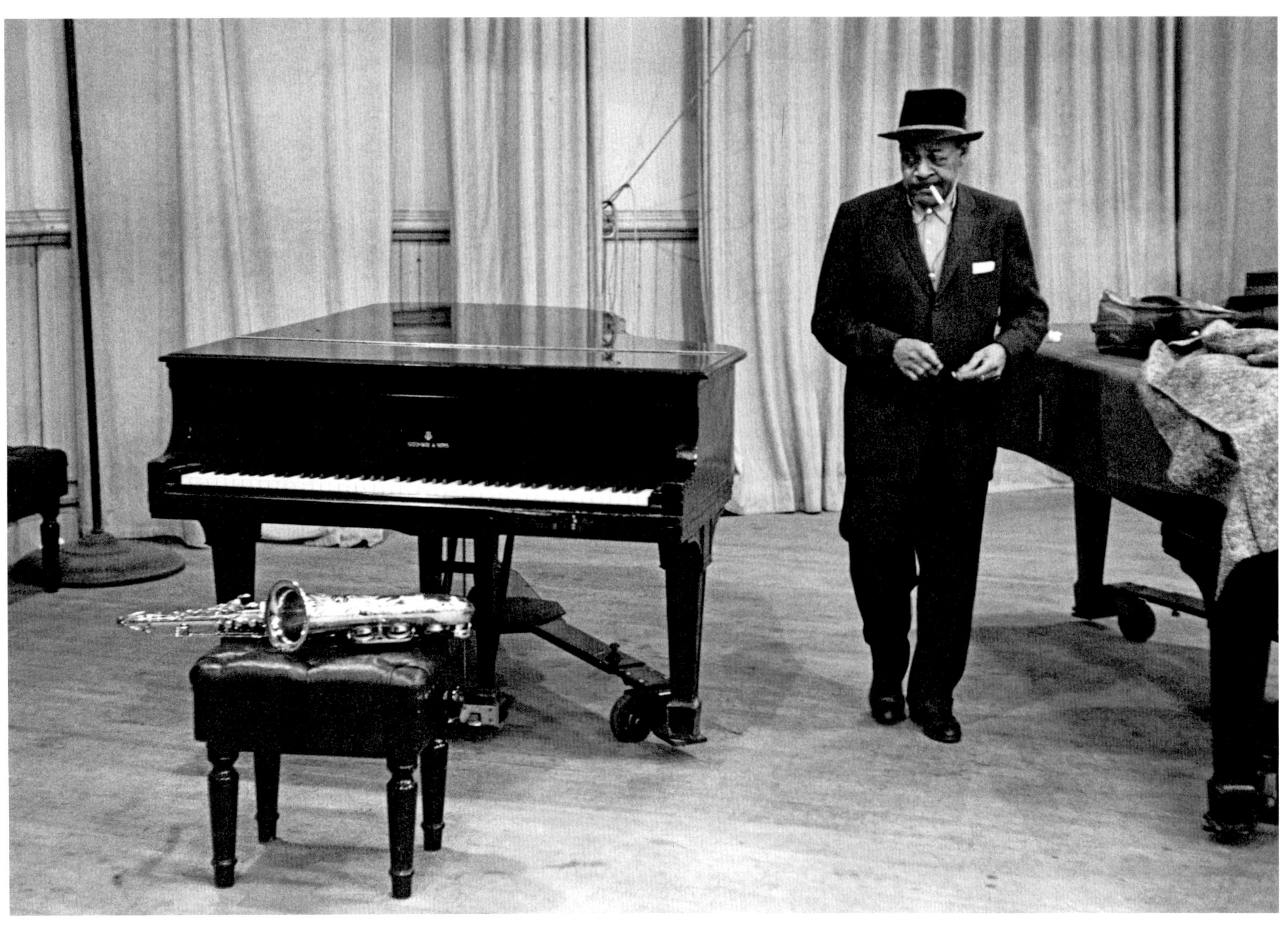

  Saxophonist Coleman Hawkins. 1958

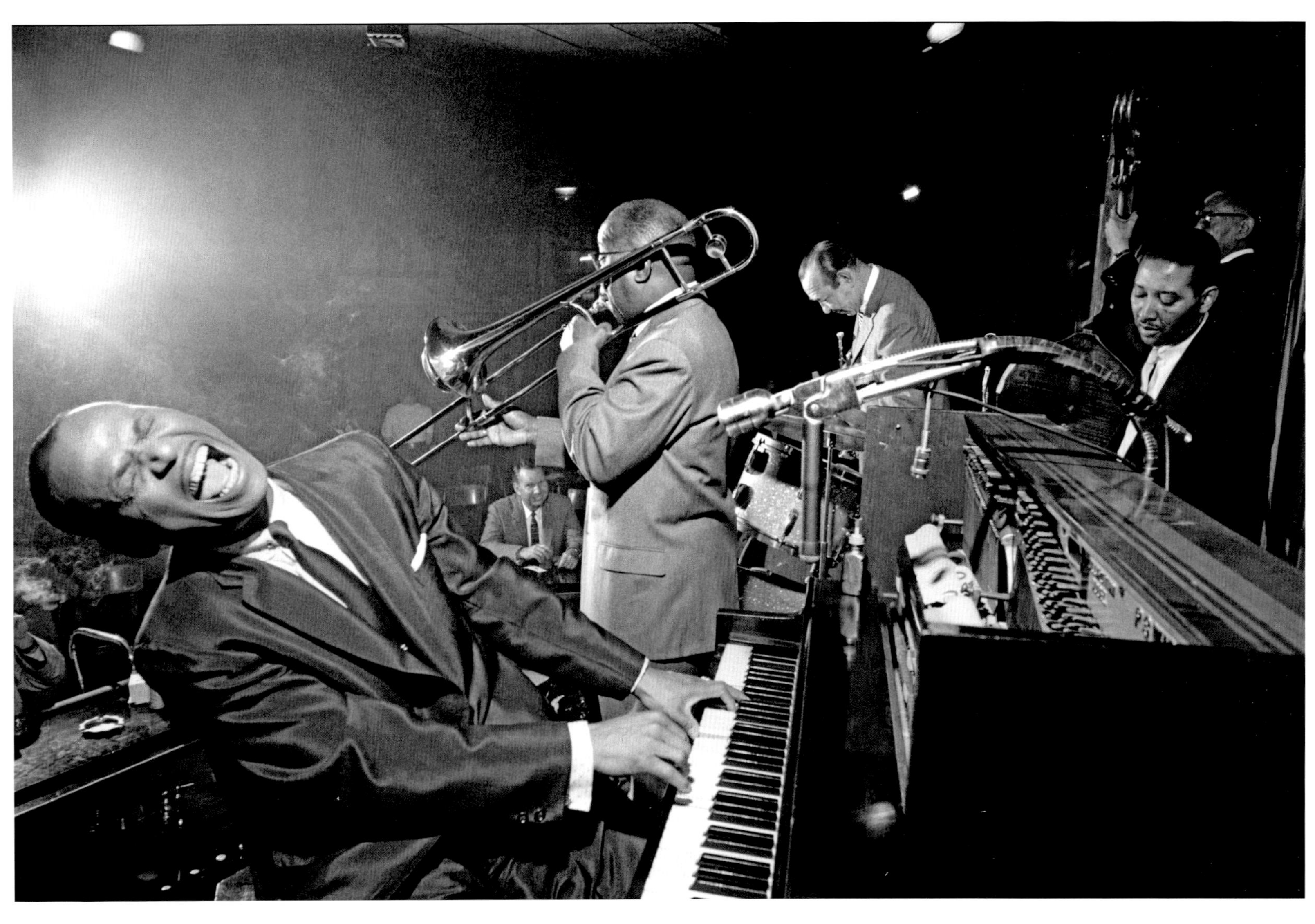

Earl Hines, pianist and bandleader; Jimmy Archey, trombonist; Francis Joseph "Muggsy" Spanier, cornet player and bandleader; Earl Watkins, drummer. San Francisco, 1958

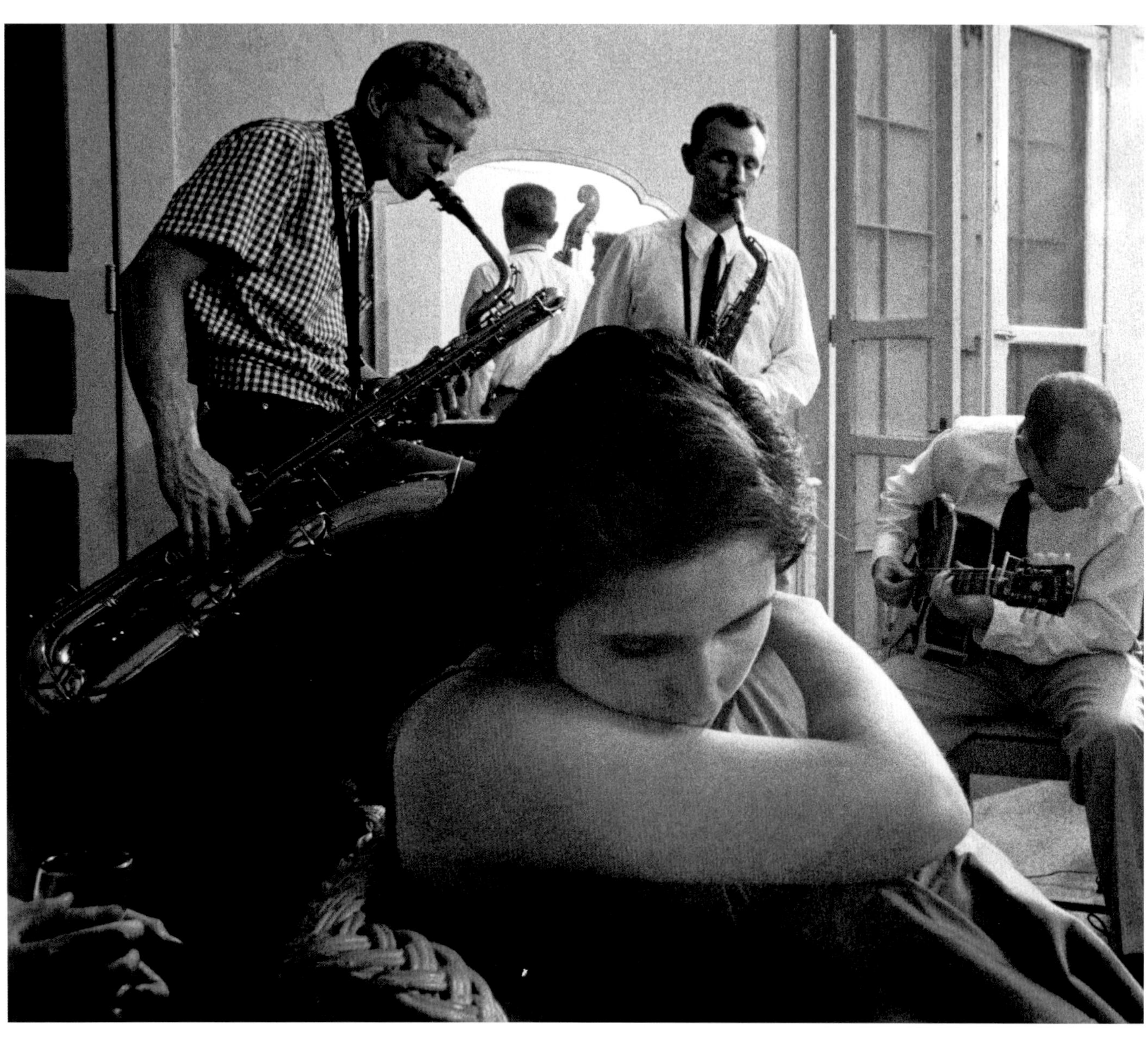

Newport Jazz Festival: Gerry Mulligan, saxophonist; Jimmy Giuffre, saxophonist; and Jim Hall, guitarist. Newport, Rhode Island, 1957

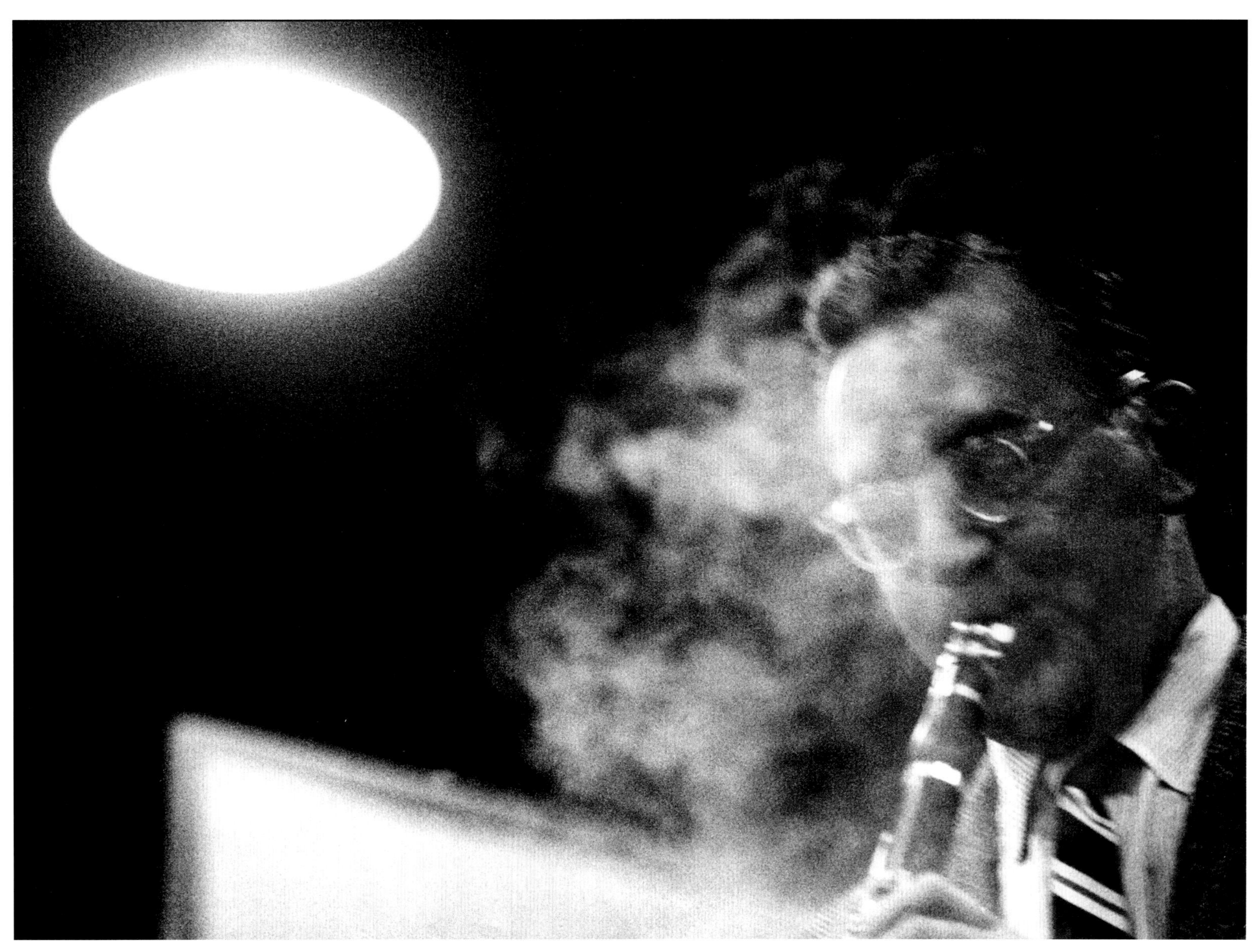

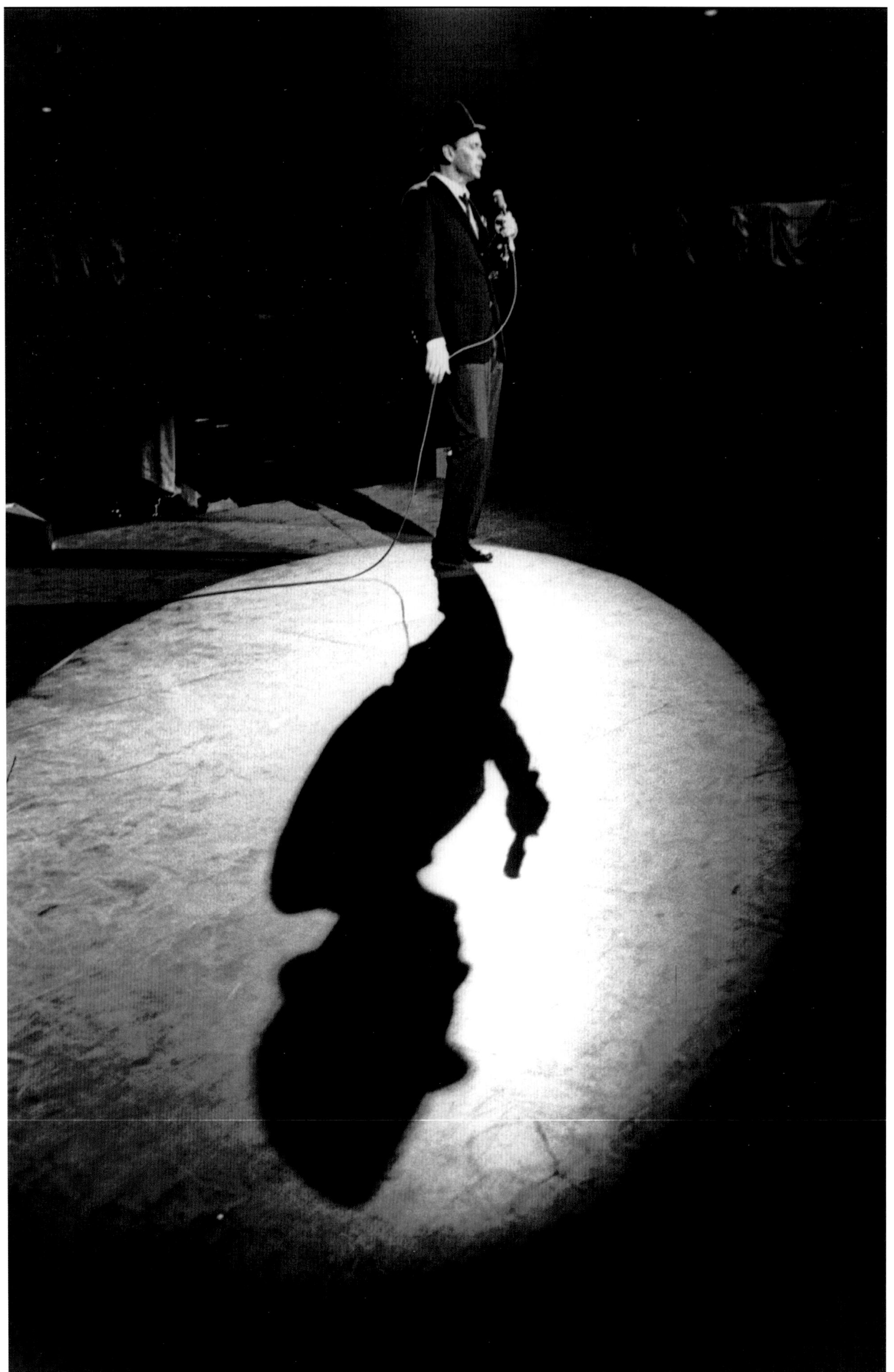

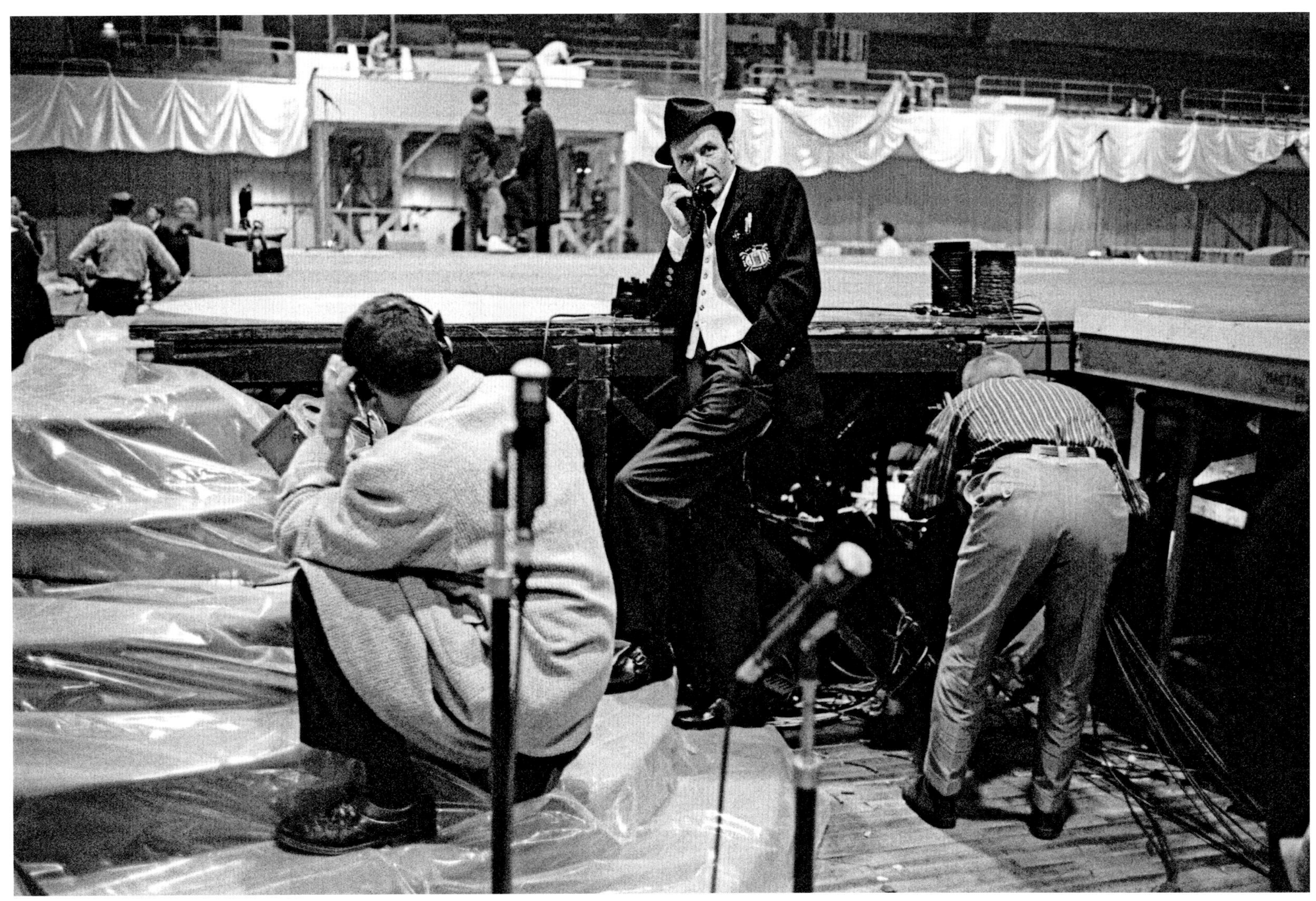

Preparations for John F. Kennedy's Presidential Inaugural Ball at the
National Guard Armory building, with a large group of entertainers from
Hollywood and the world of show business, under the conductorship
of Leonard Bernstein. Washington, DC, January 1961

above
For JFK's inaugural ball, Frank Sinatra was responsible for the vocal groups.
Washington, DC, January 1961

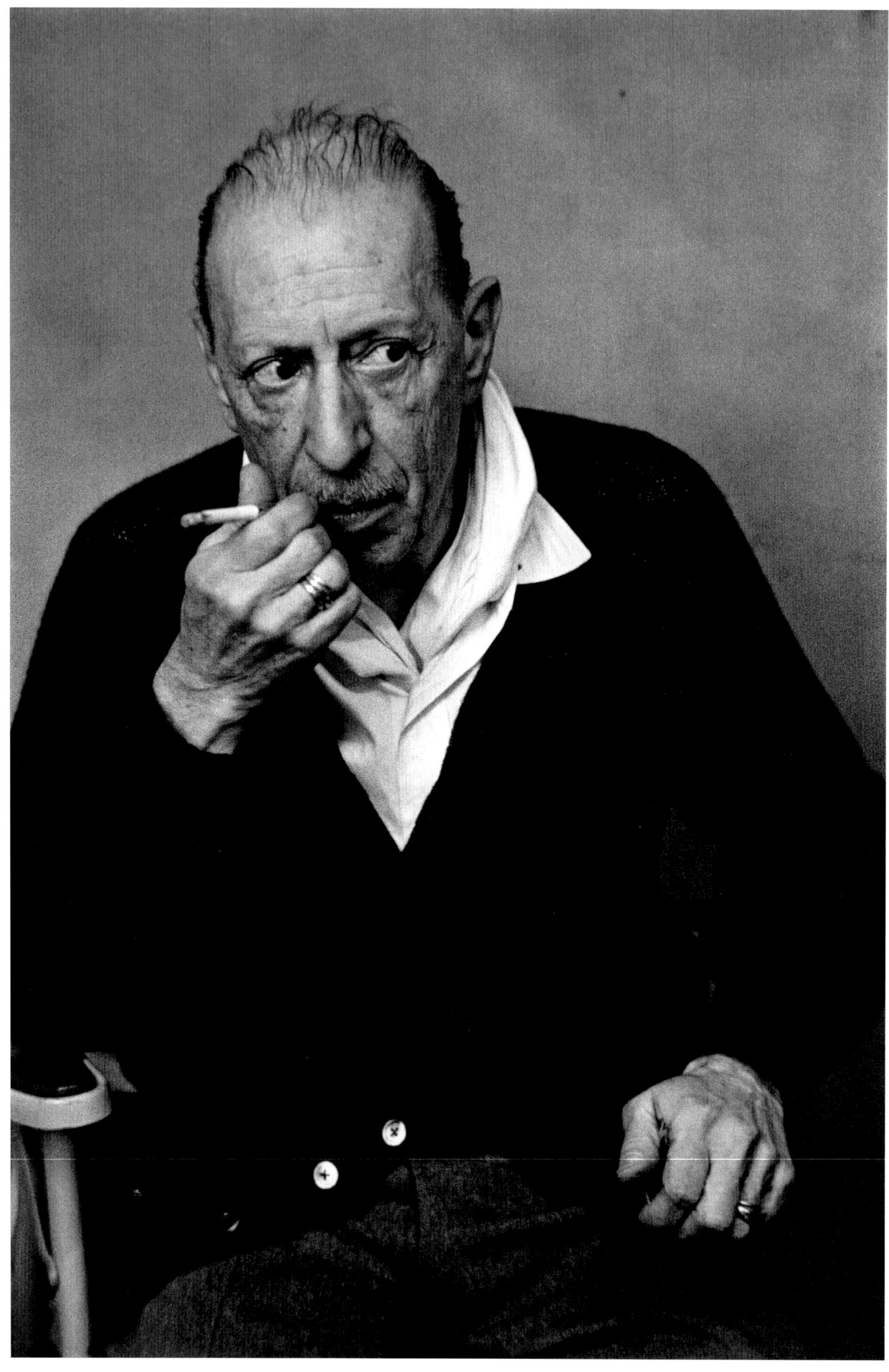

  Igor Stravinsky recording session at Columbia Studios. New York City, 1957

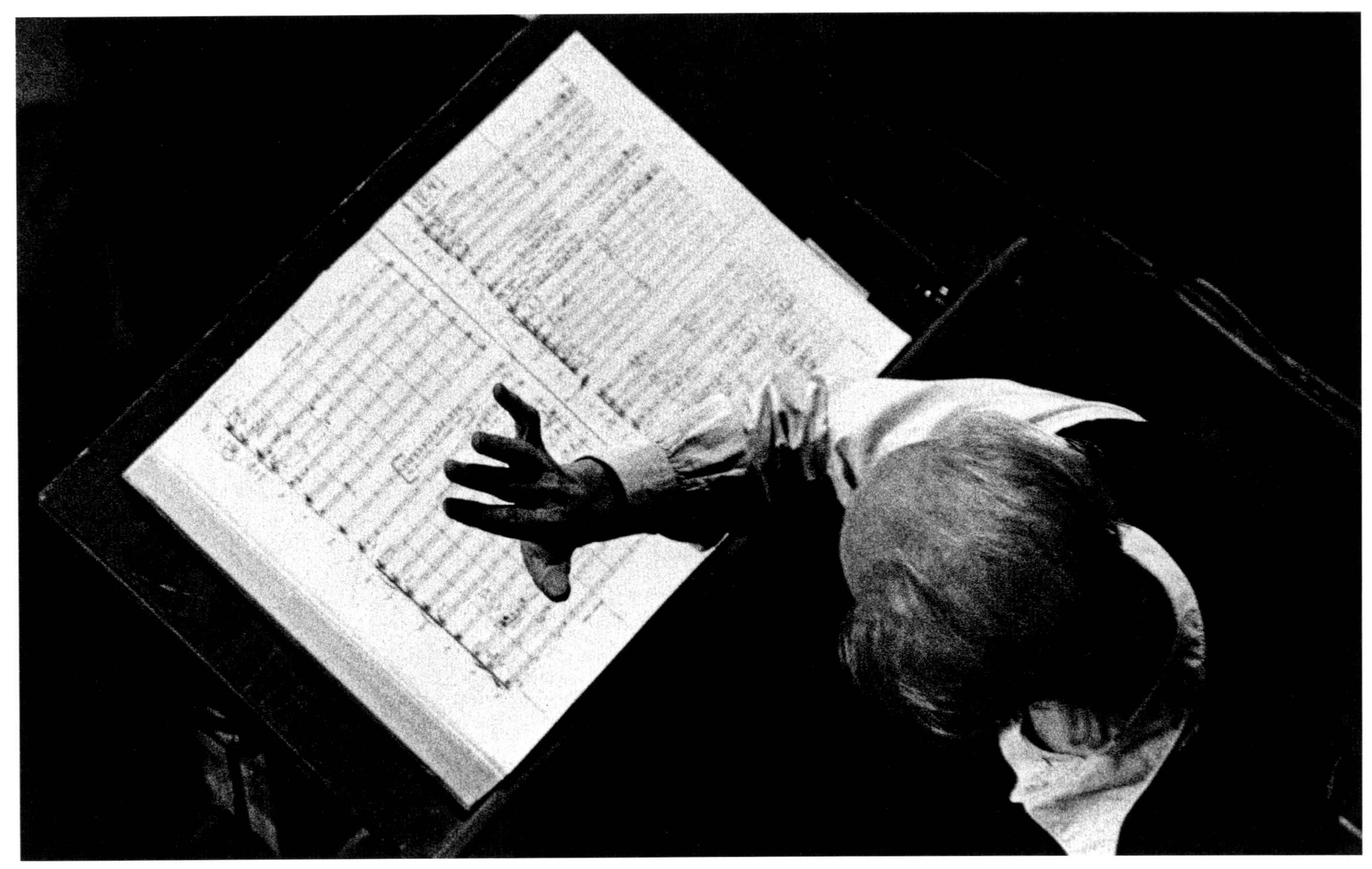

Leopold Stokowski rehearsing TURANDOT at the Metropolitan Opera. New York City, 1961 **065**

Laurence Olivier in a television
production of POWER AND GLORY. 1961

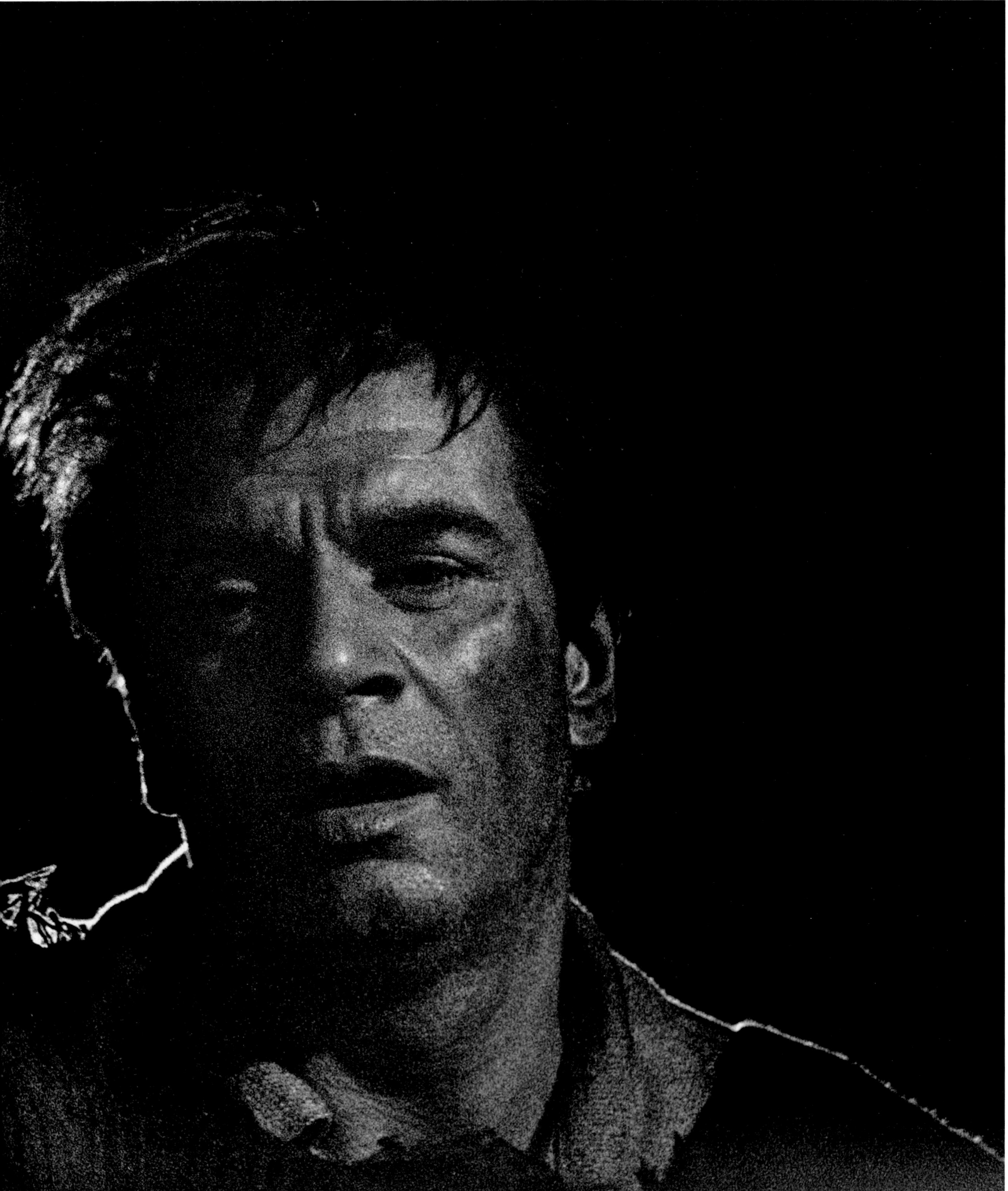

Arthur Miller and his wife Inge Morath waiting backstage at the Lincoln Center Repertory Theater on the opening night of AFTER THE FALL. New York City, 1964

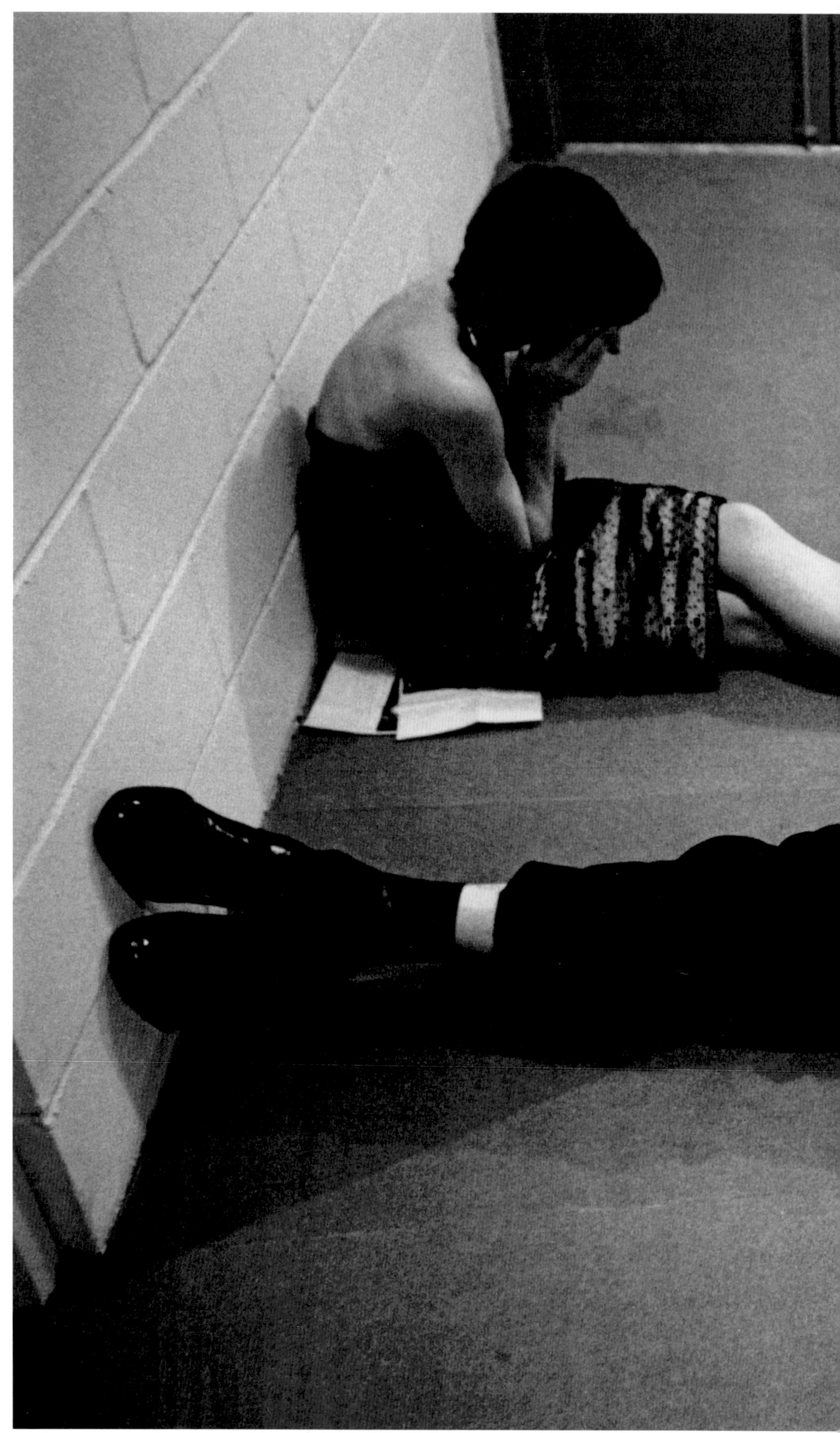

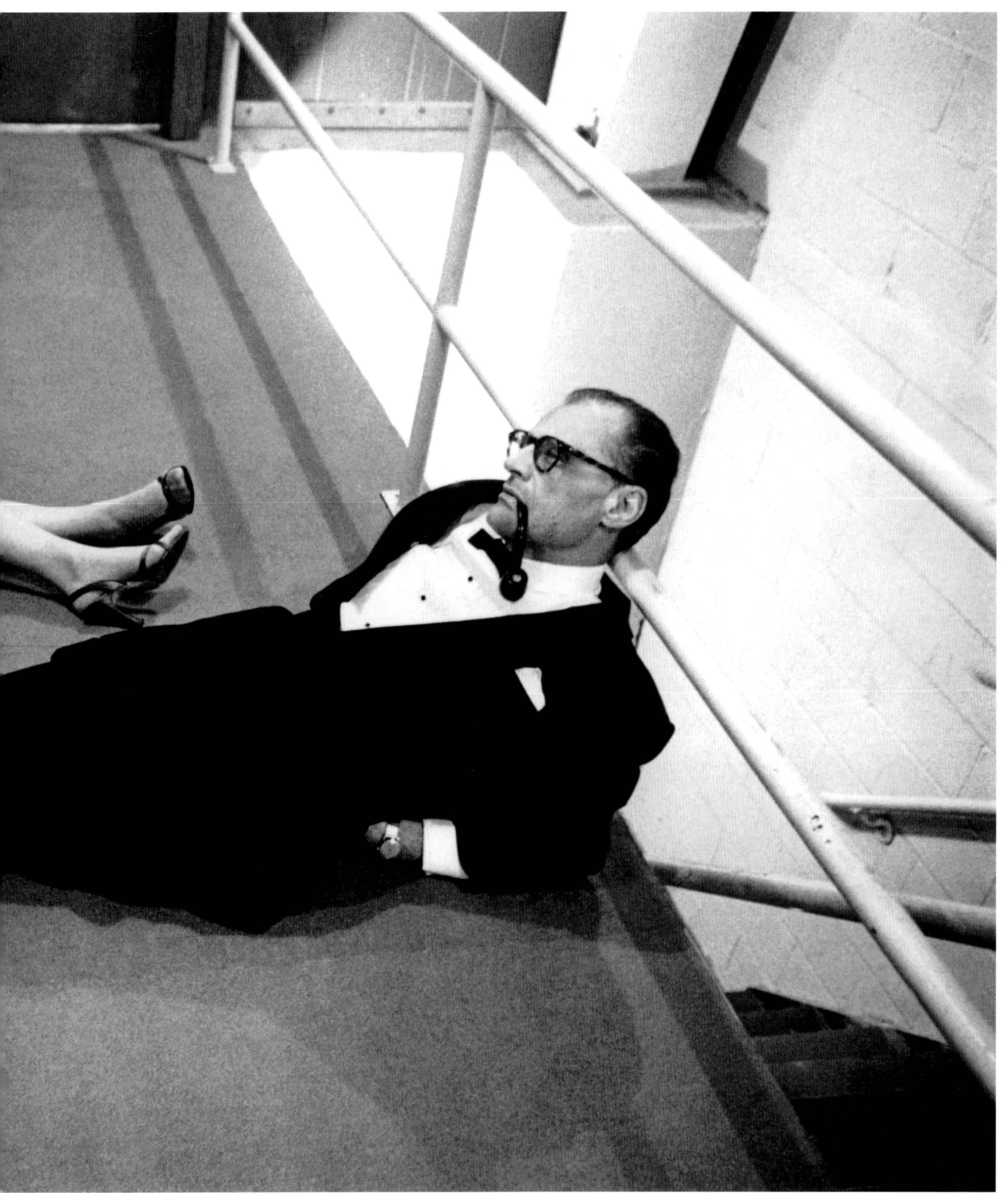

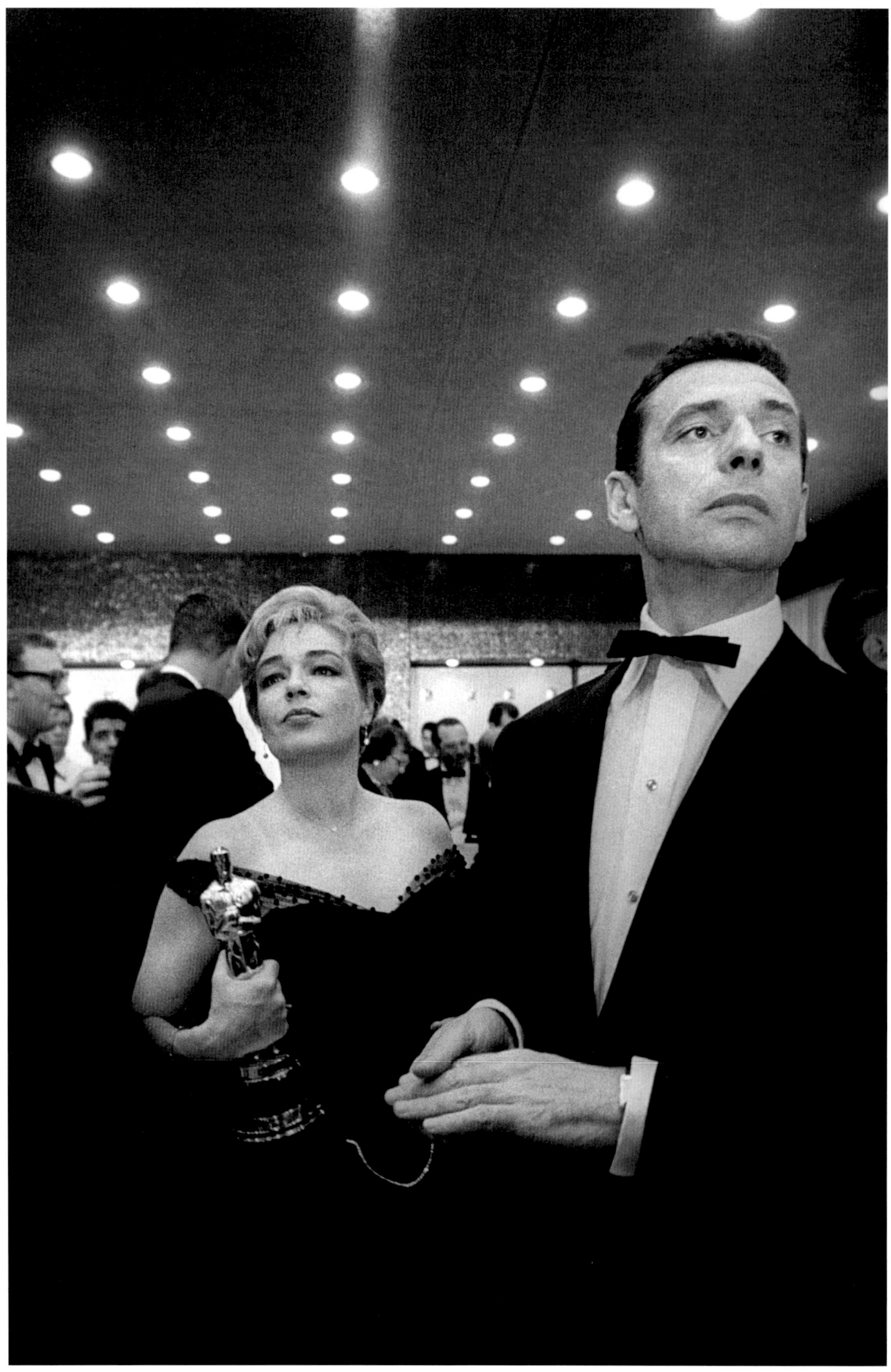

 Simone Signoret receives an Oscar for the film ROOM AT THE TOP, directed by Jack Clayton. Los Angeles, 1959

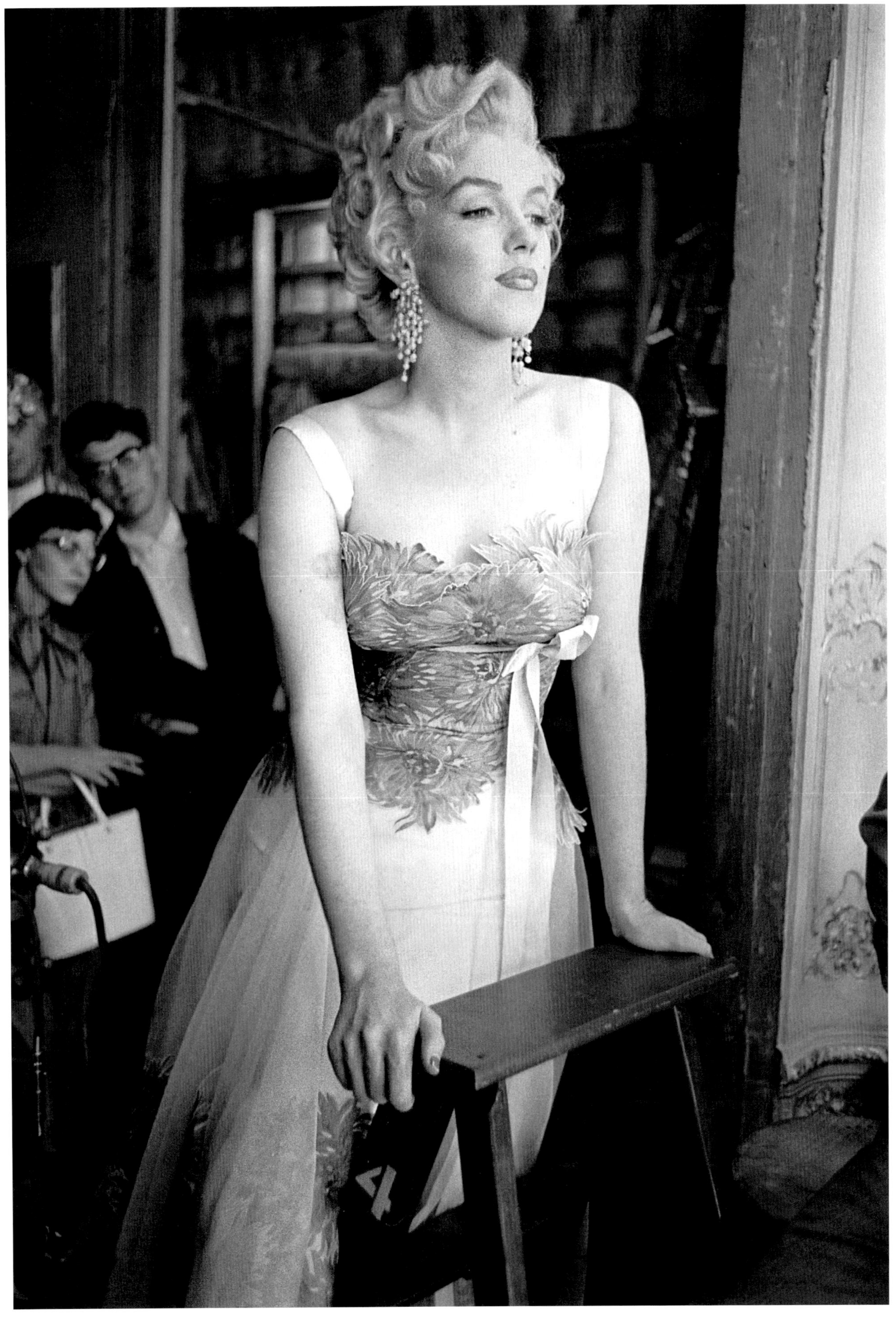

Marilyn Monroe watching the shooting of DÉSIRÉE, directed by Henry Koster. California, 1954

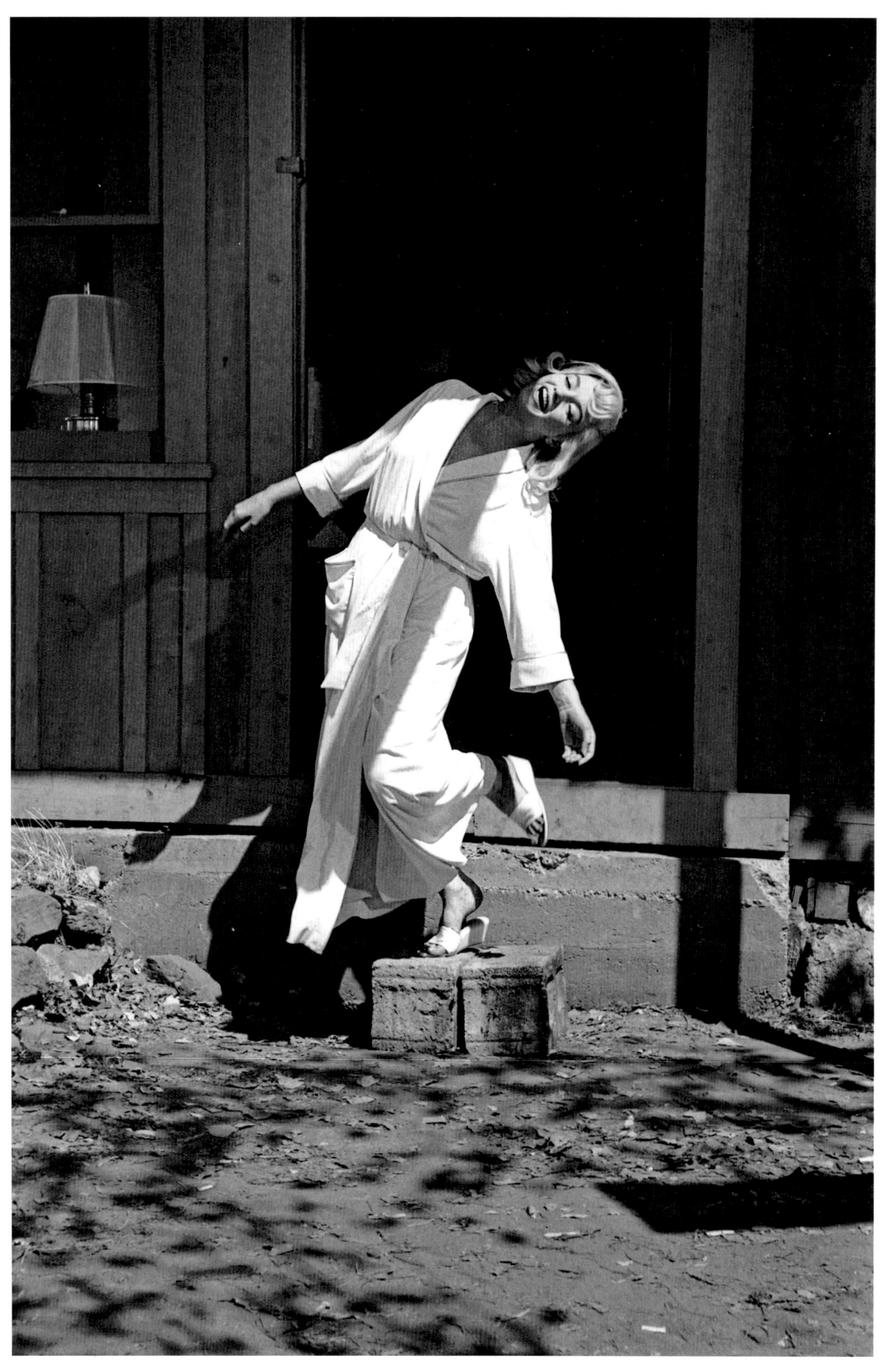

Marilyn Monroe during the shooting of THE MISFITS, directed by John Huston
and written by Arthur Miller. Nevada, 1960

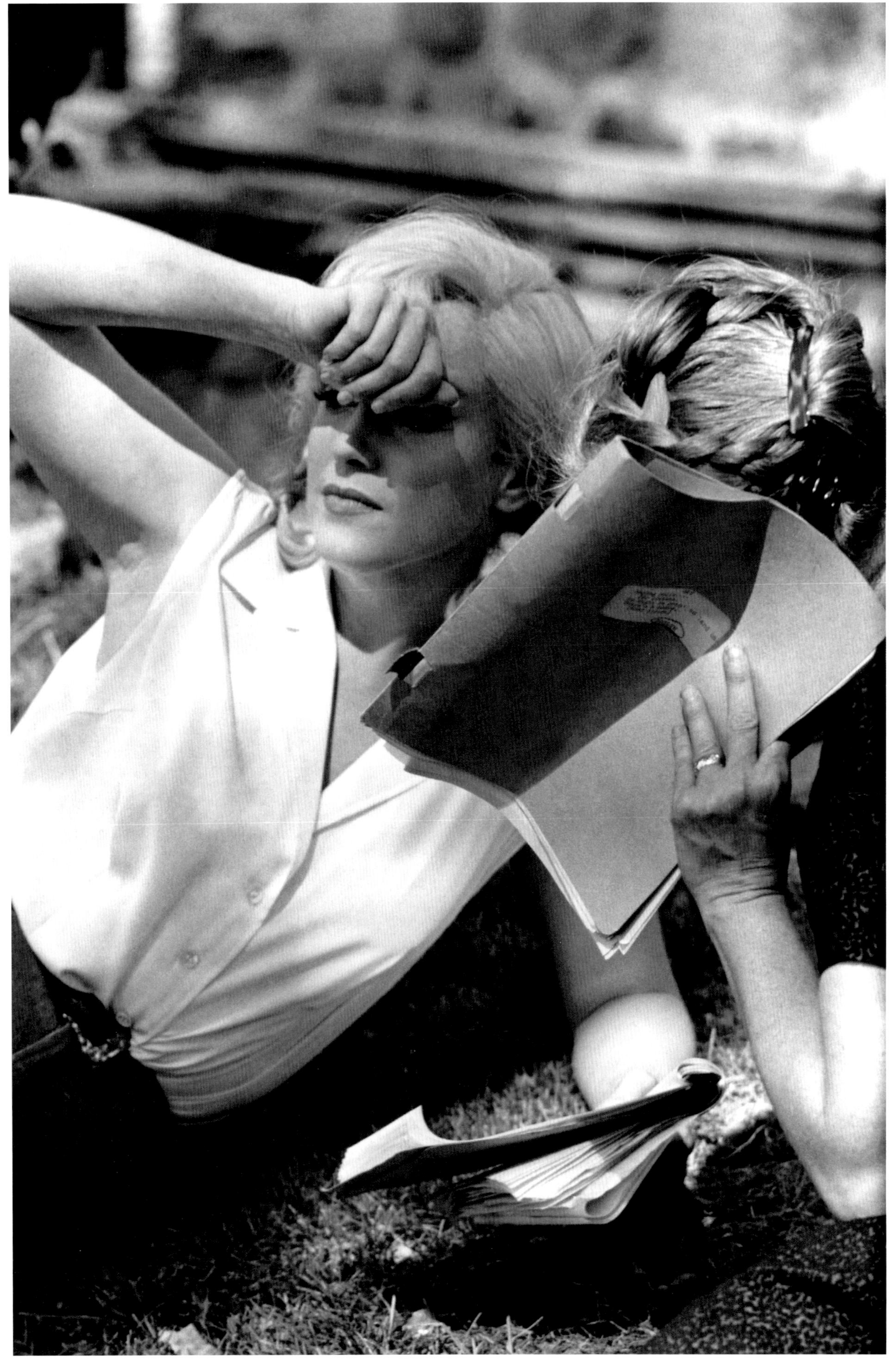

Marilyn Monroe working on her dialogue with coach Paula Strasberg for the film THE MISFITS. 1960

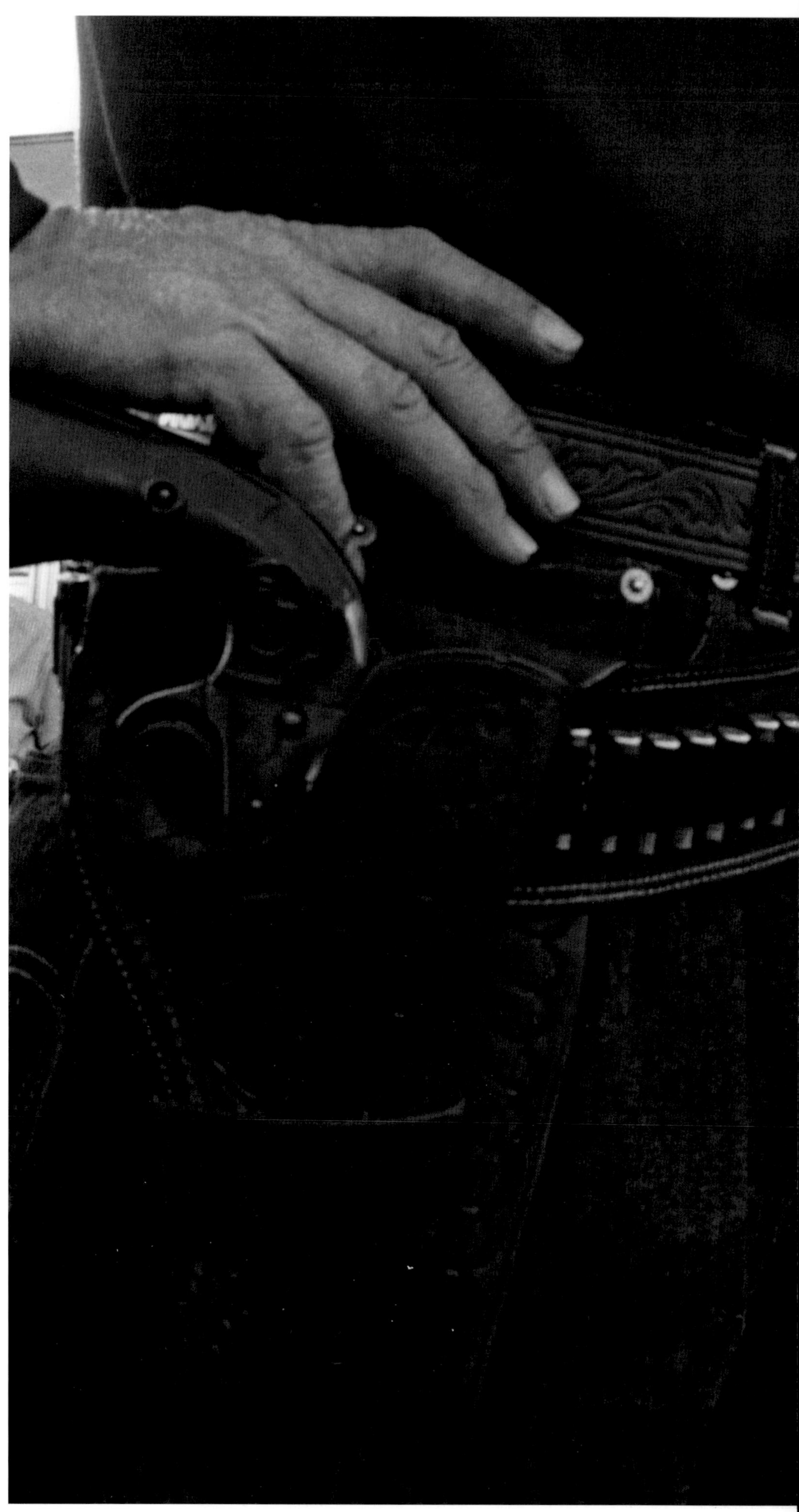

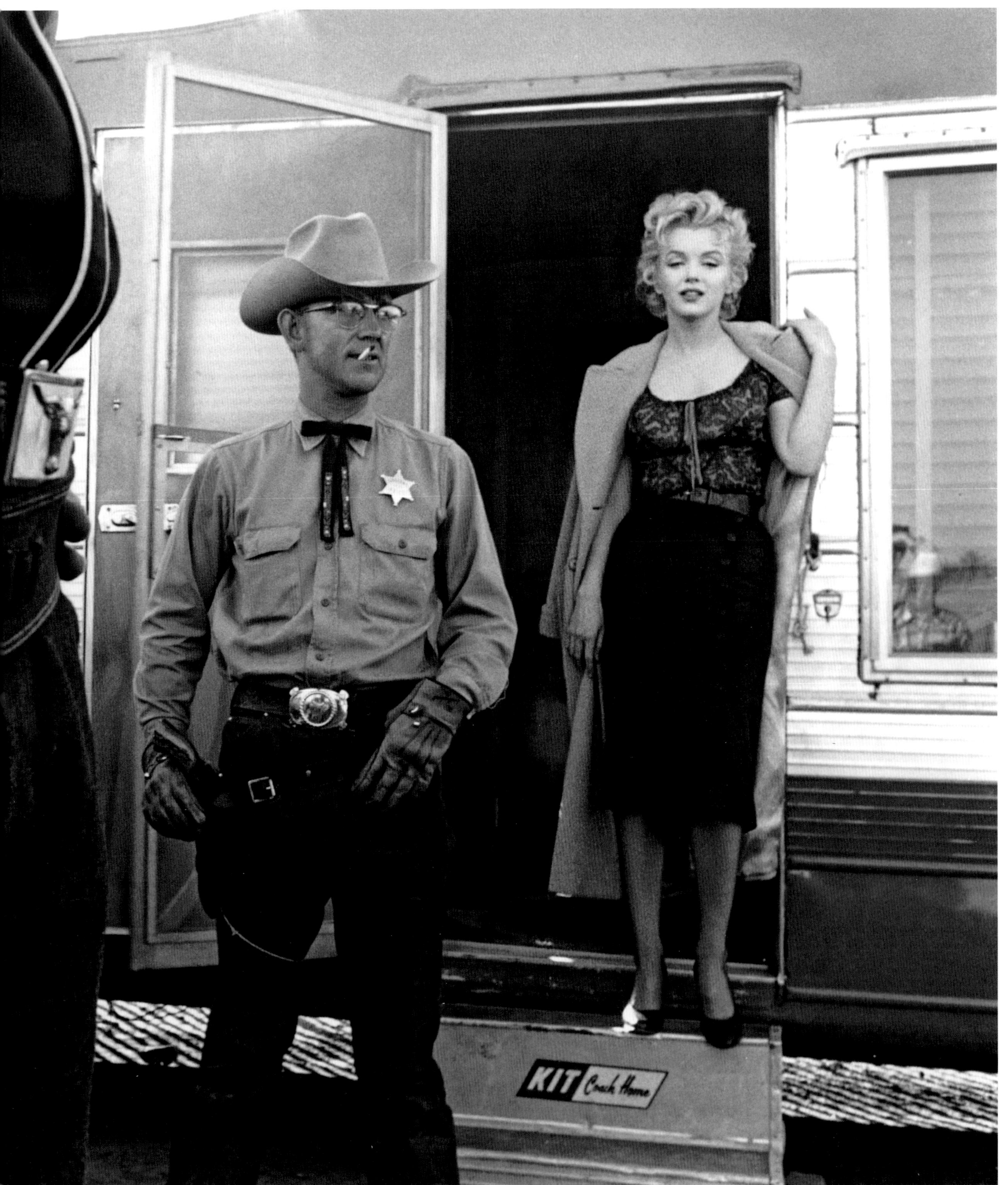

KIT Coach Home

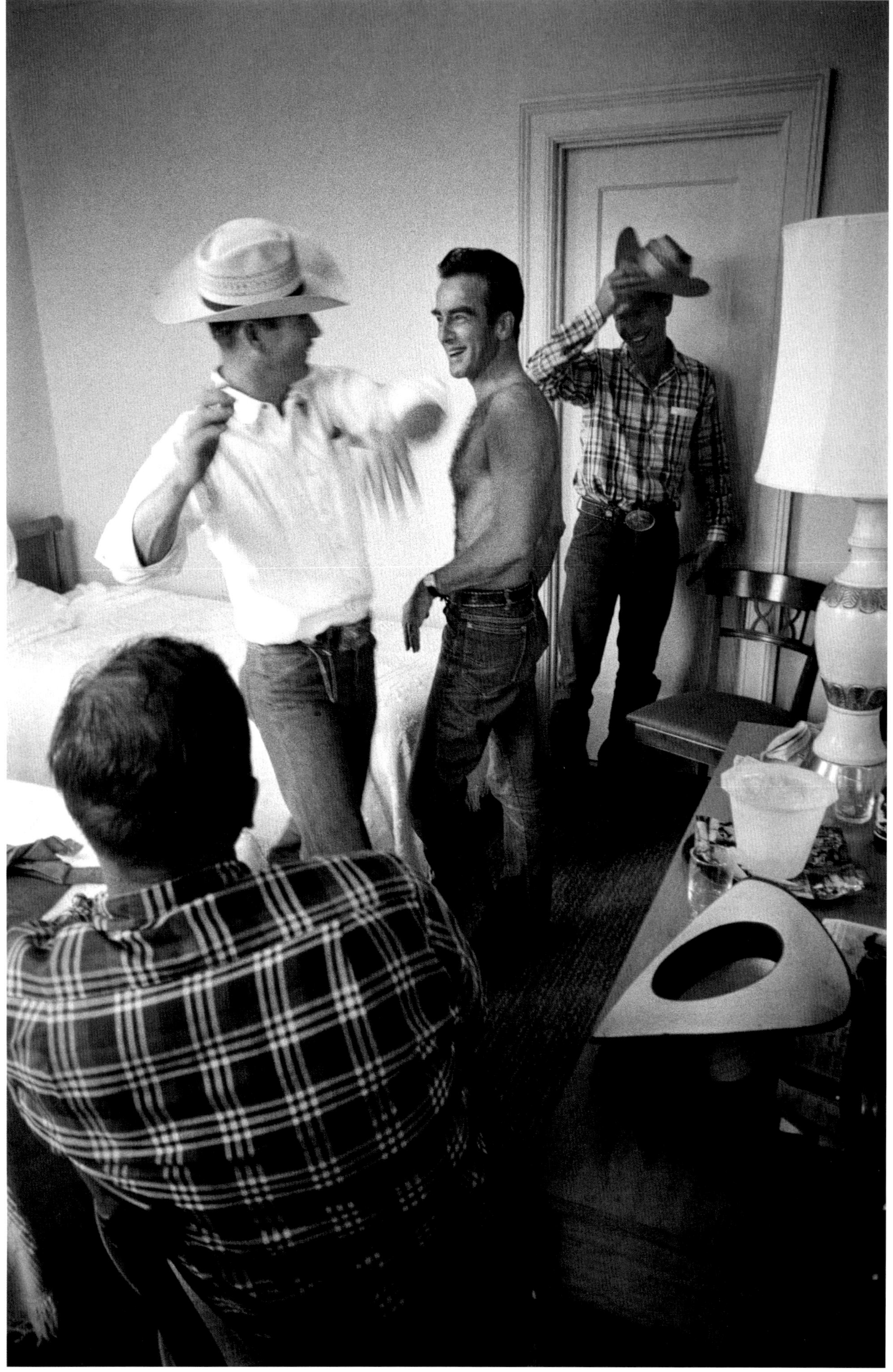

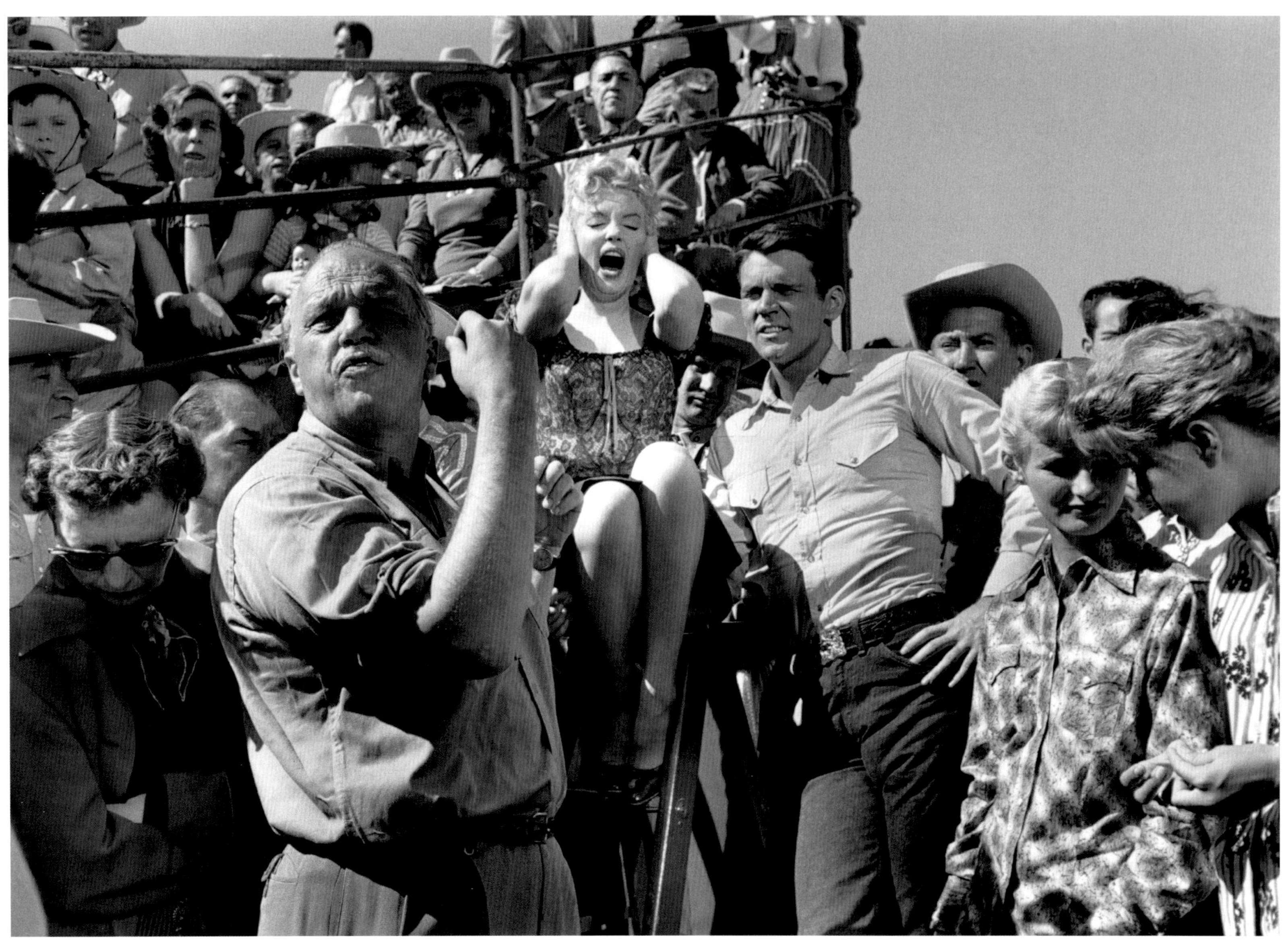

 Marilyn Monroe and co-star Don Murray in the film BUS STOP. Hollywood, 1956

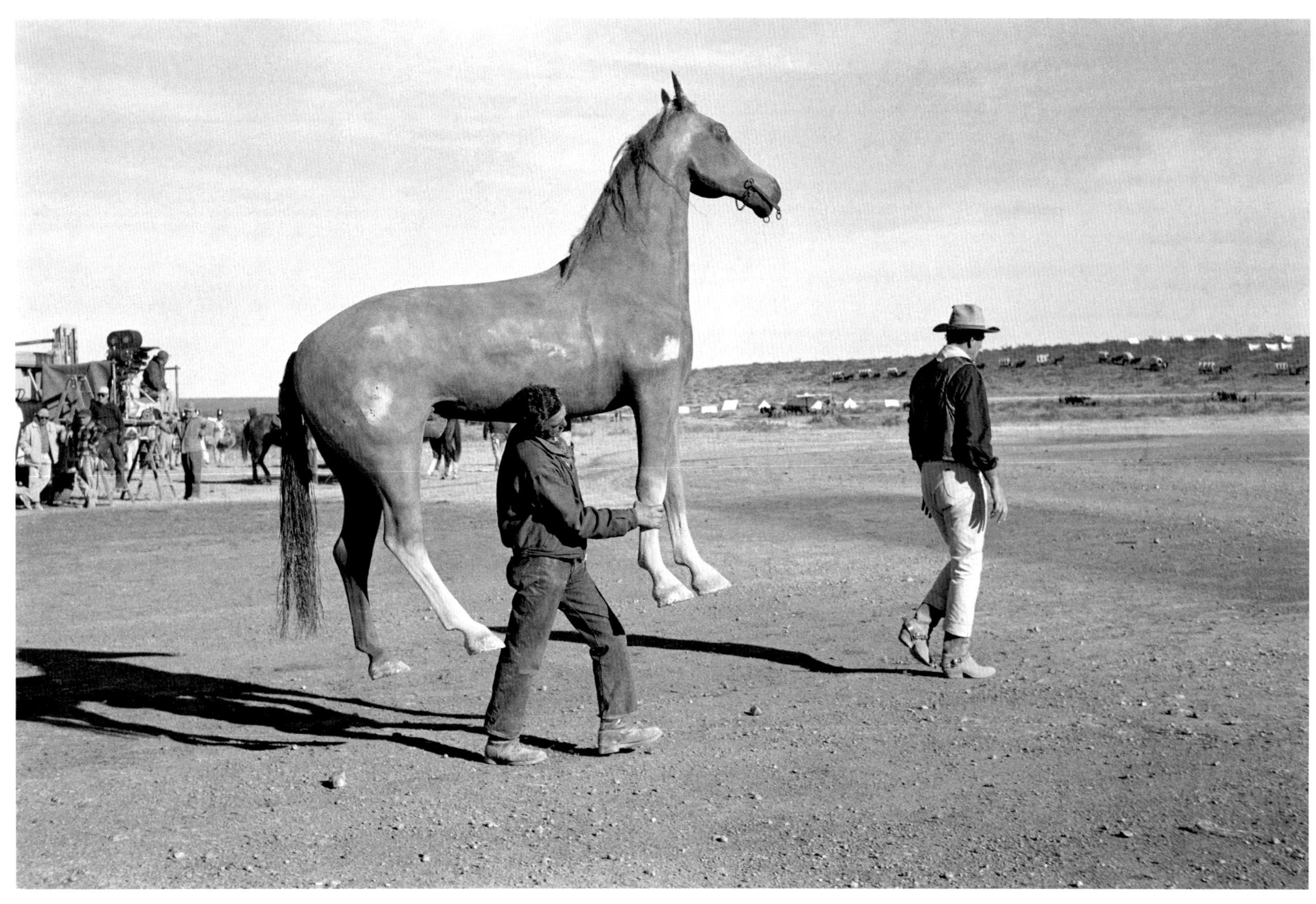

John Wayne on the set of the movie THE ALAMO. 1959

John Wayne on the set of the
movie THE ALAMO. 1959

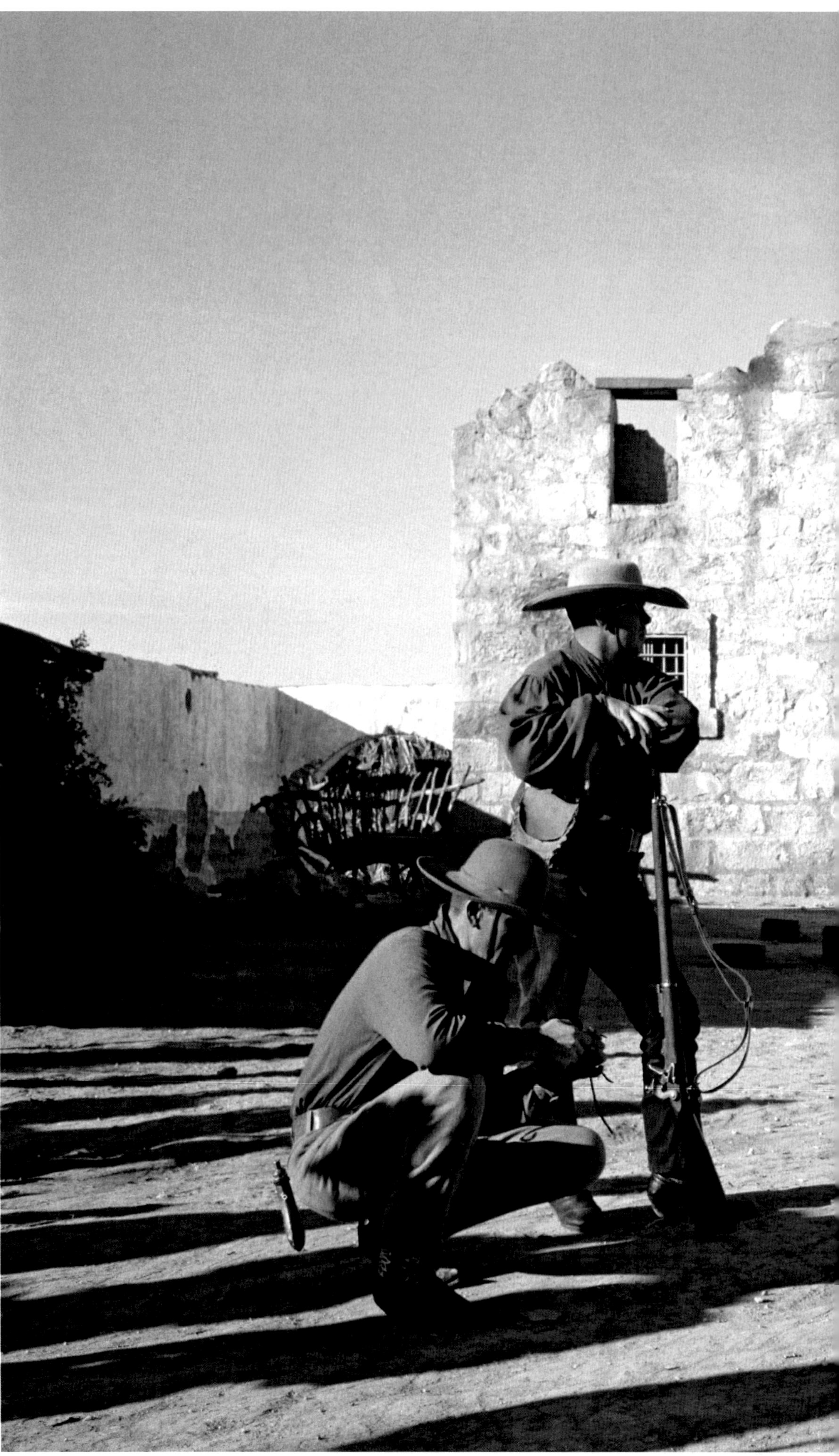

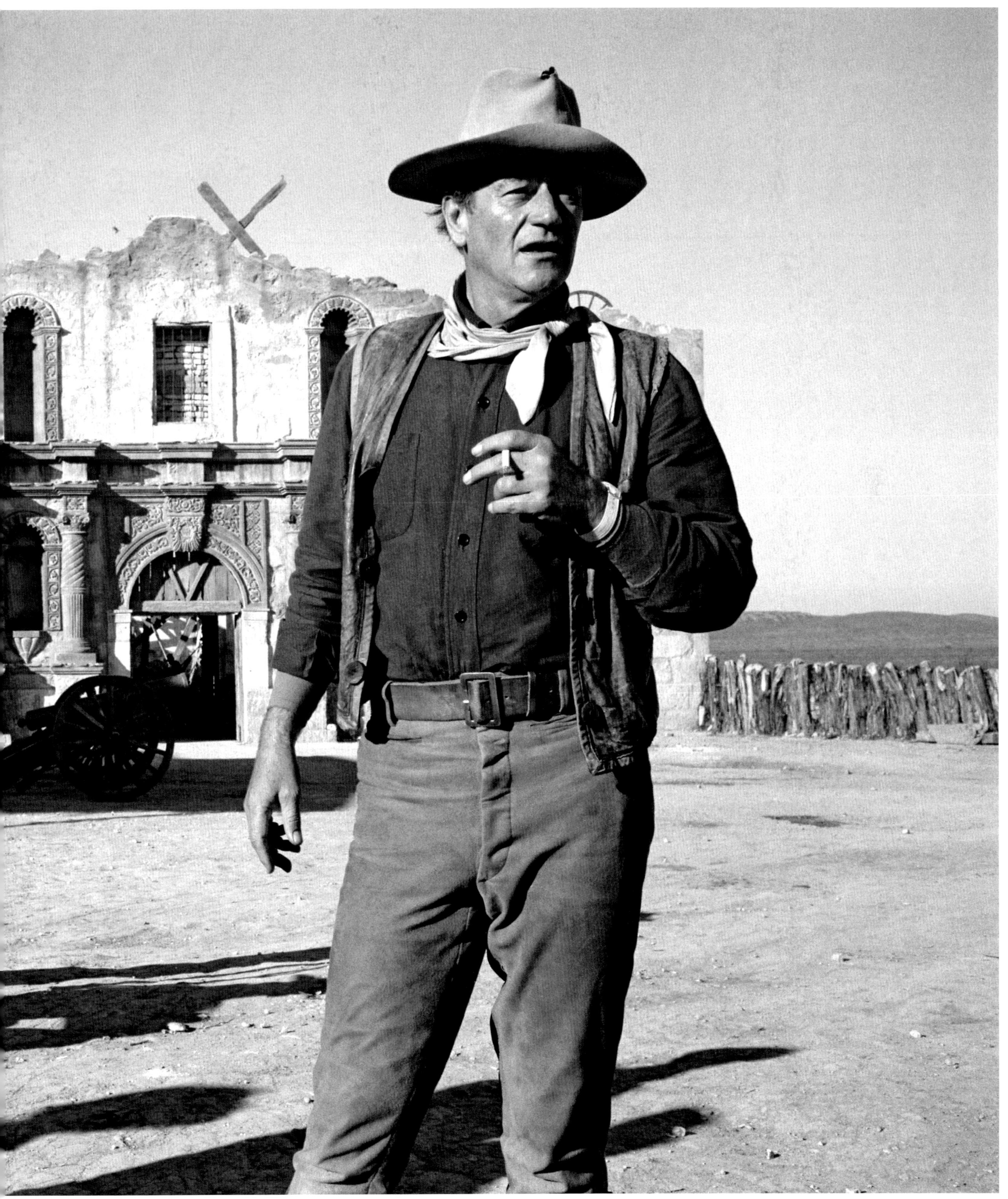

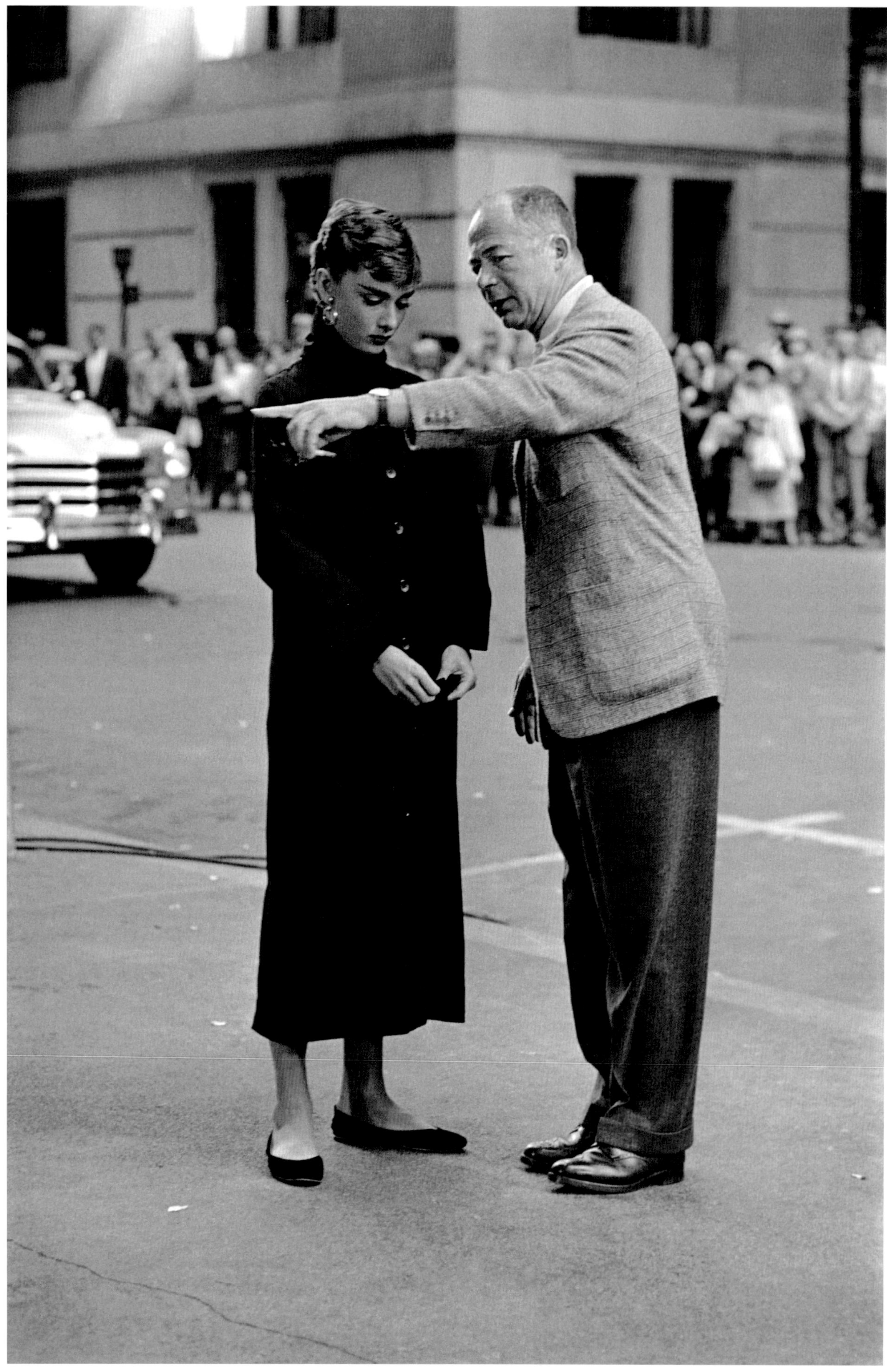

 Audrey Hepburn and Billy Wilder during the filming of SABRINA. New York City, 1954

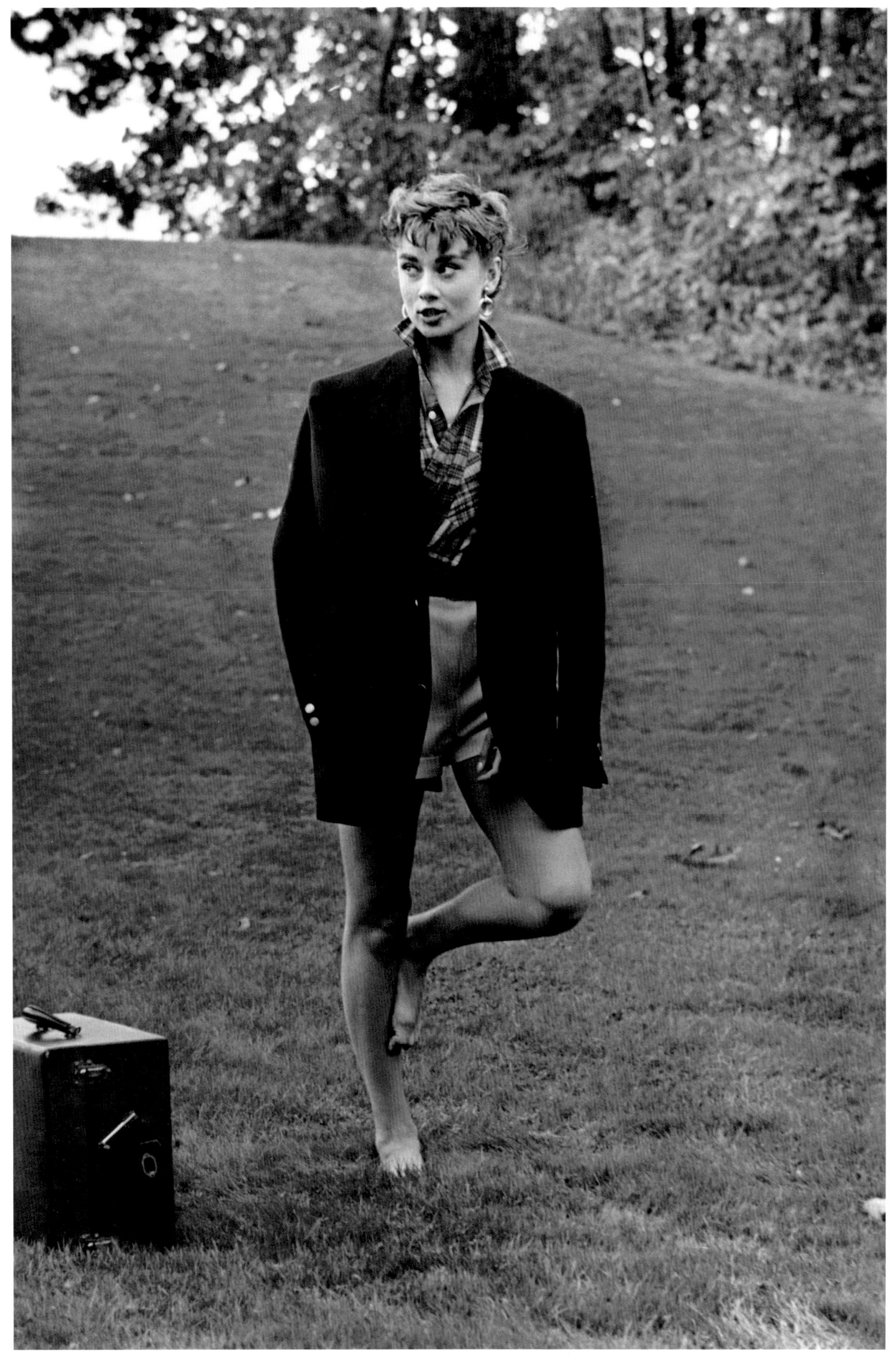

Audrey Hepburn during the filming of SABRINA. Long Island, New York, 1954

Audrey Hepburn during the filming of SABRINA,
directed by Billy Wilder. New York City, 1954

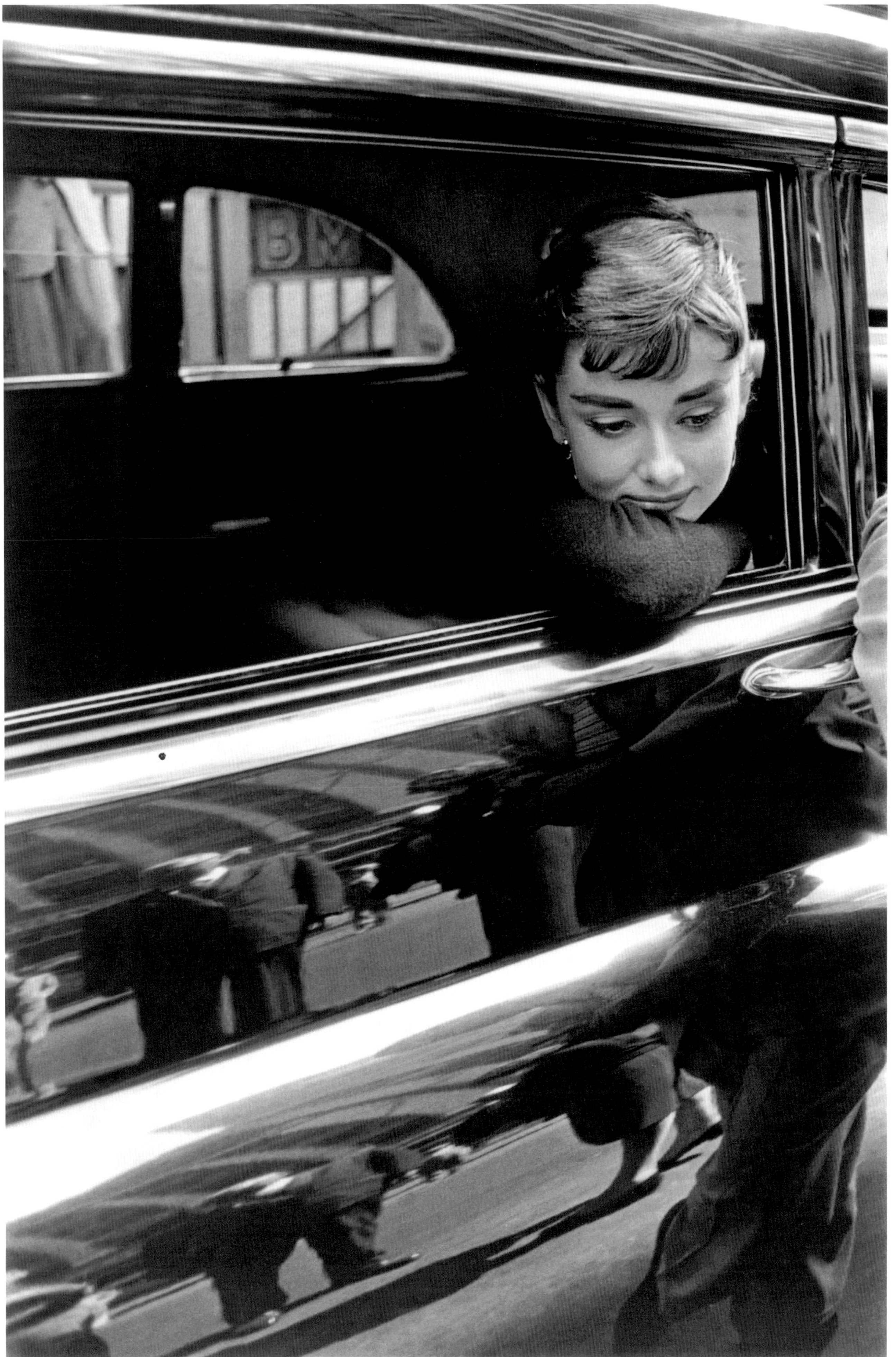

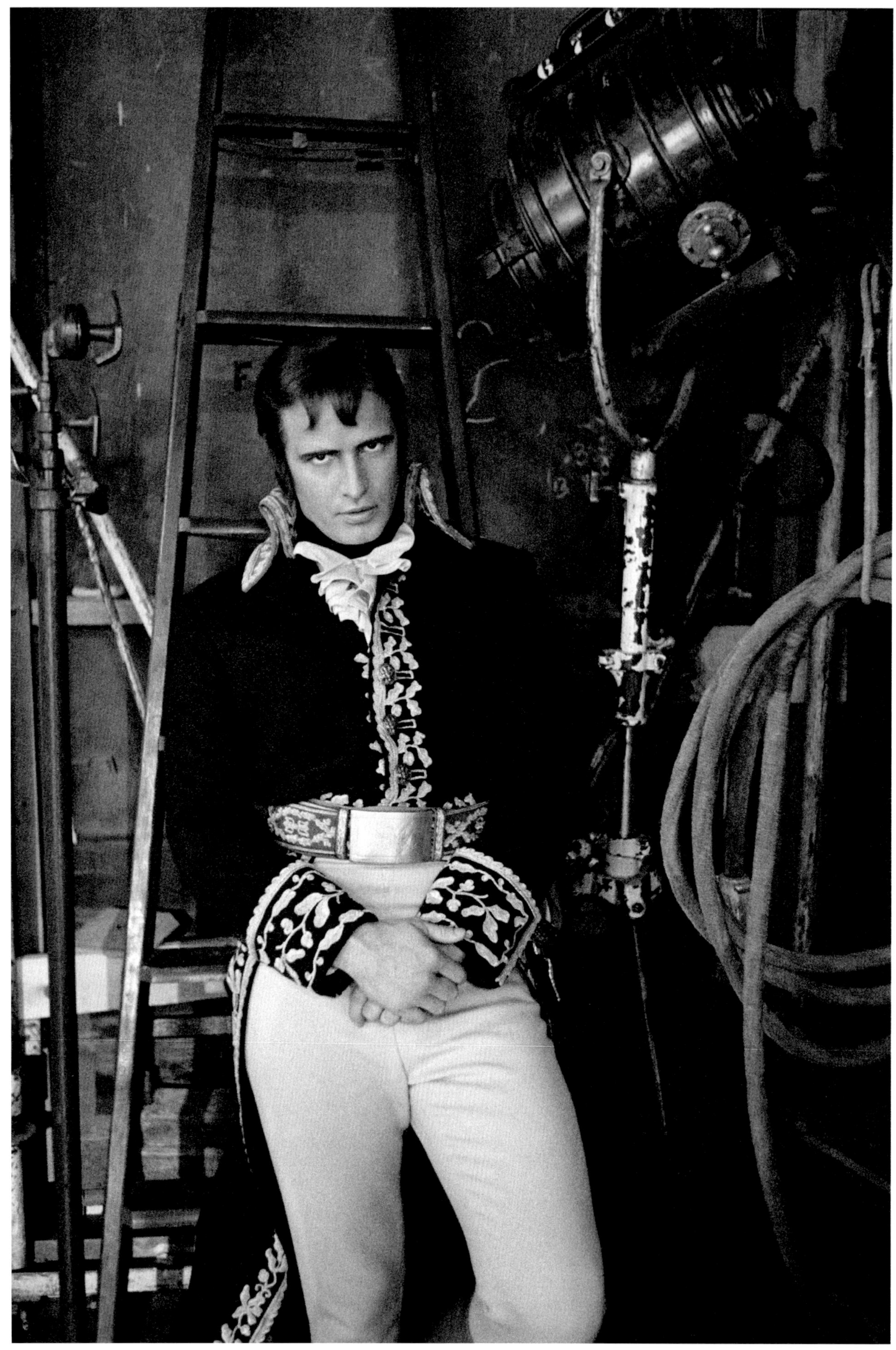

 Marlon Brando as Napoleon during the filming of DÉSIRÉE, directed by Henry Koster. 1954

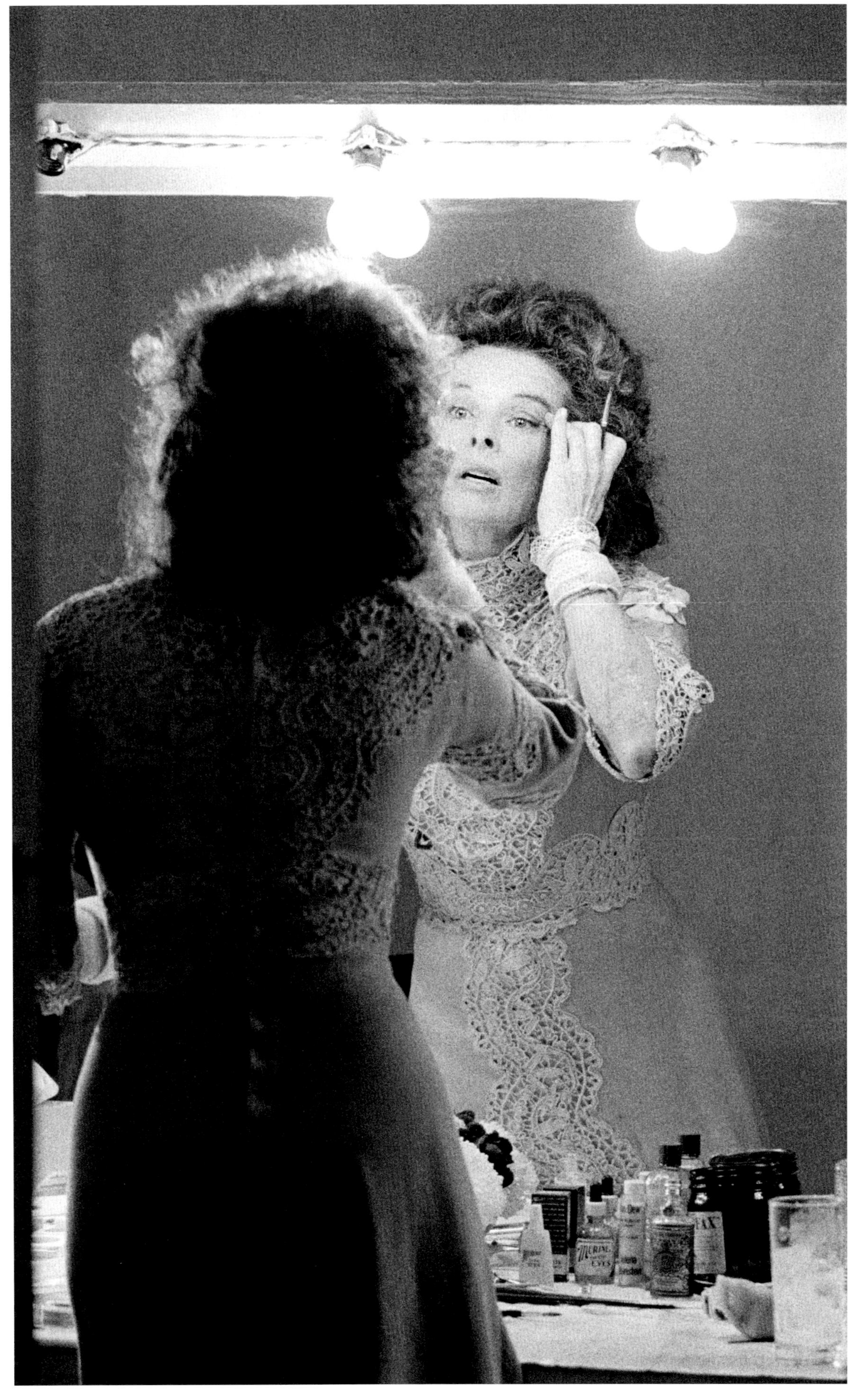

Katharine Hepburn in the make-up room on the set of LONG DAY'S JOURNEY INTO NIGHT. New York City, 1961 **087**

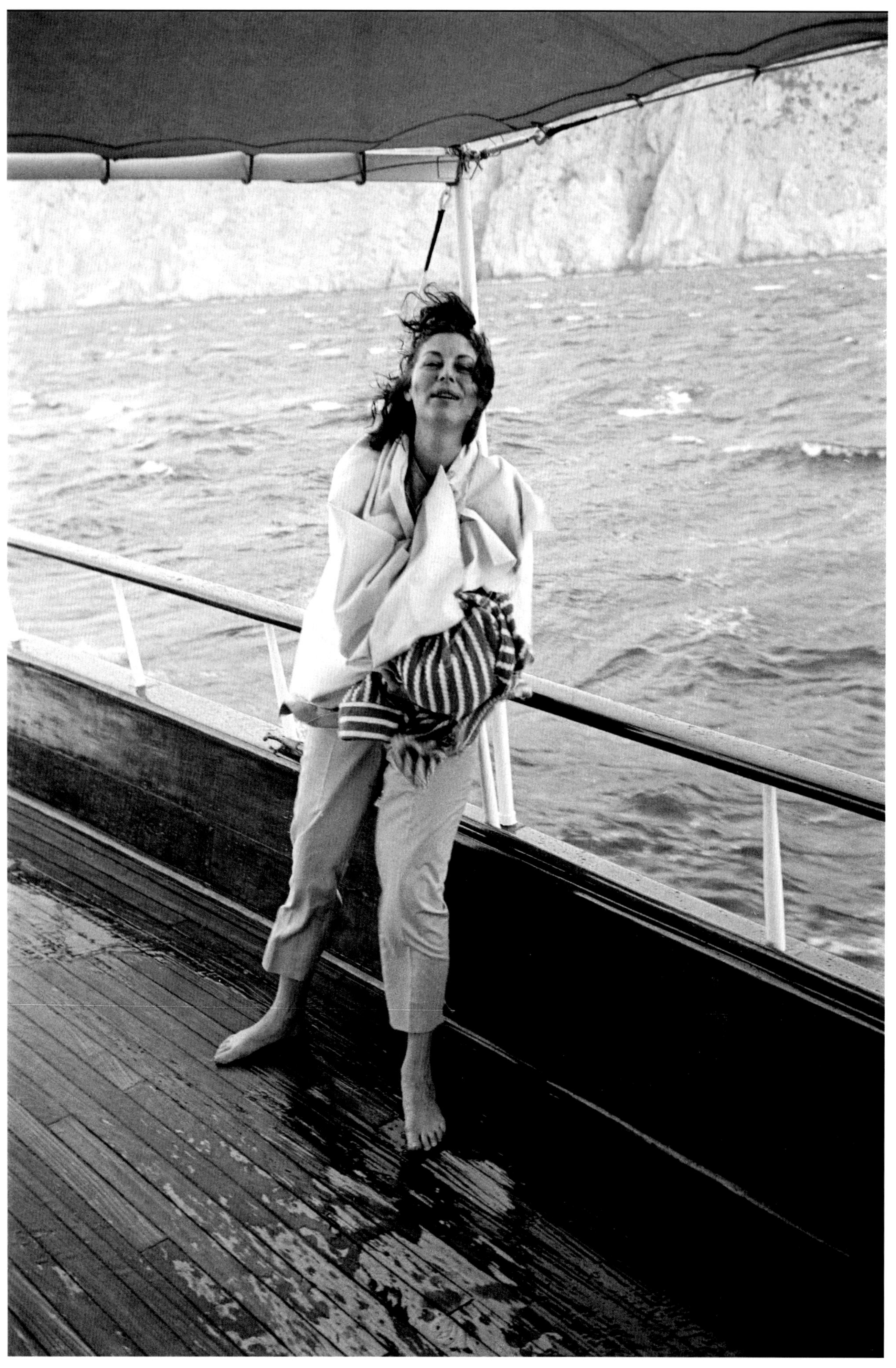

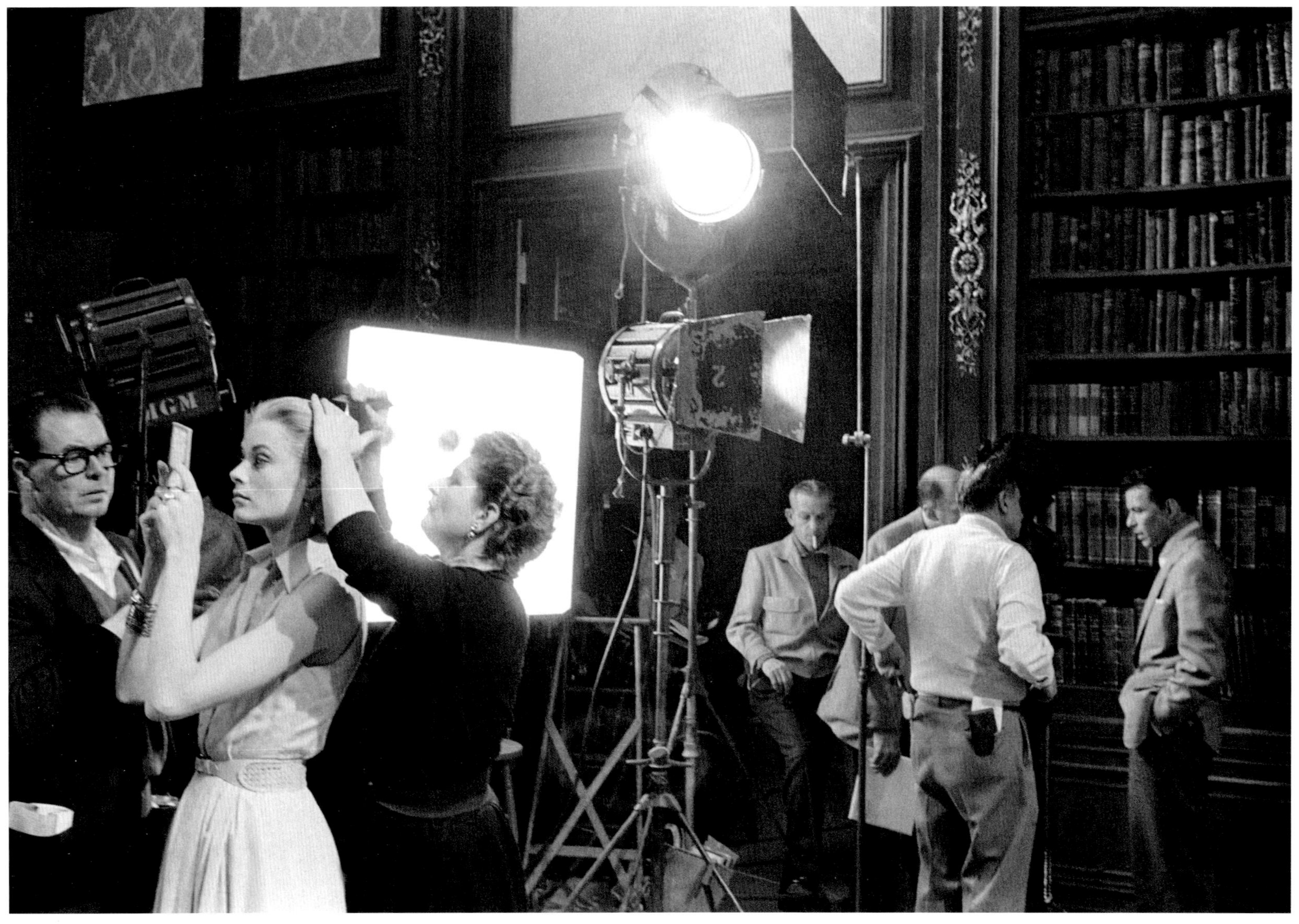

left
Ava Gardner on the yacht of Samuel Bronston in the waters around Mallorca, during
the filming of 55 DAYS AT PEKING, directed by Nicholas Ray. Mallorca, Spain, 1962

above
The shooting of the film HIGH SOCIETY, directed by Charles Walters, which featured
Bing Crosby, Frank Sinatra, Grace Kelly, Celeste Holm, and Louis Armstrong. Here, a scene
with Grace Kelly playing a rich girl. Hollywood, 1956

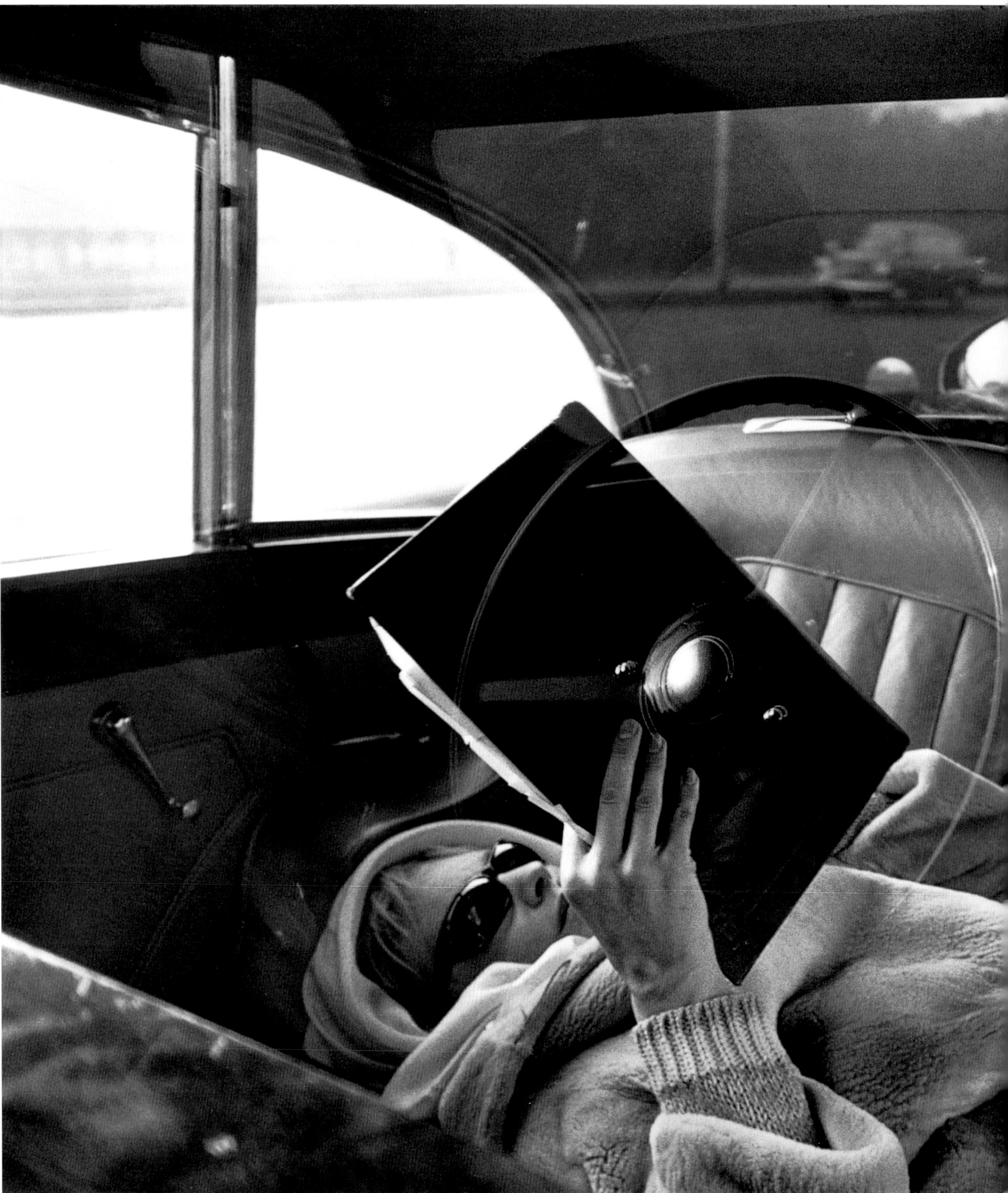

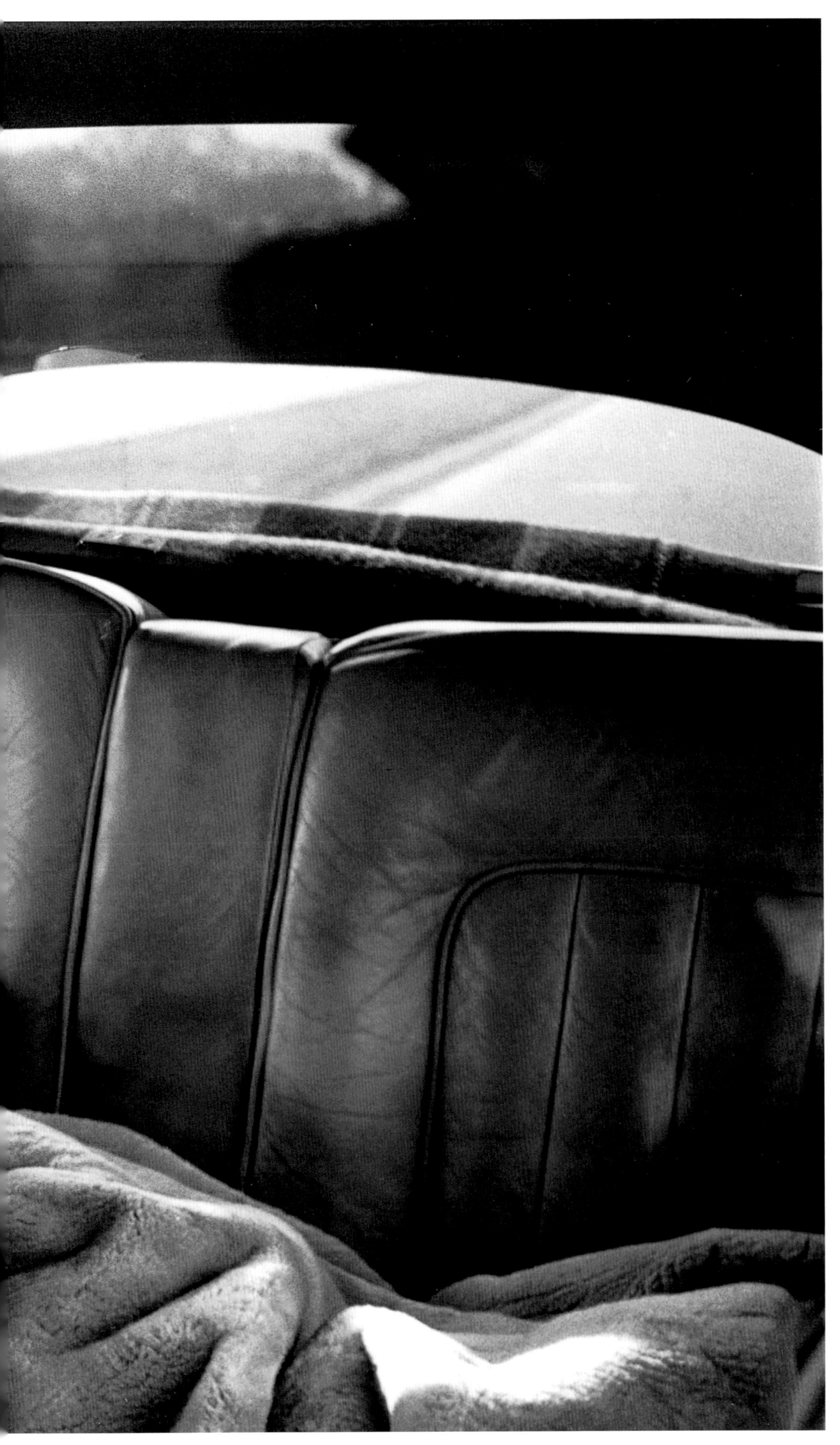

Swedish actress Ingrid Thulin.
England, 1965

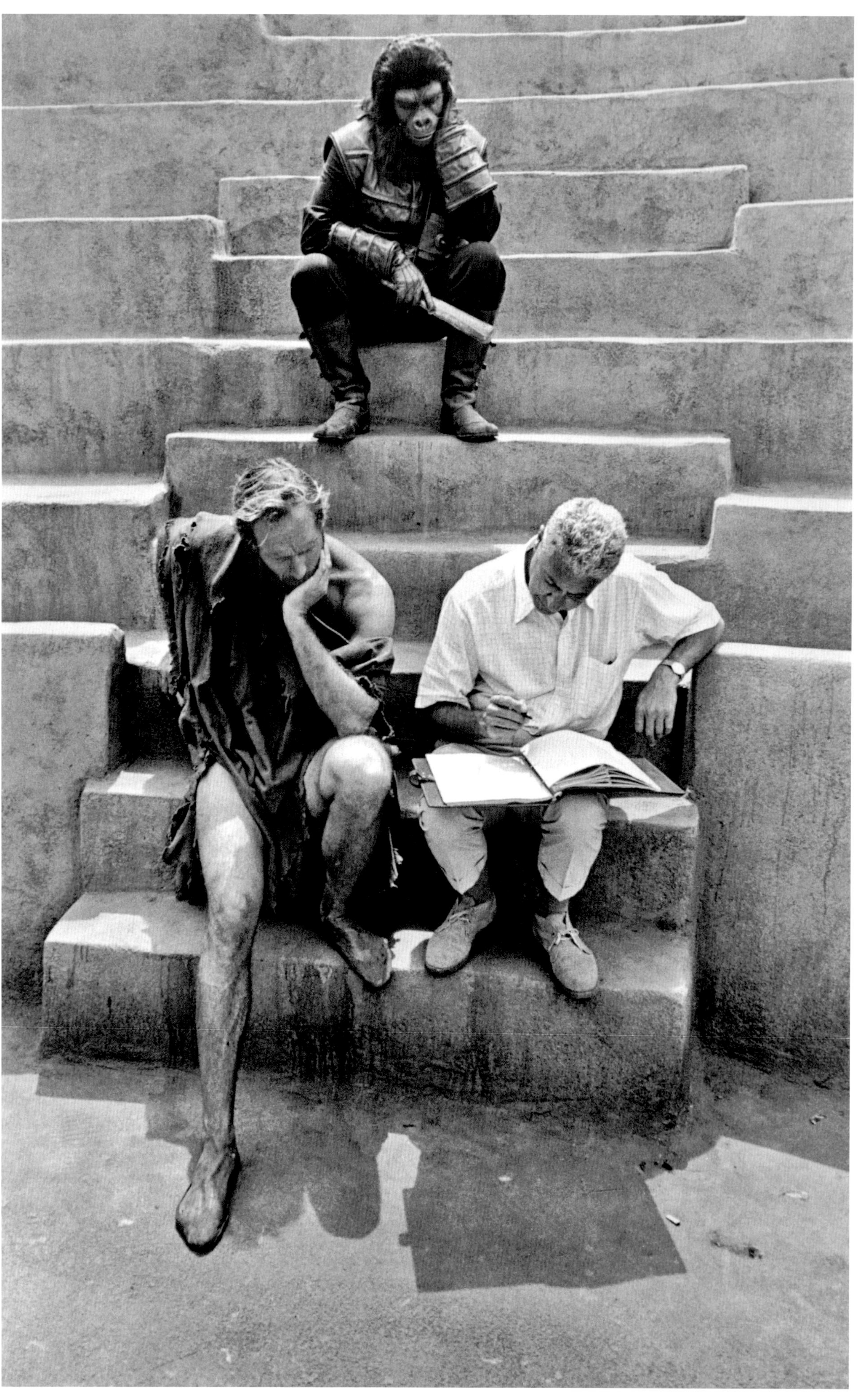

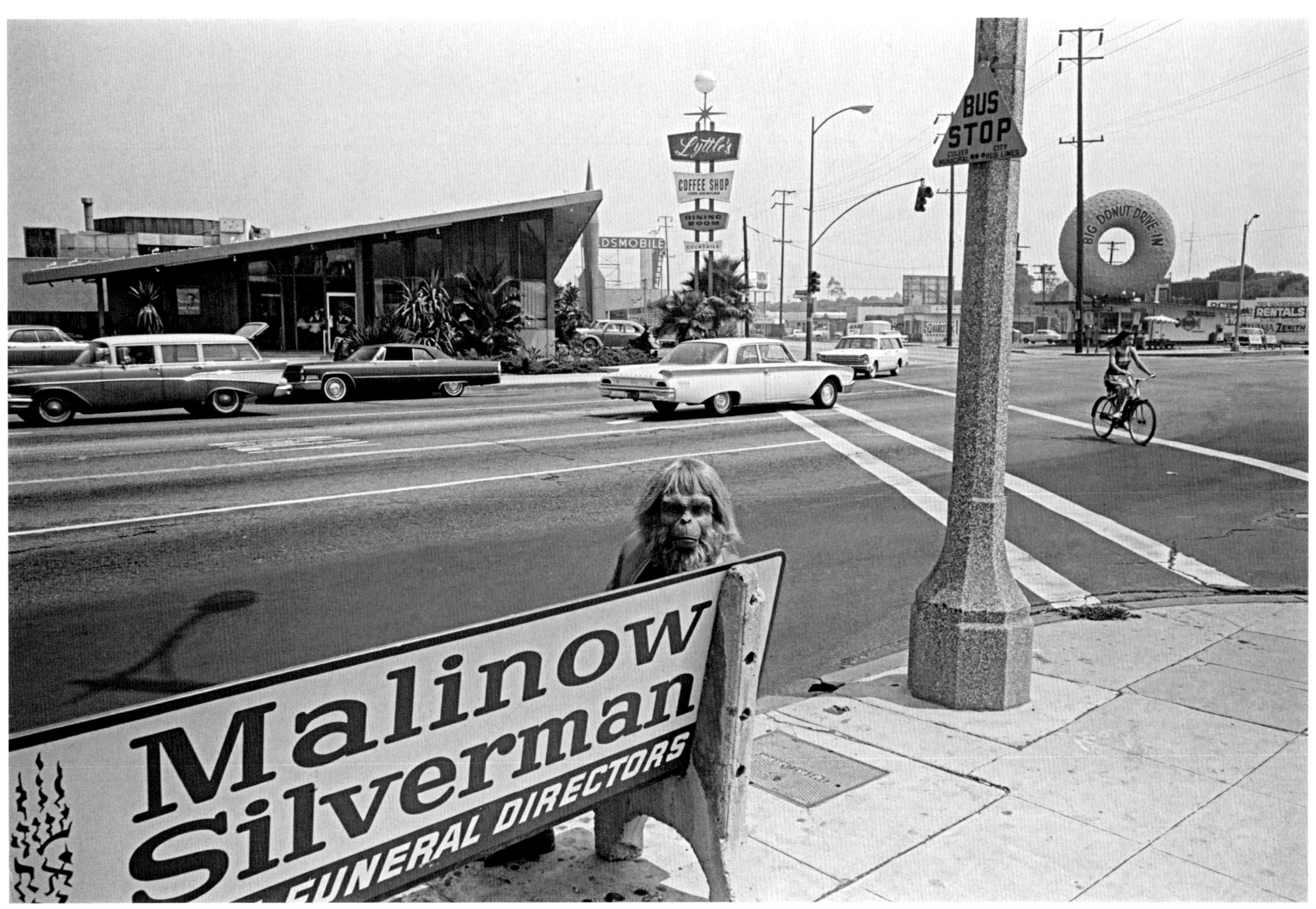

left
PLANET OF THE APES, directed by Franklin J. Schaffner,
featuring Charlton Heston (left), Roddy McDowall, Kim Hunter,
and Maurice Evans. California, 1967

above
PLANET OF THE APES. 1967

FAIRS &
FESTIVAL

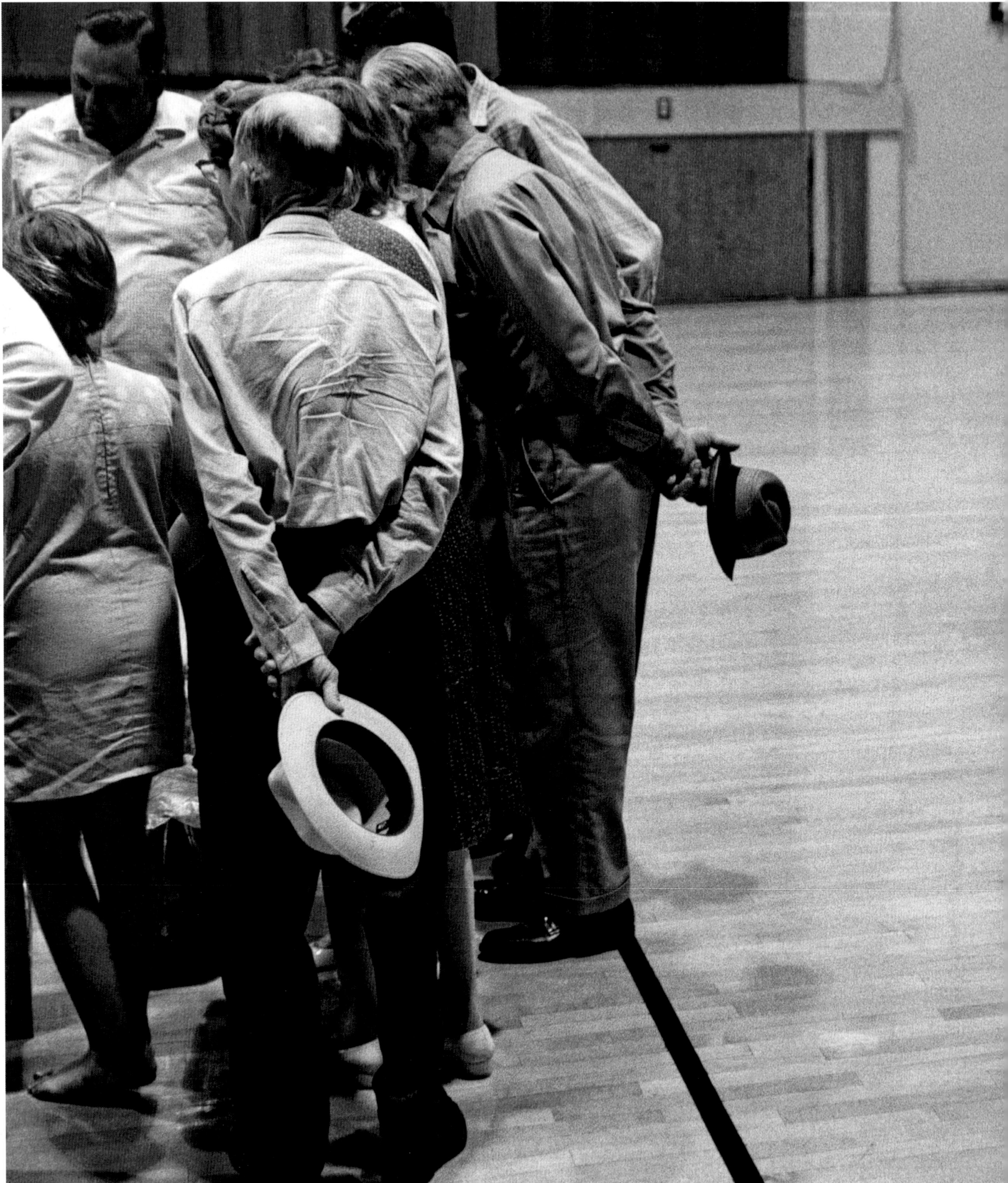

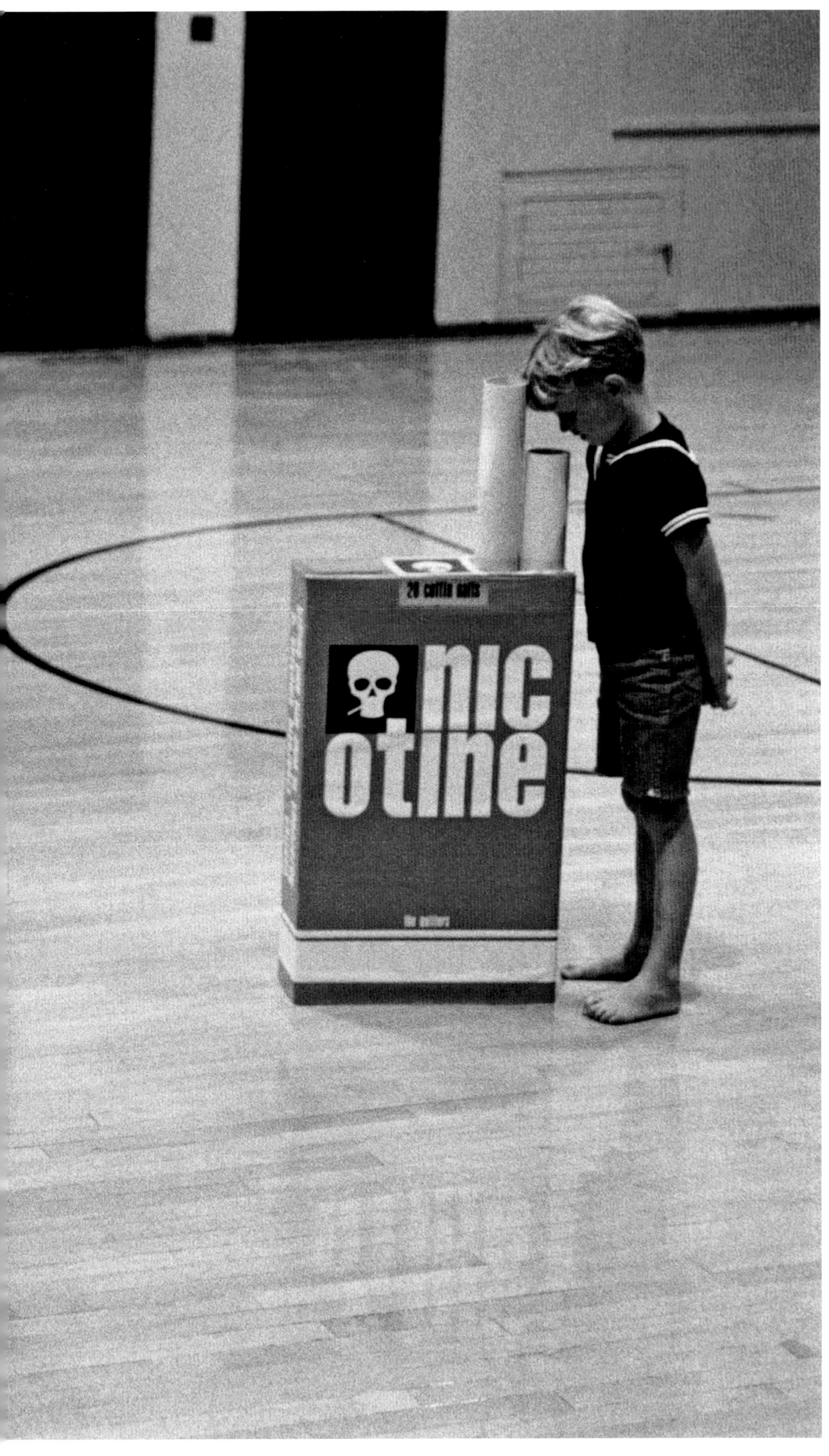
20 coffin nails
nic
otine
the antidote

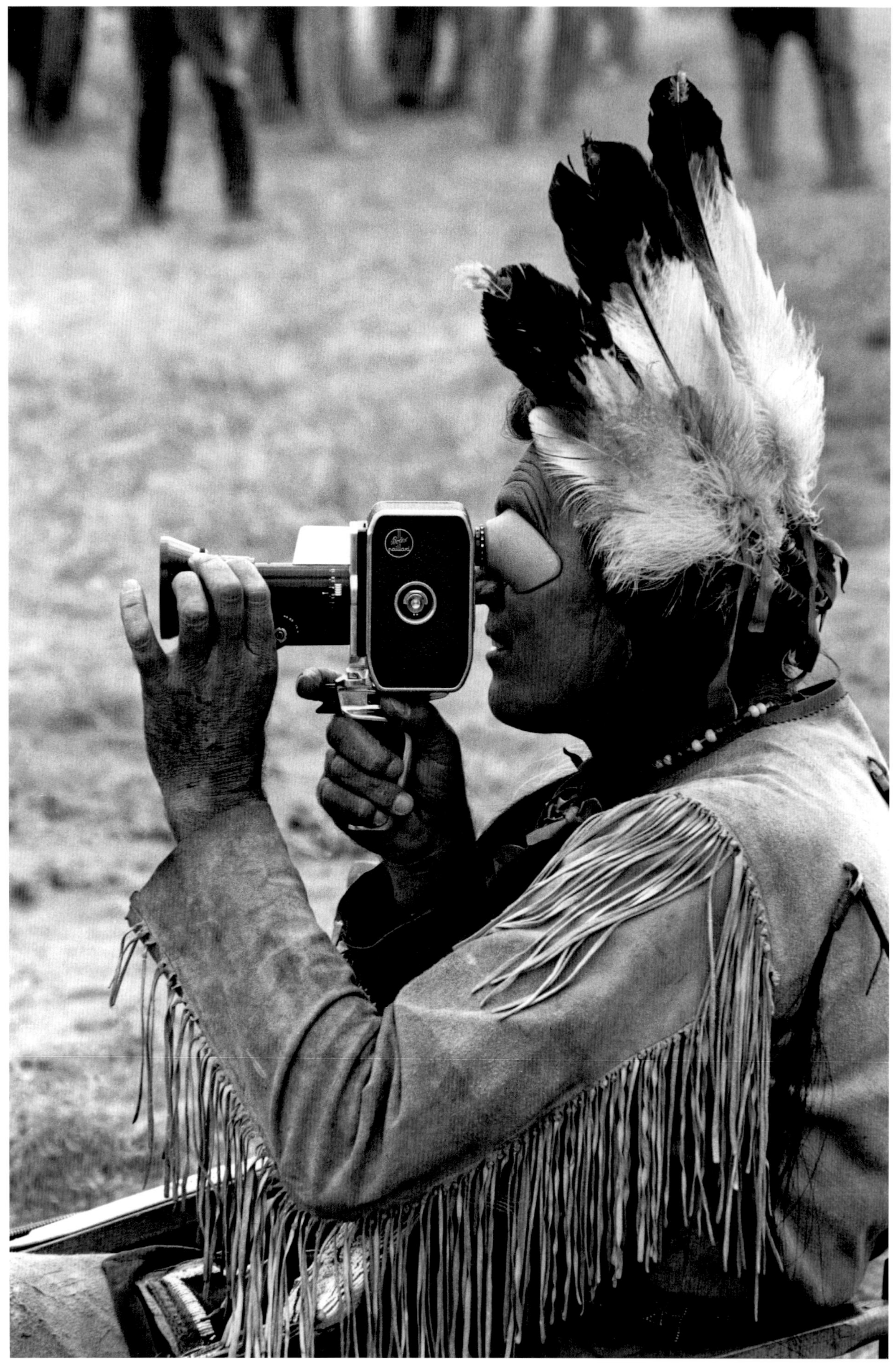

  Native American powwow. 1964

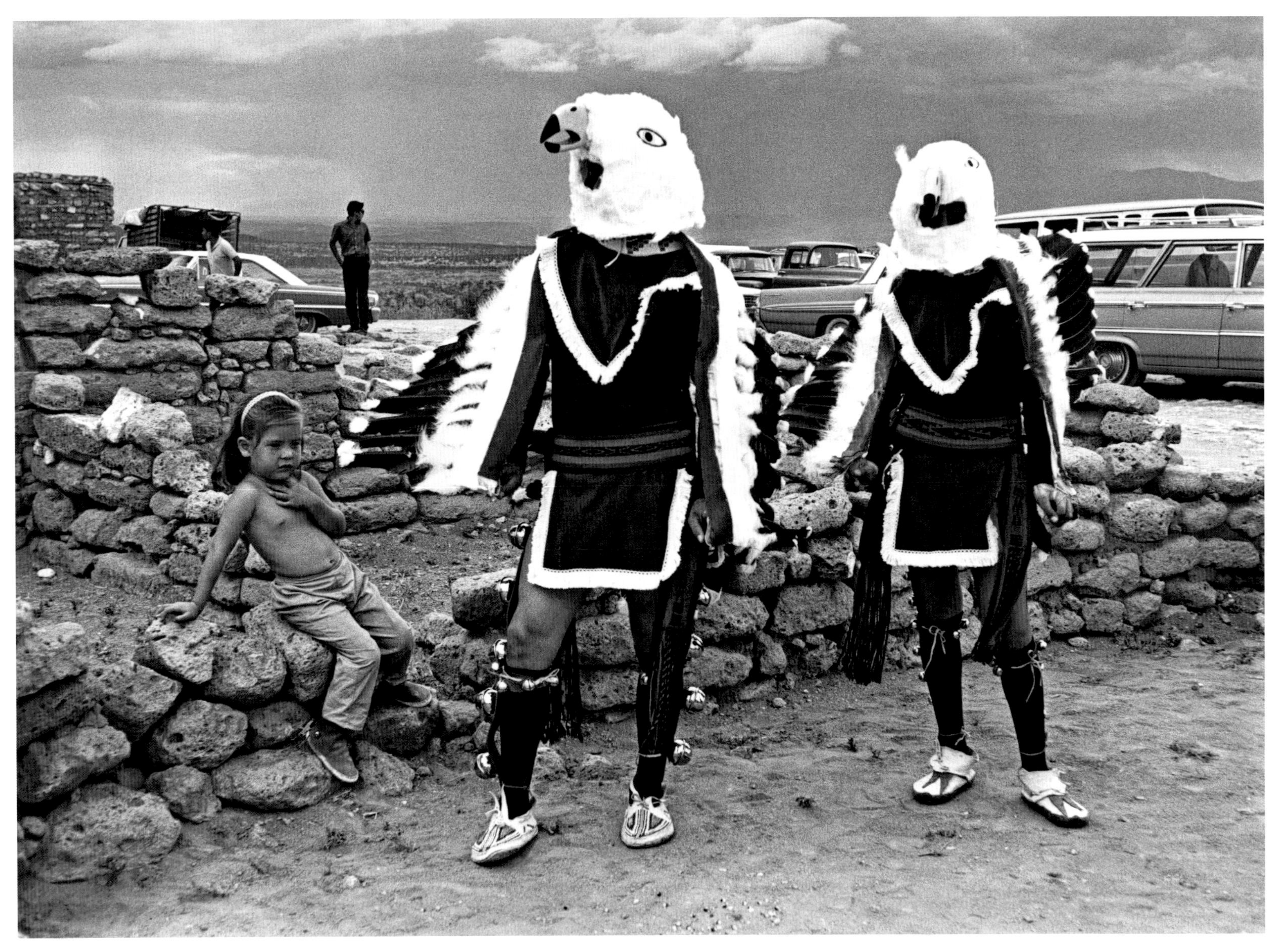

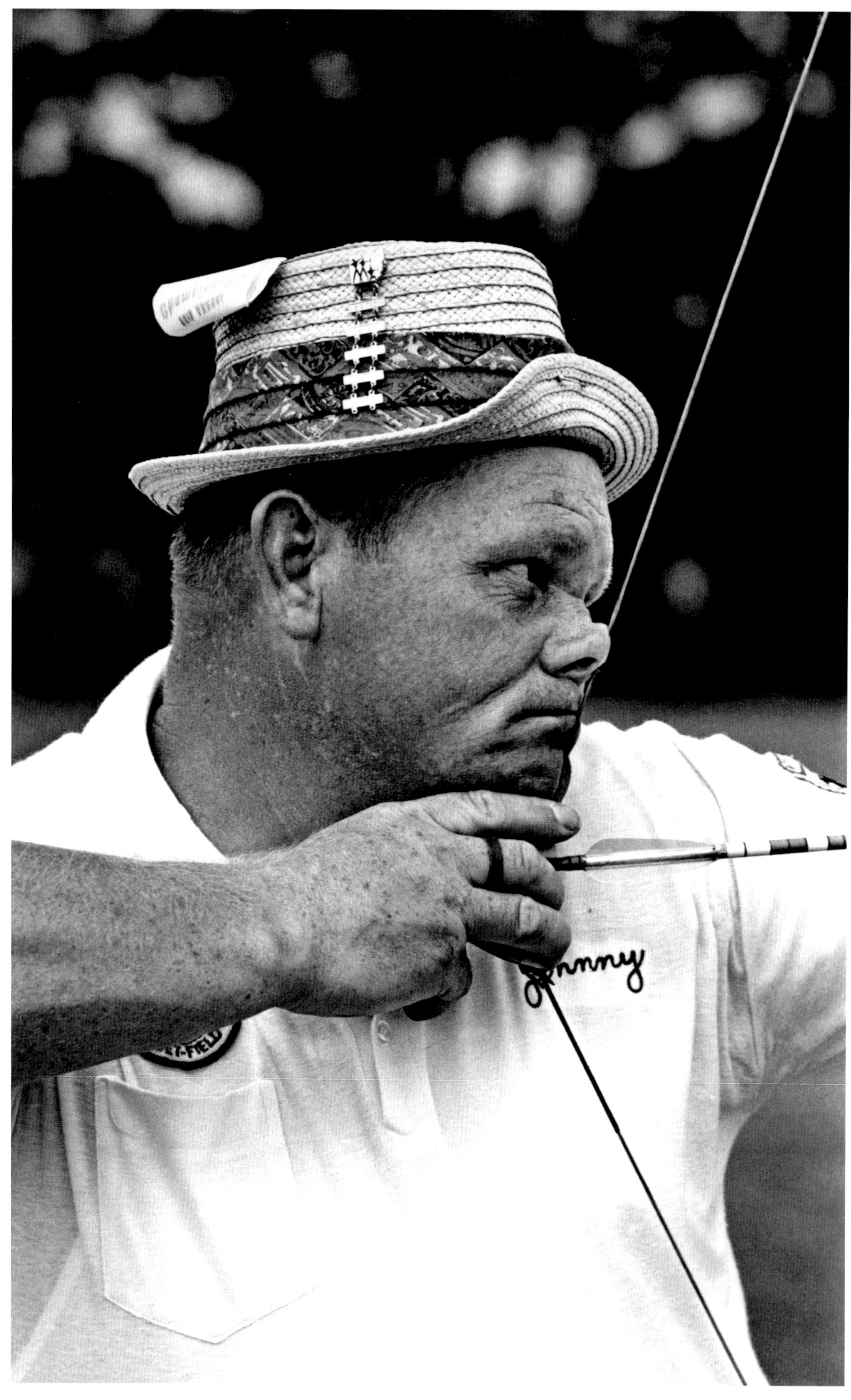

 Archery contestant. 1964

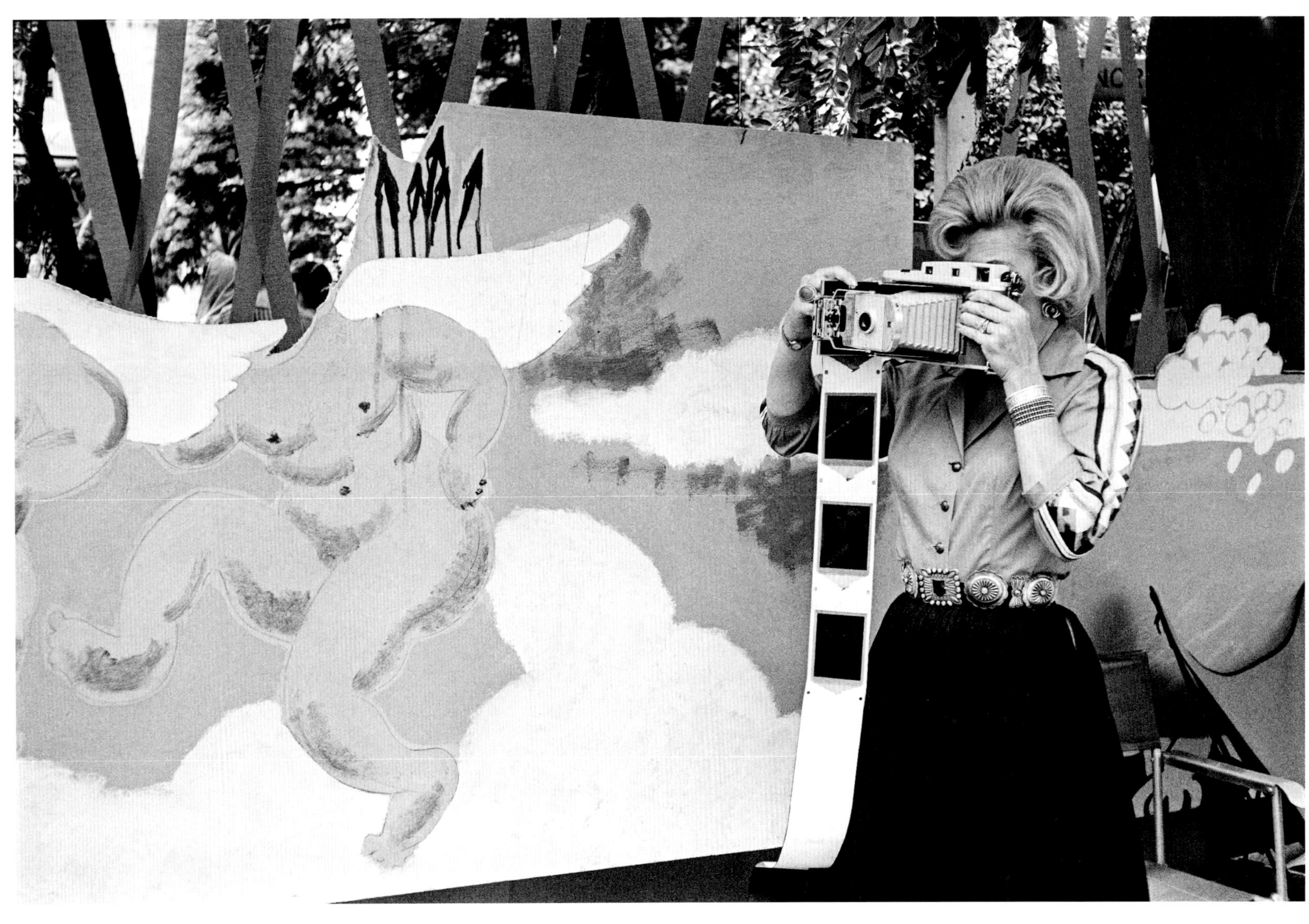

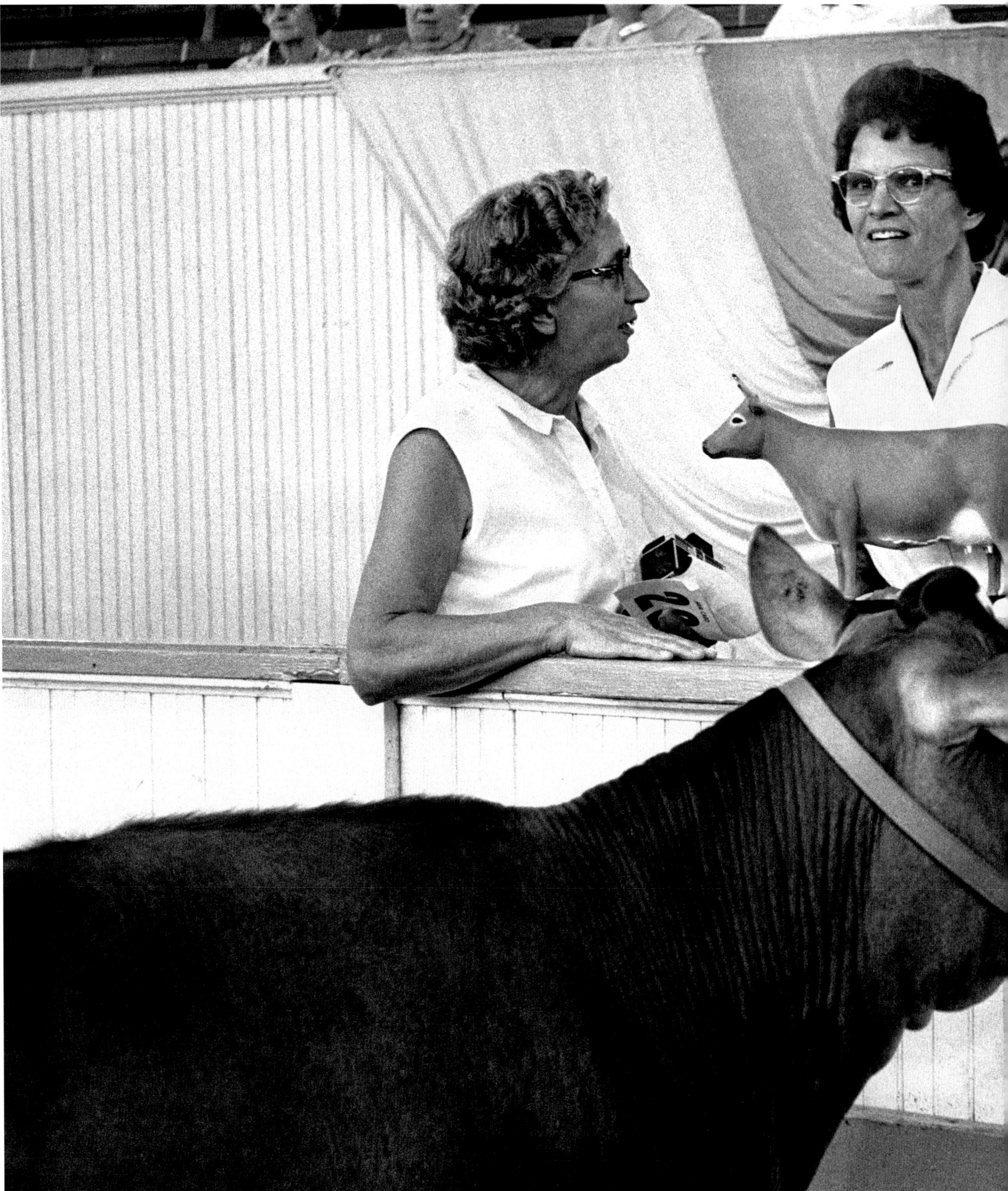

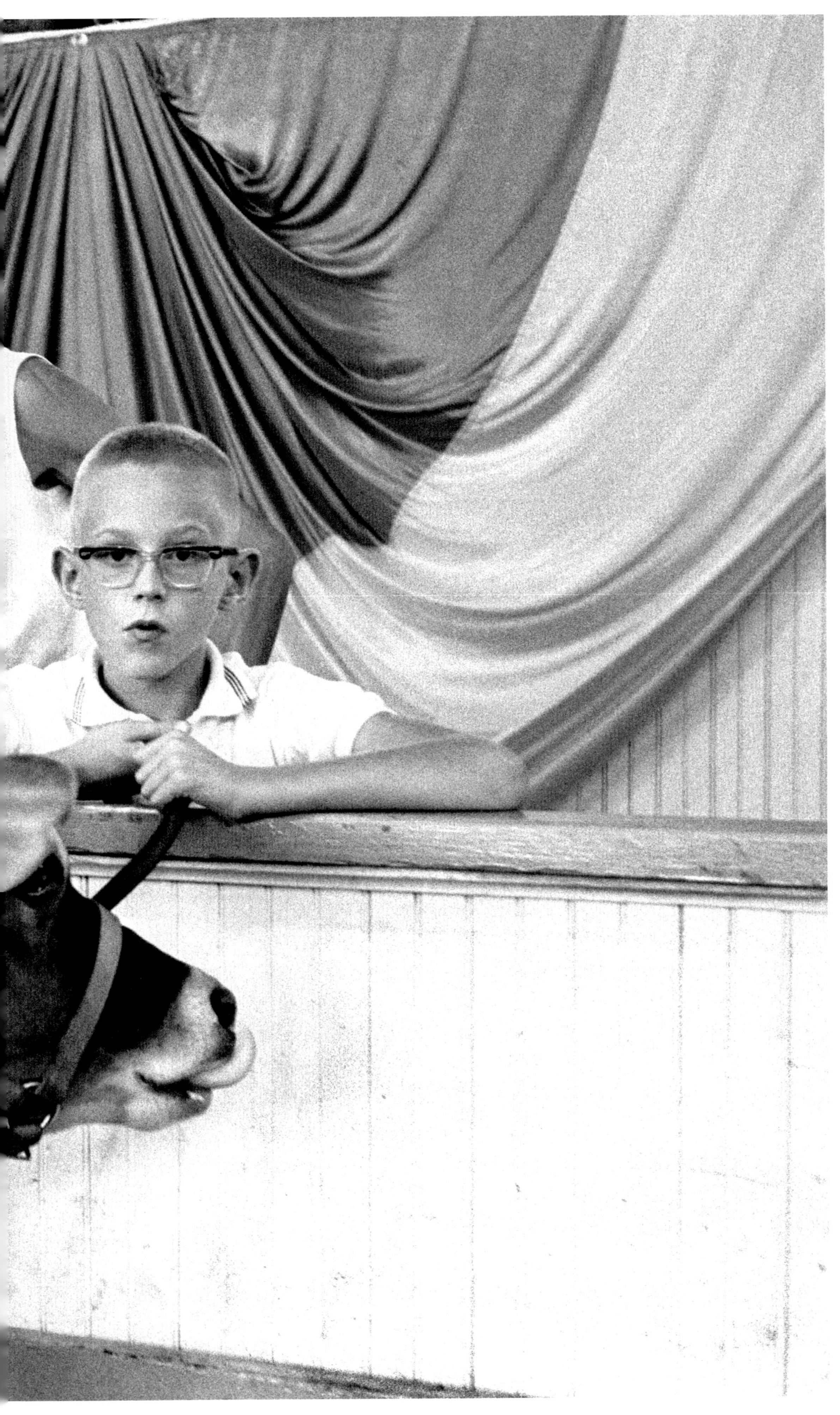

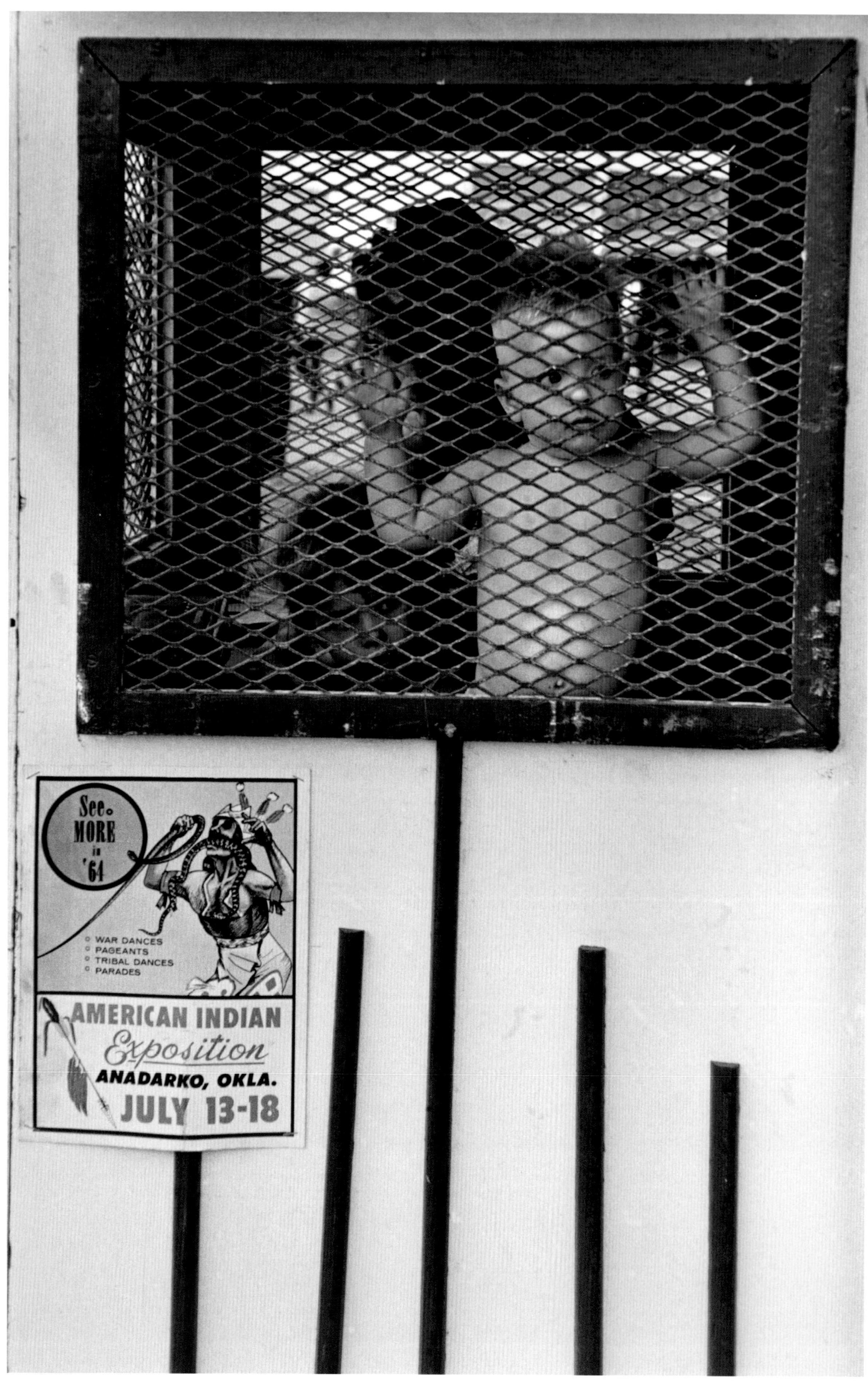

  State fair. Anadarko, Oklahoma, 1964

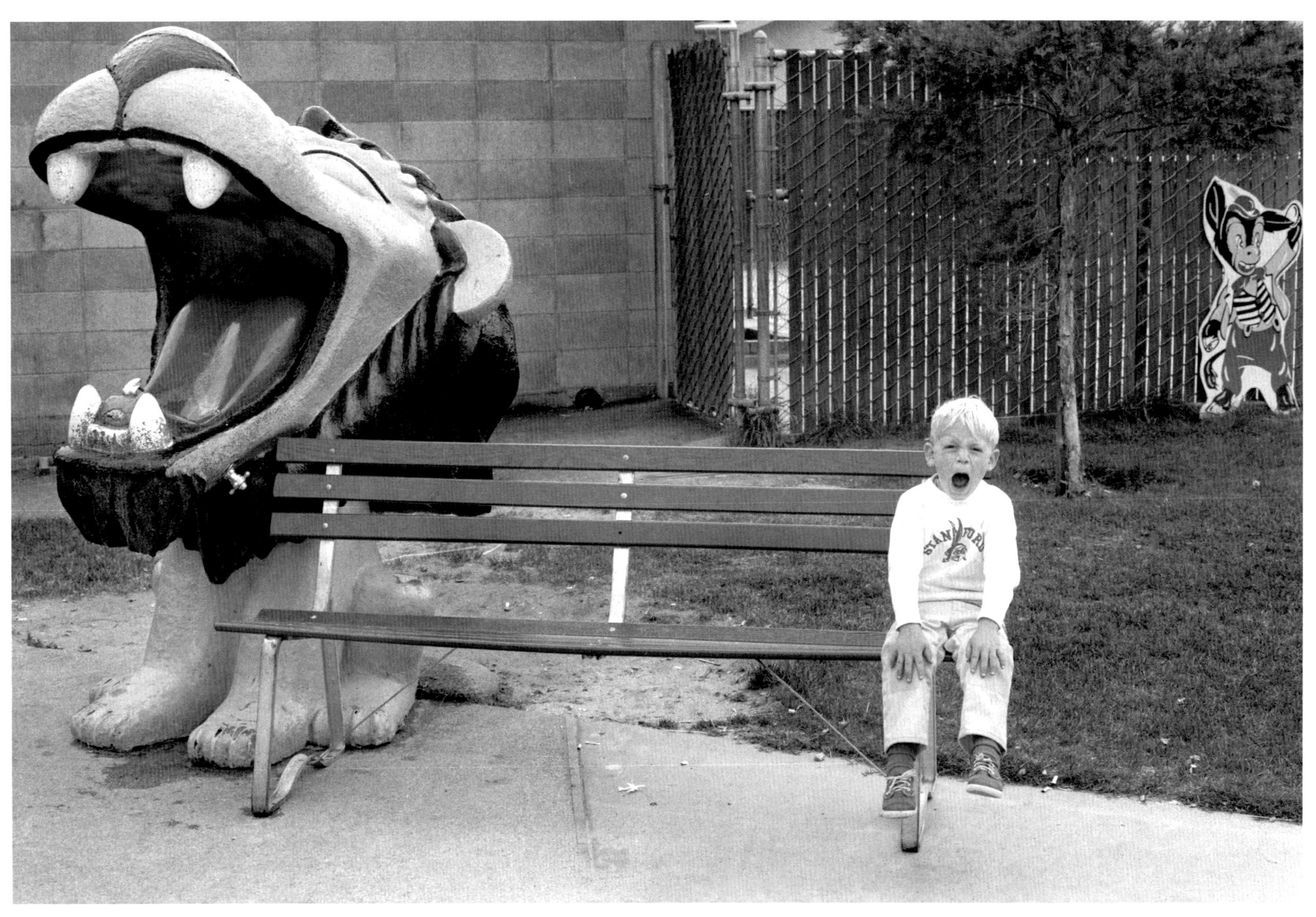

At Dennis the Menace Park. Monterey, California, 1964 **105**

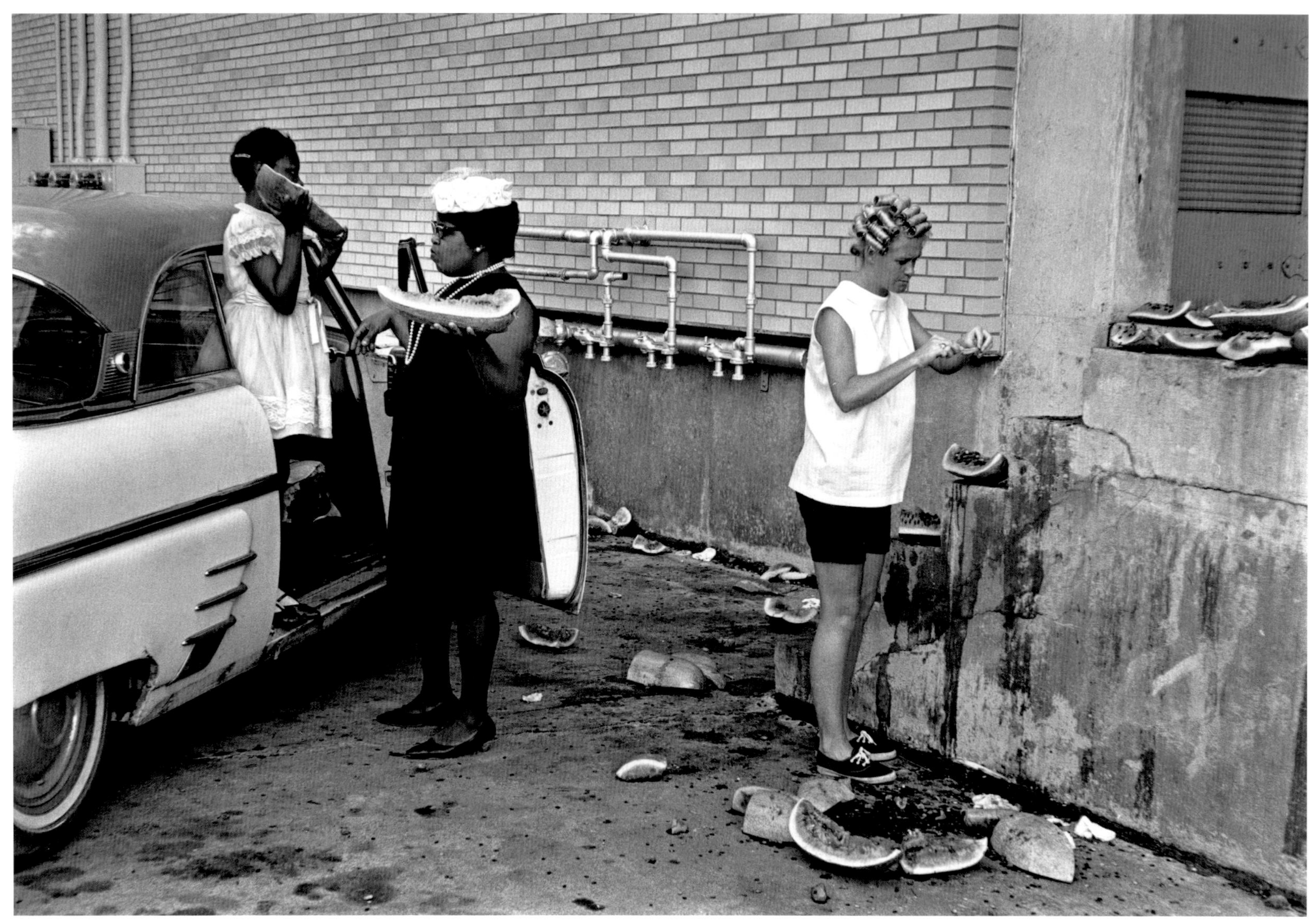

above
Watermelon Festival. Atlanta, 1964

right
Thousands of spectators line the streets
and the parking buildings along the
route near Los Angeles, waiting to see
the Soviet Leader Nikita Khrushchev.
California, 1959

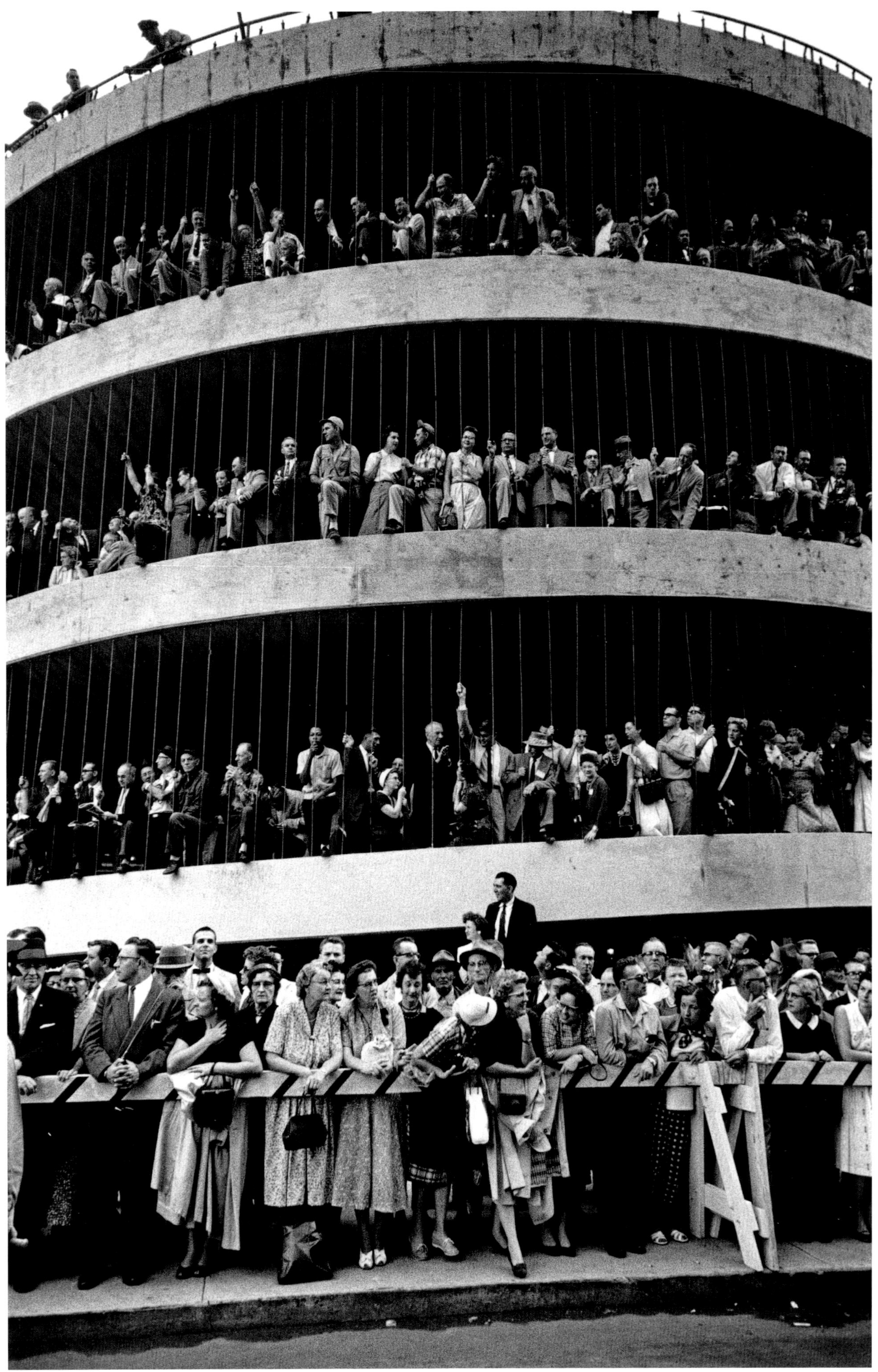

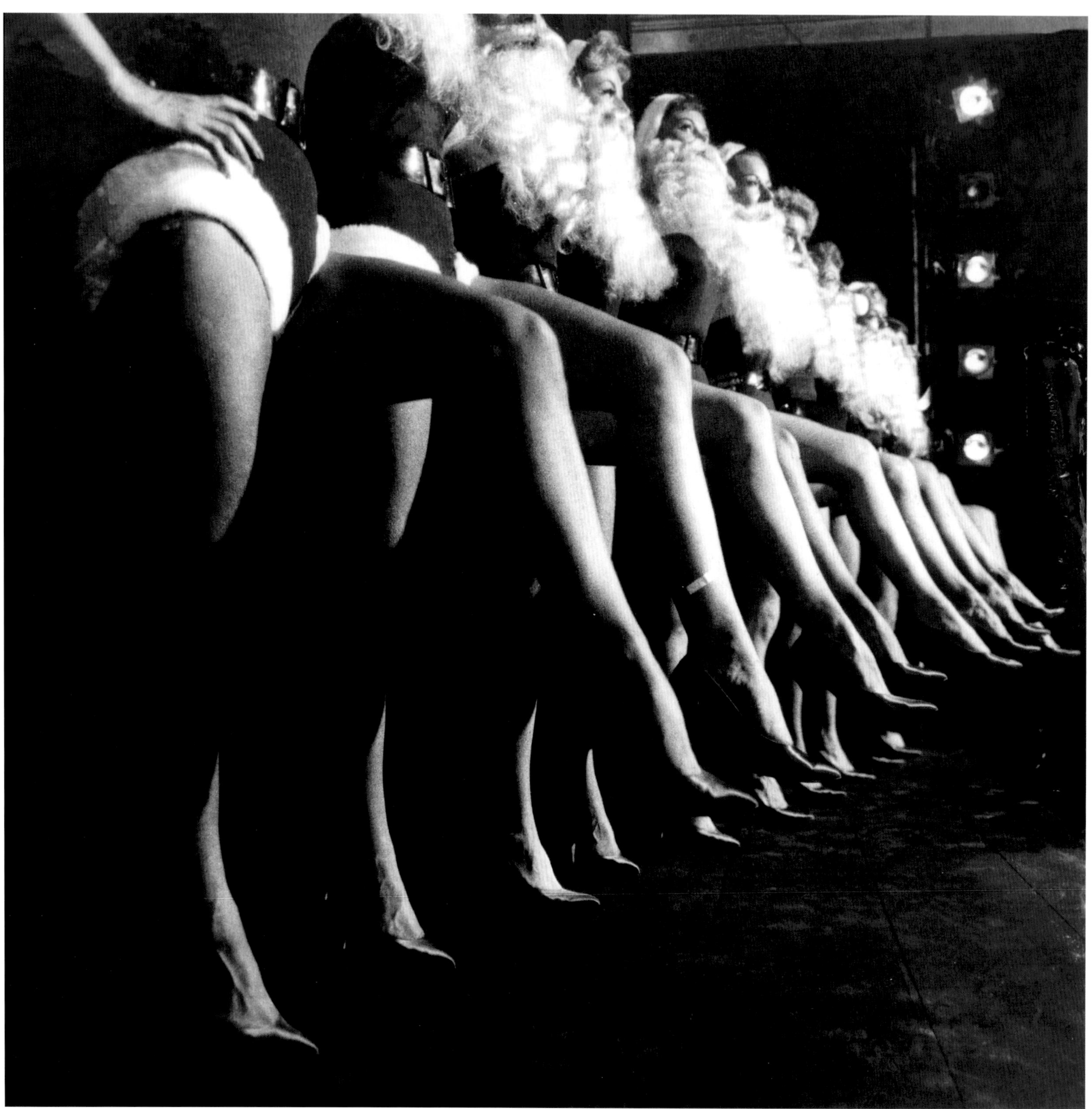

108   The legs of dancers at Radio City Music Hall. New York City, 1959

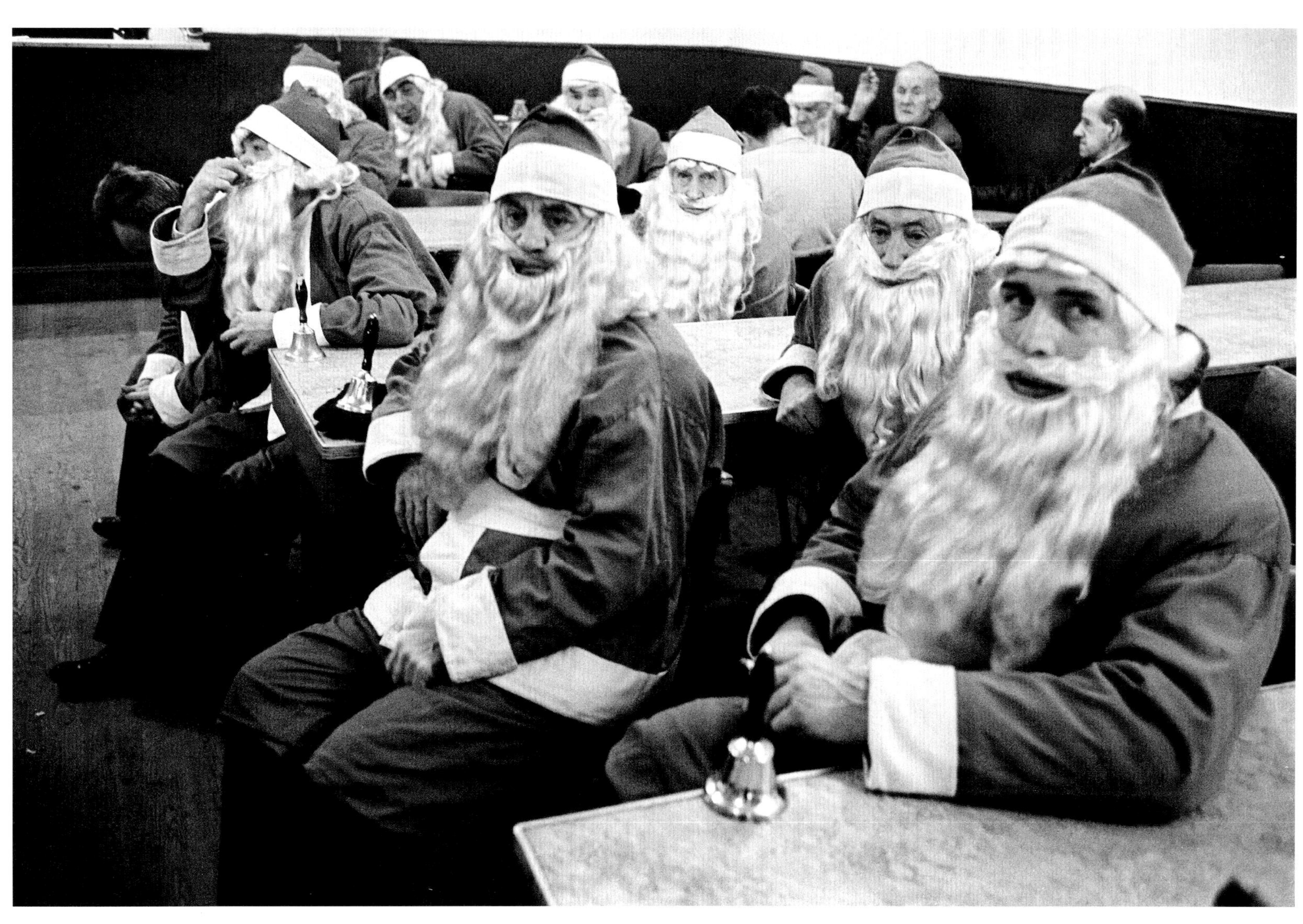

School for Santas. New York City, 1961   **109**

CALIFORNIA

Military display at state fair.
Sacramento, 1968.

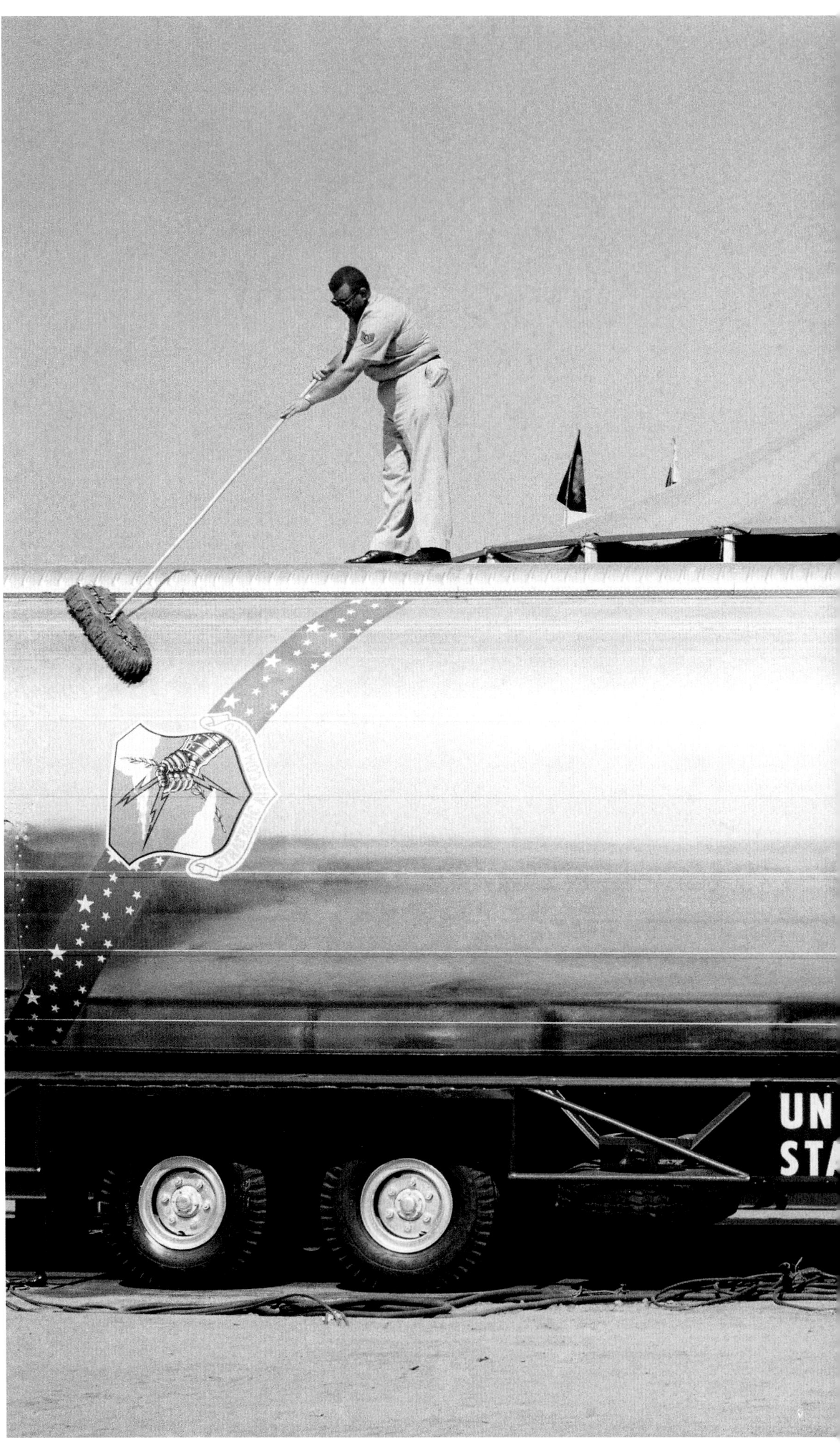

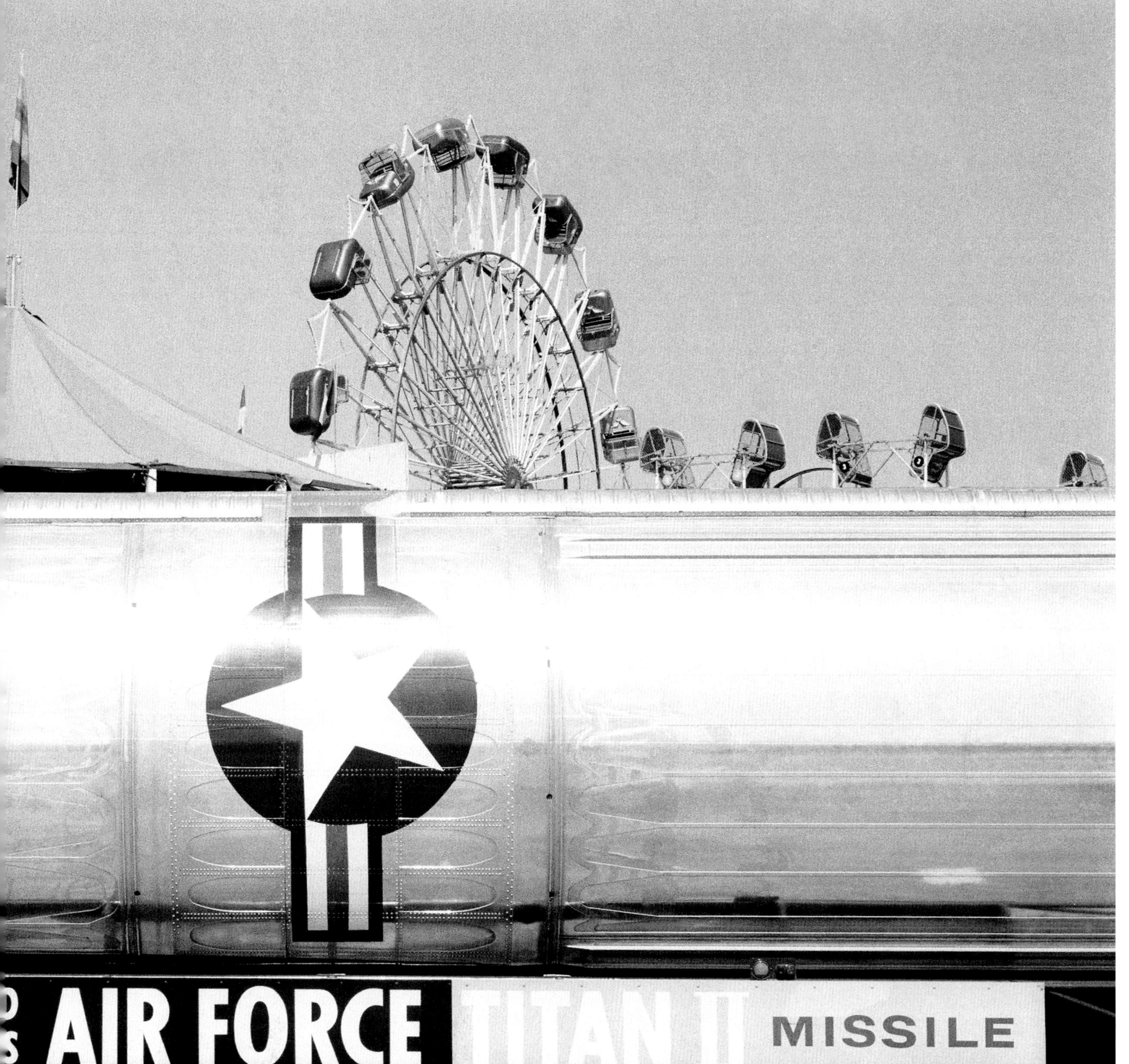

AIR FORCE TITAN II MISSILE

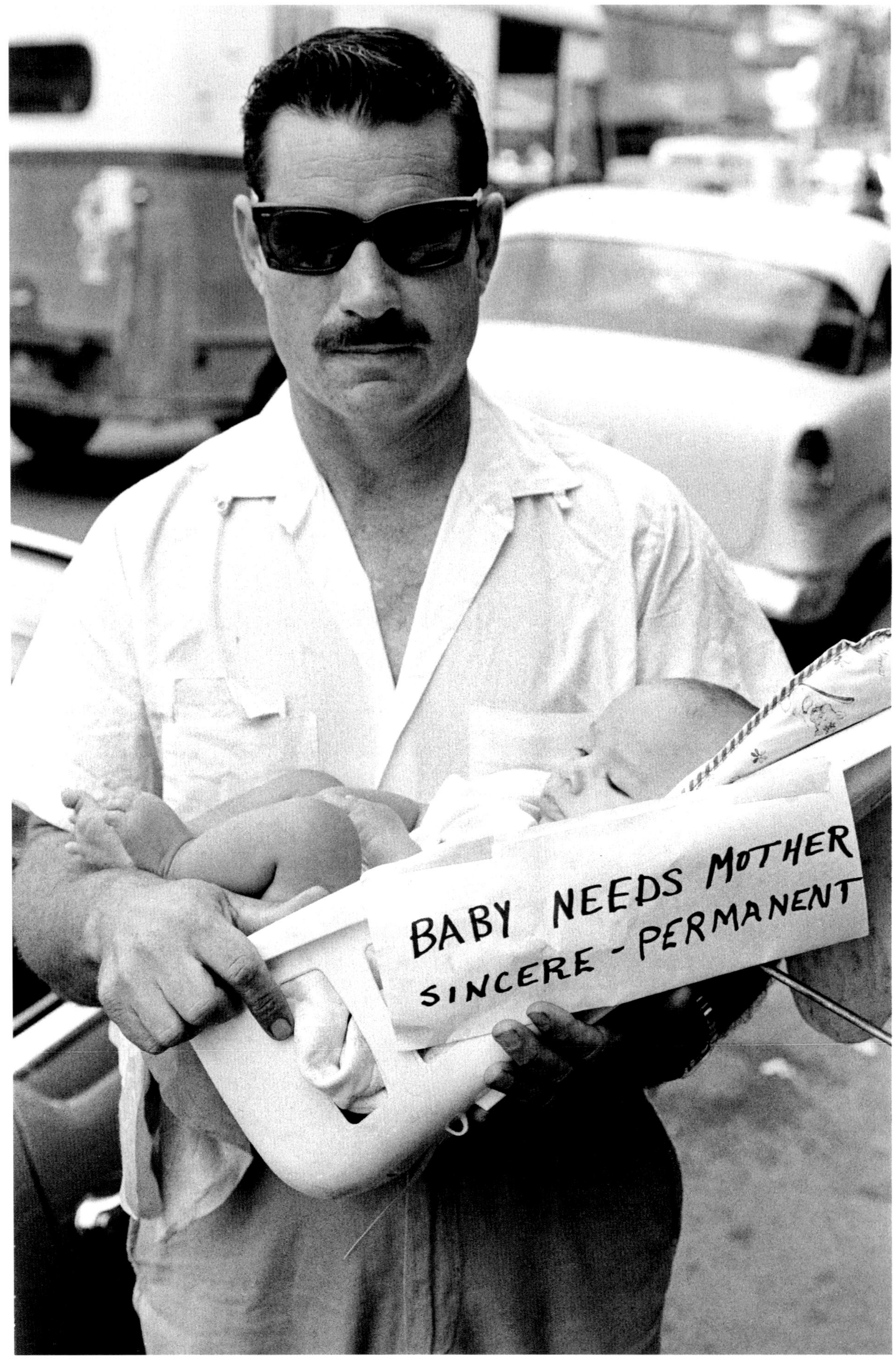

   A father. Berkeley, California, 1968

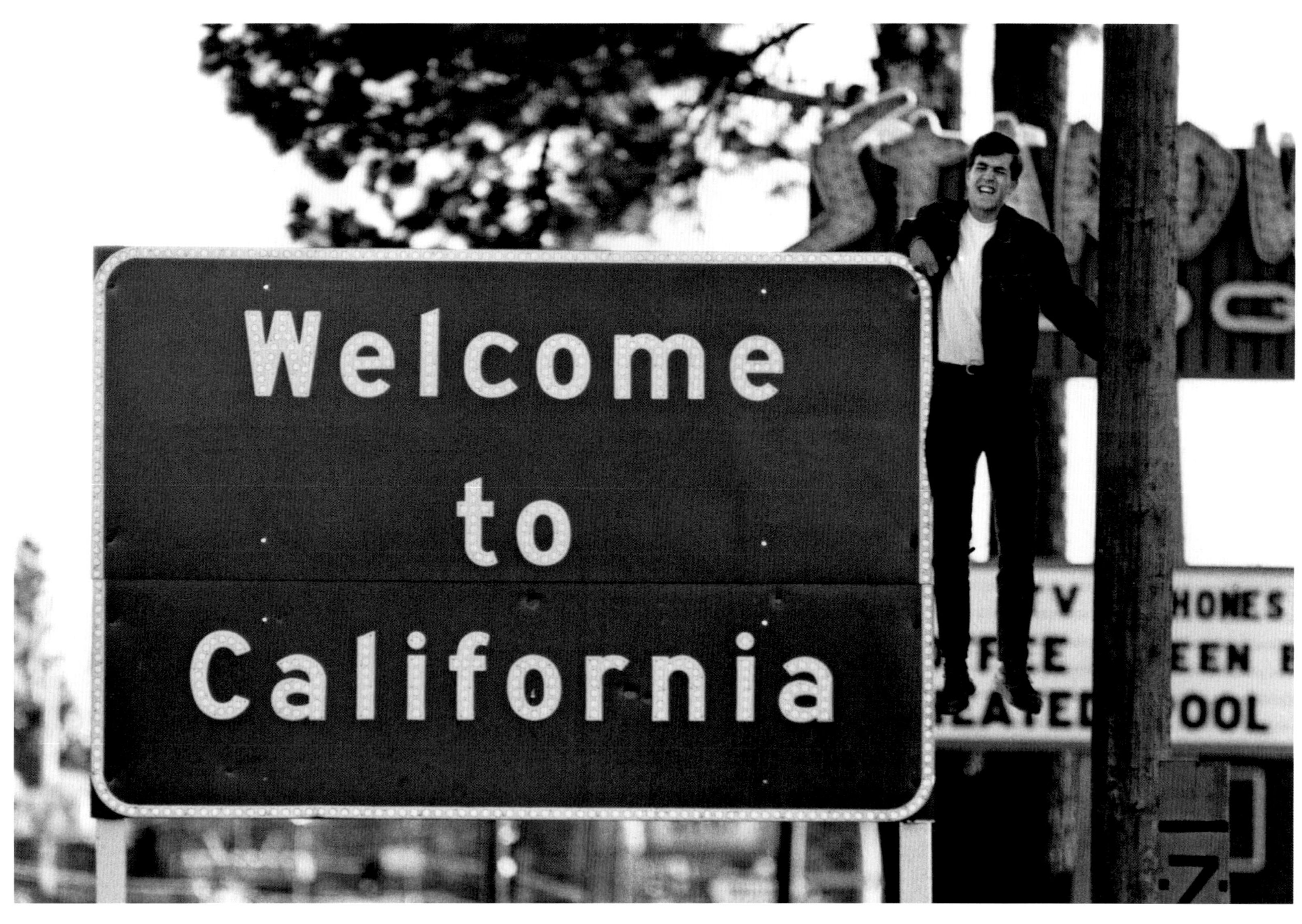
Welcome
to
California

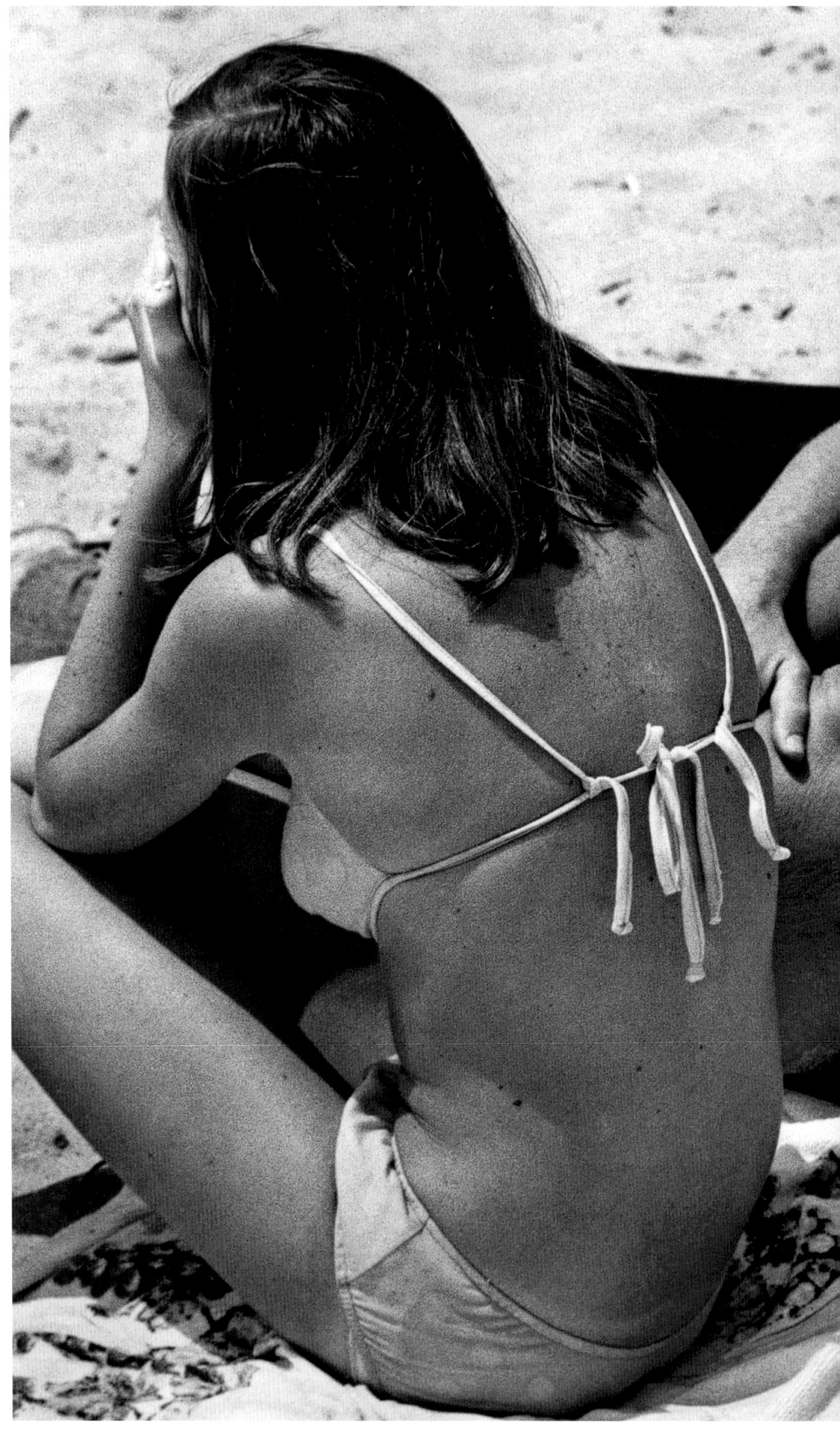

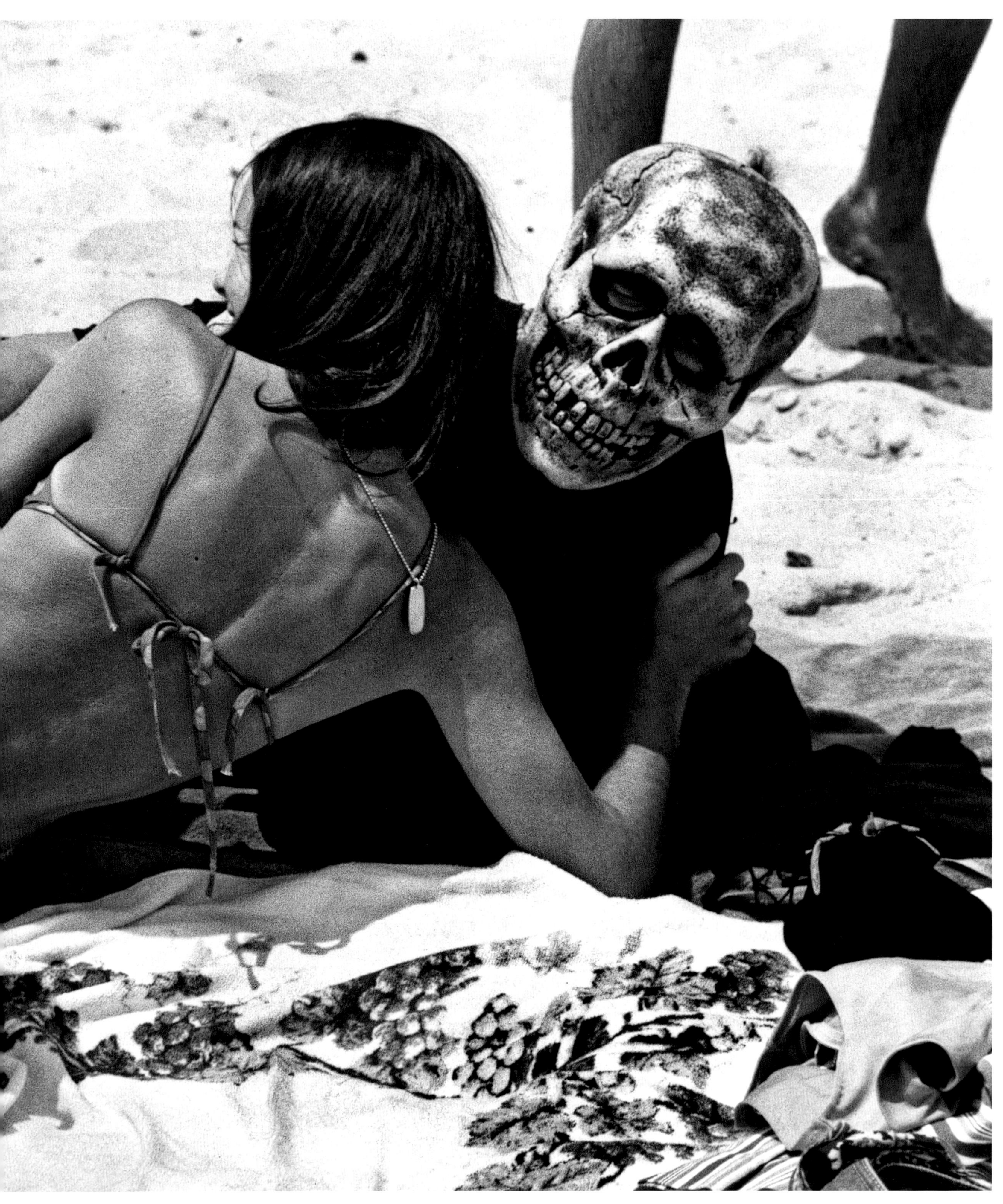

Man holding a surfboard on beach steps. Corona del Mar, California, 1968

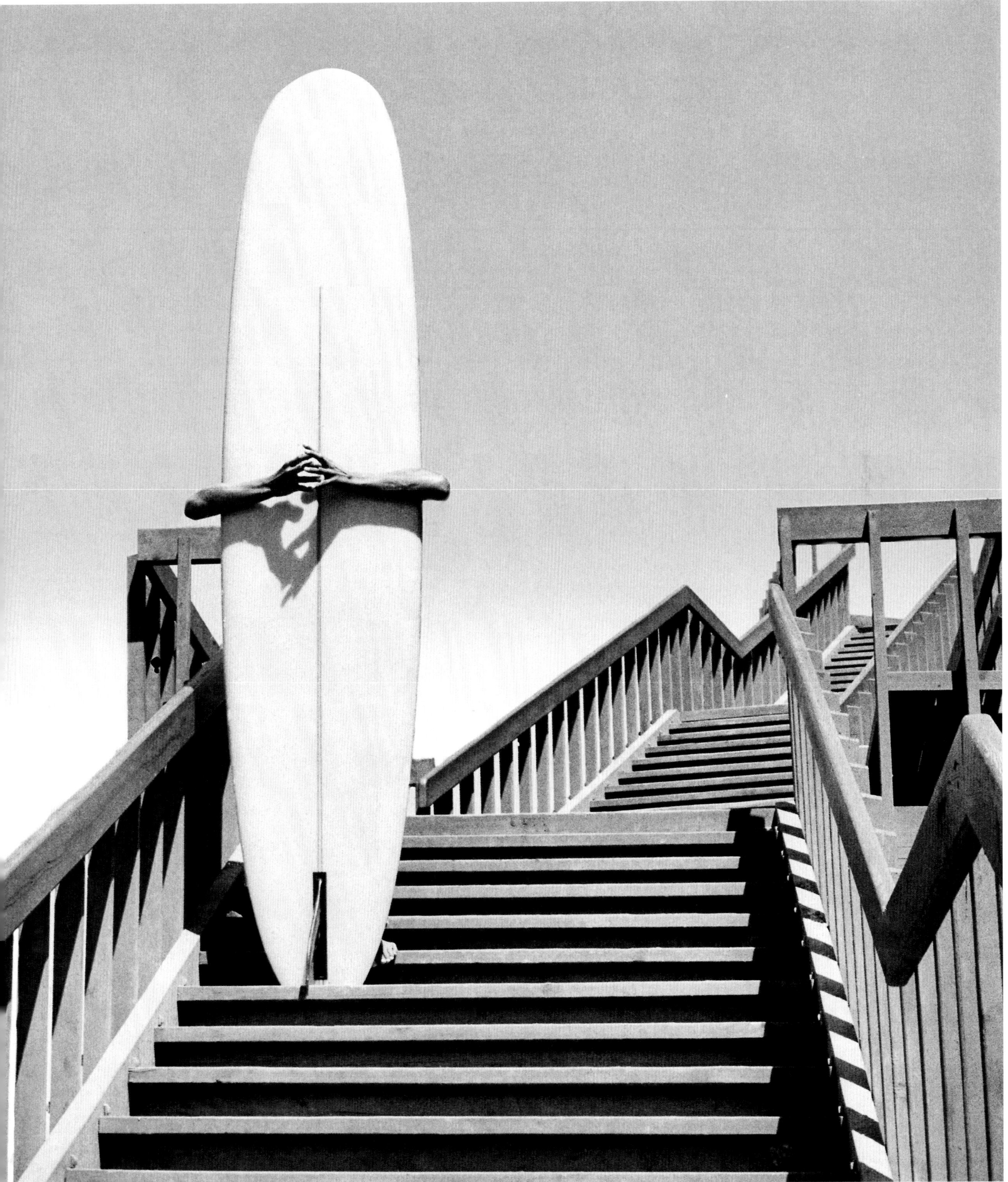

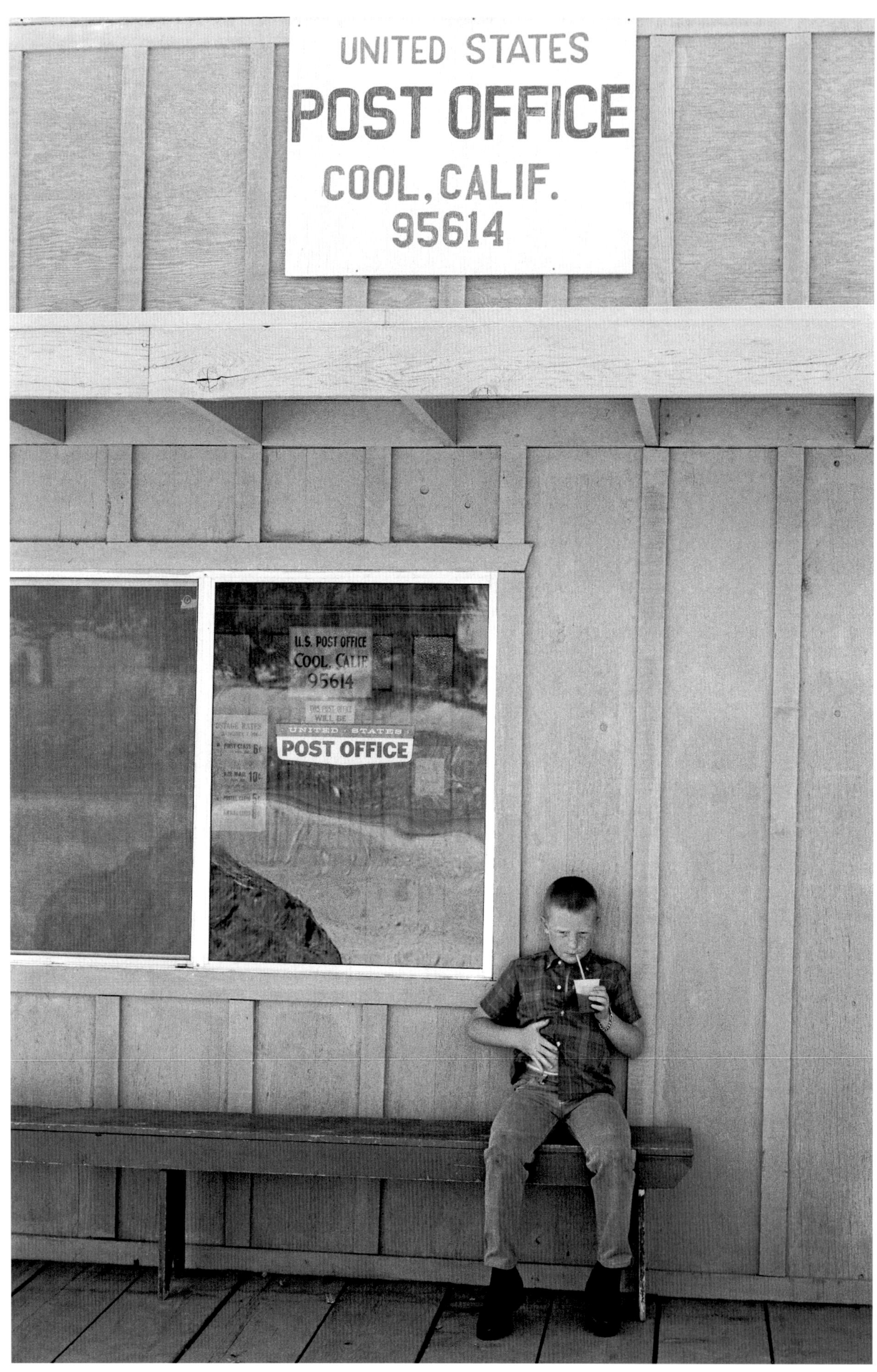

    Outside the post office. Cool, California, 1968

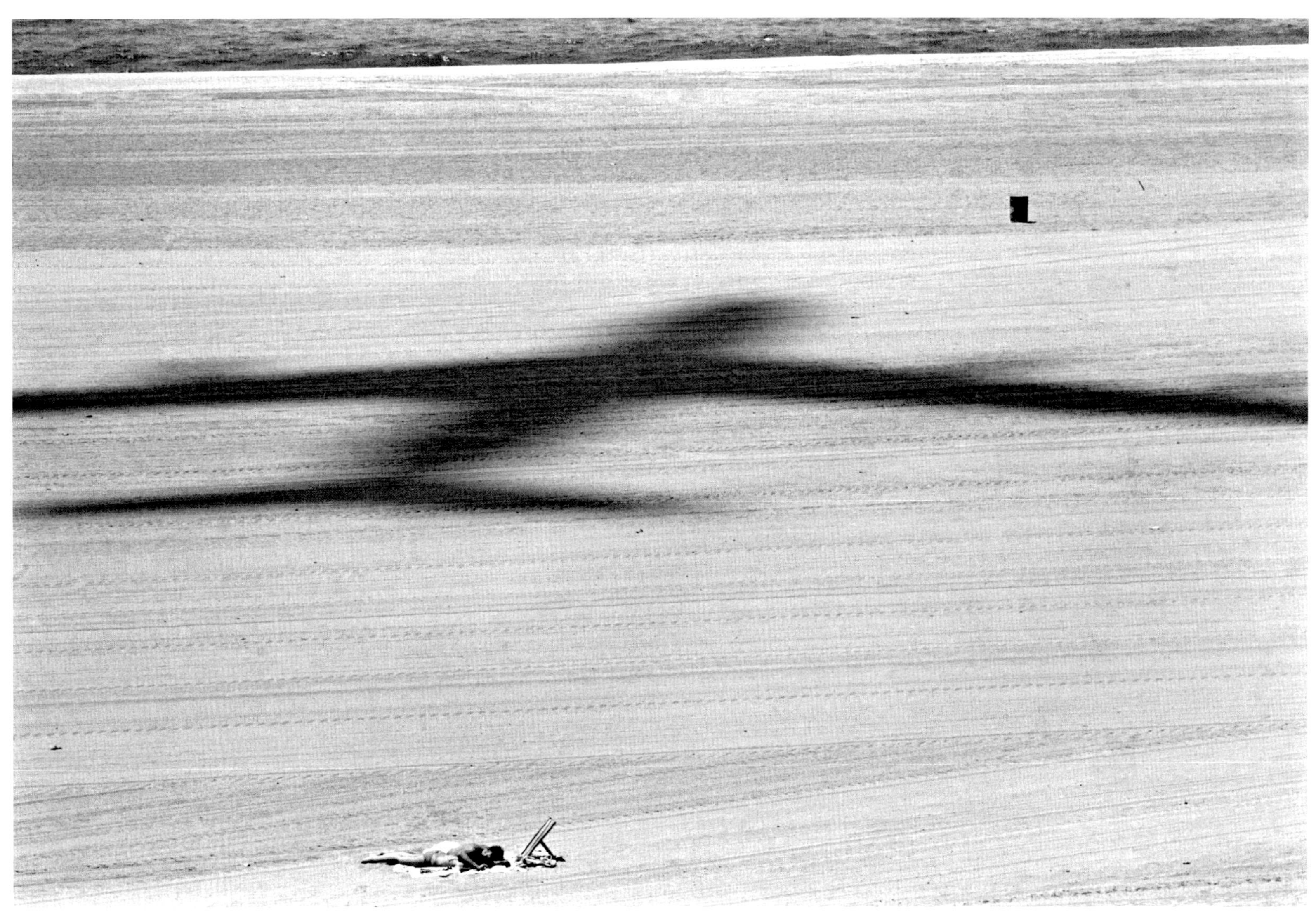

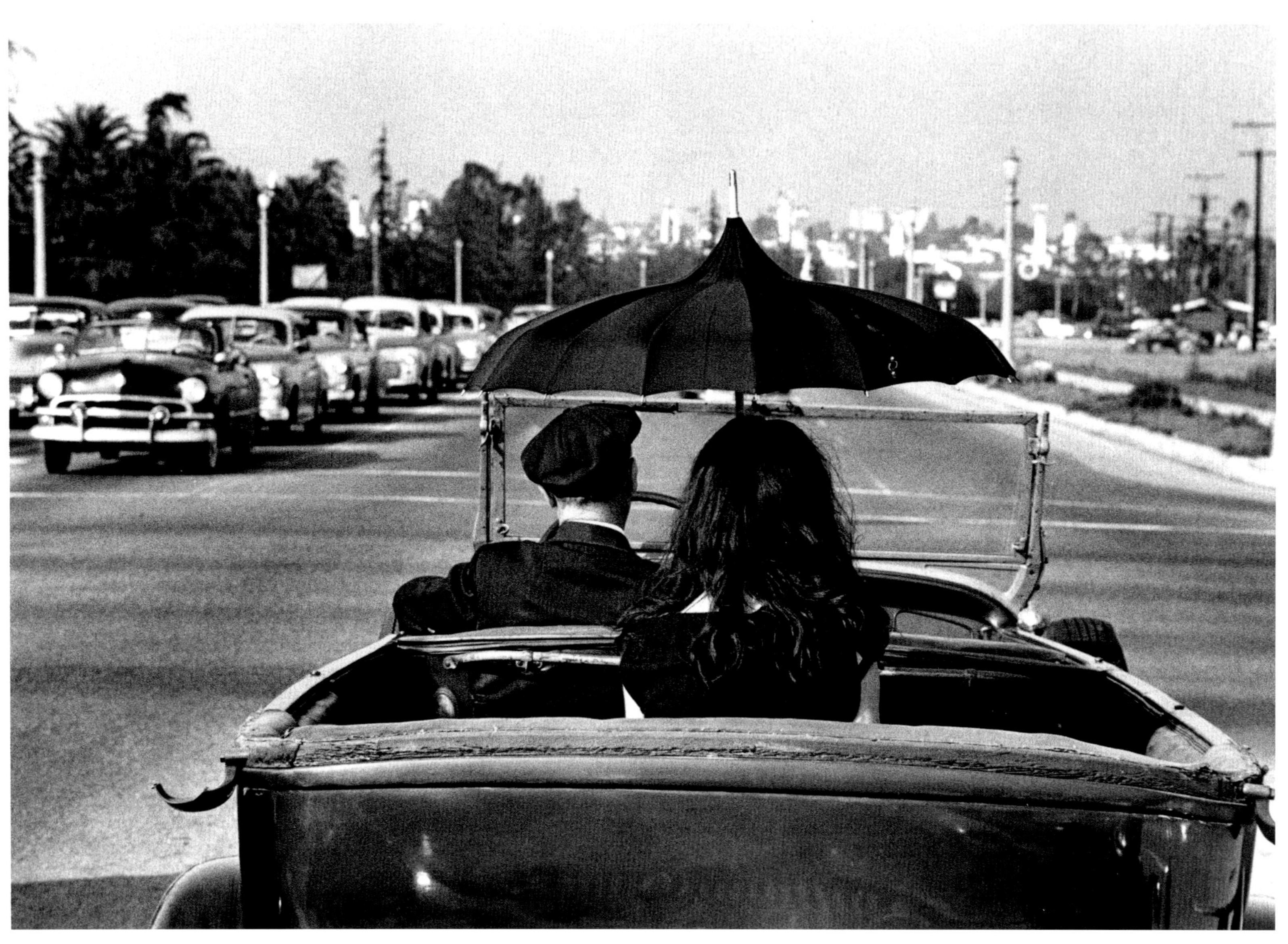

122   Maila Nurmi, star of THE VAMPIRA SHOW. Hollywood, 1954

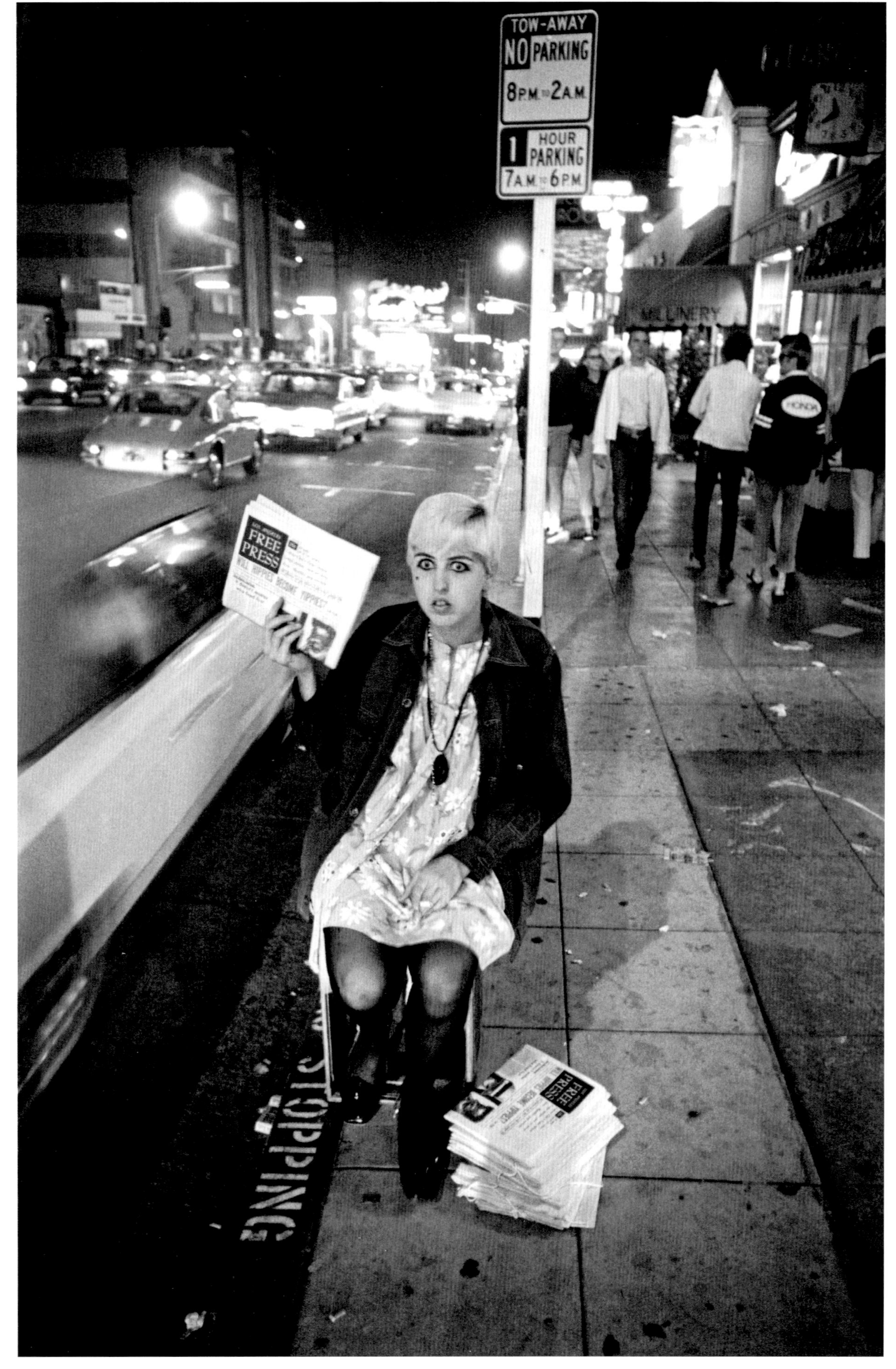

Militant selling the FREE PRESS, an alternative newspaper, on Sunset Boulevard. Los Angeles, 1968

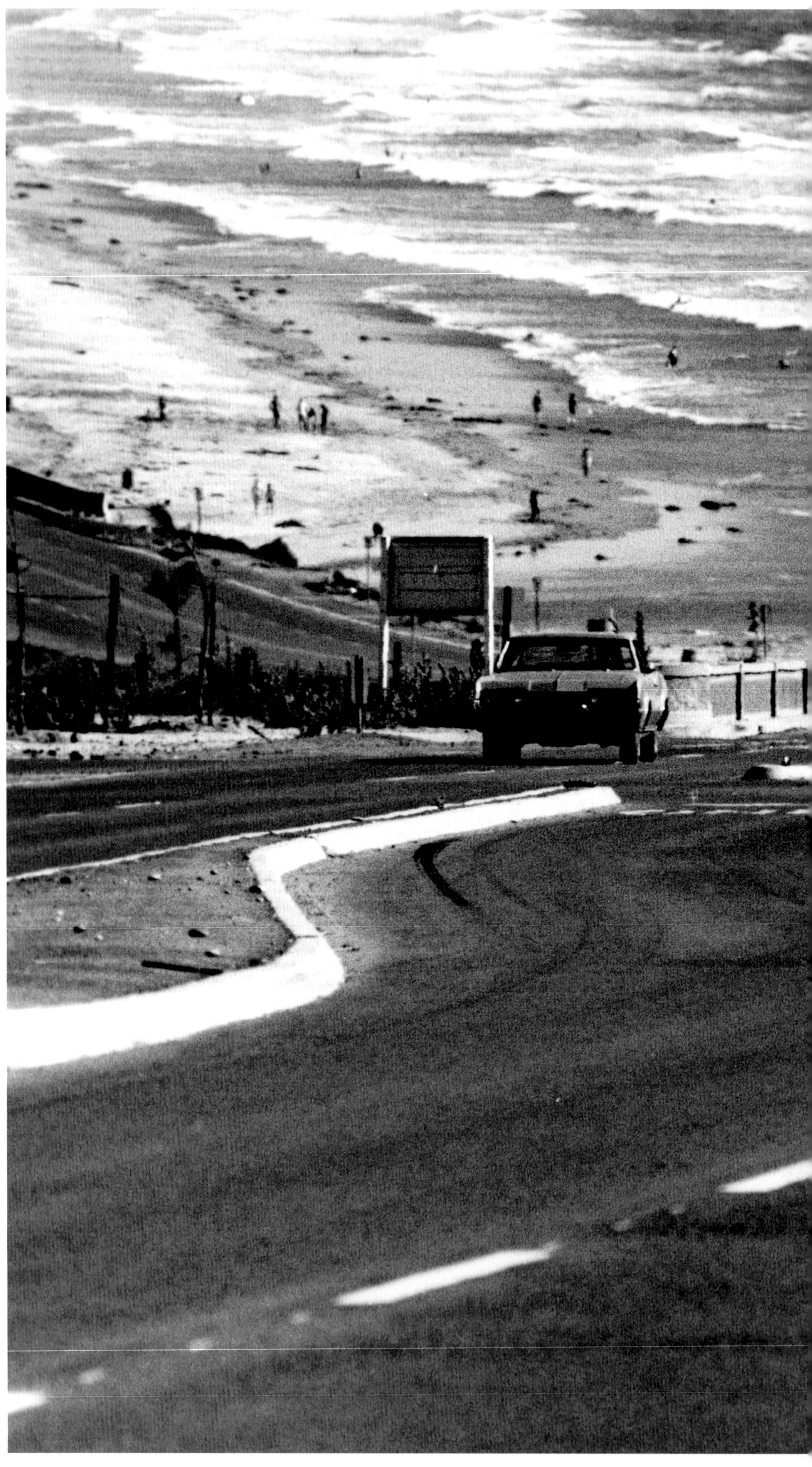

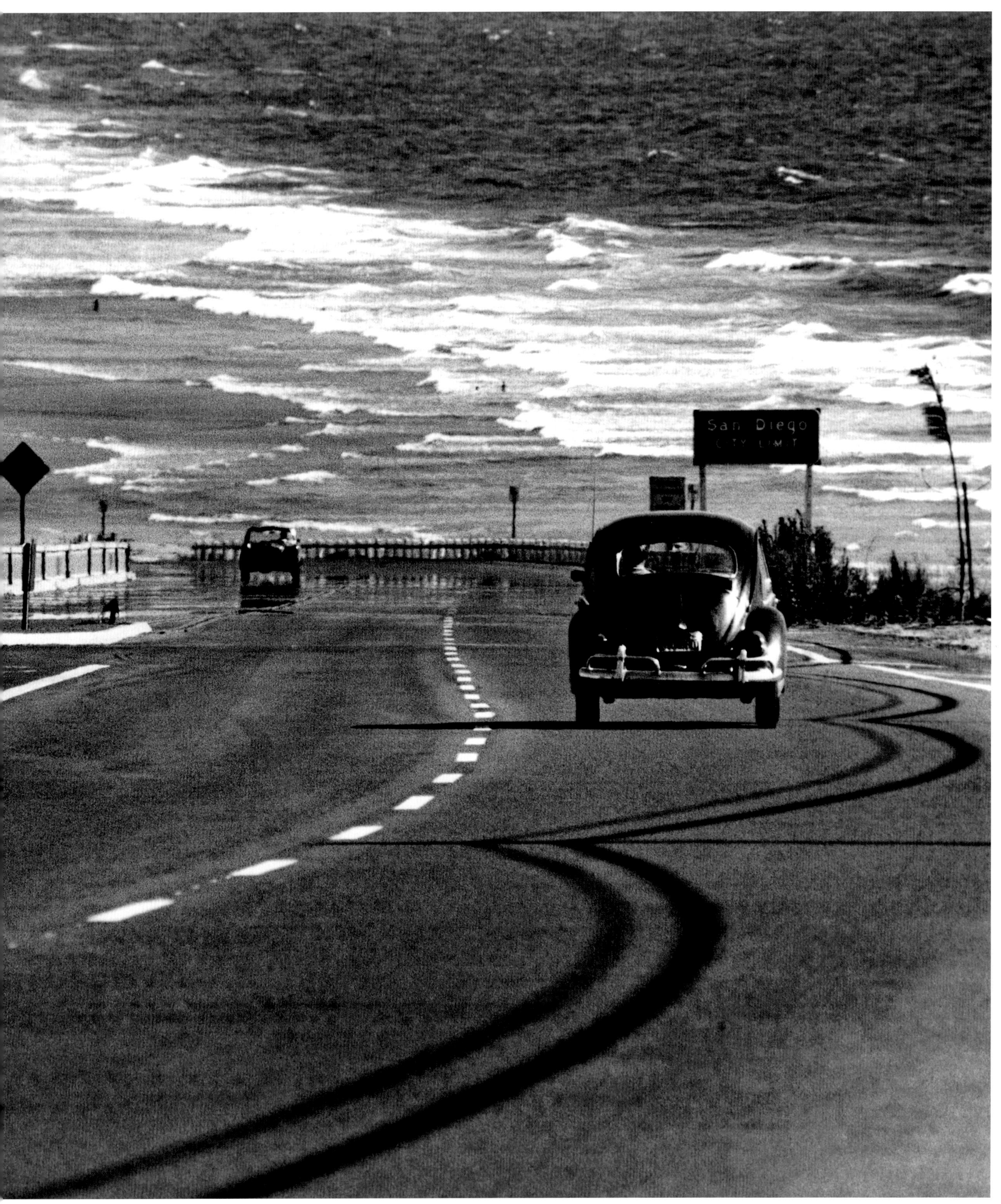

San Diego
CITY LIMIT

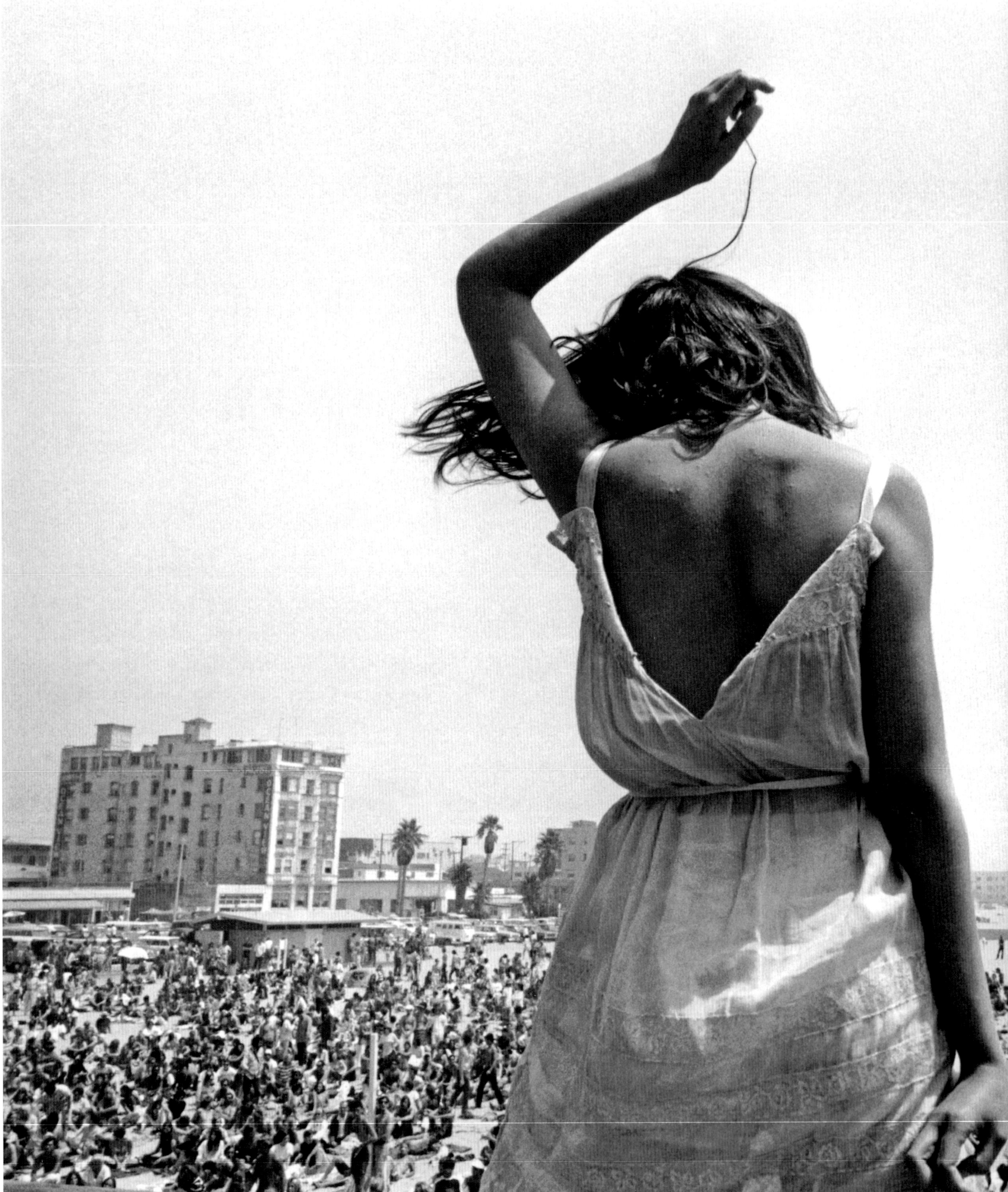

HIPPIES

ROAD PEO

Portrait of a couple in "American Gothic style."
New Mexico, 1969

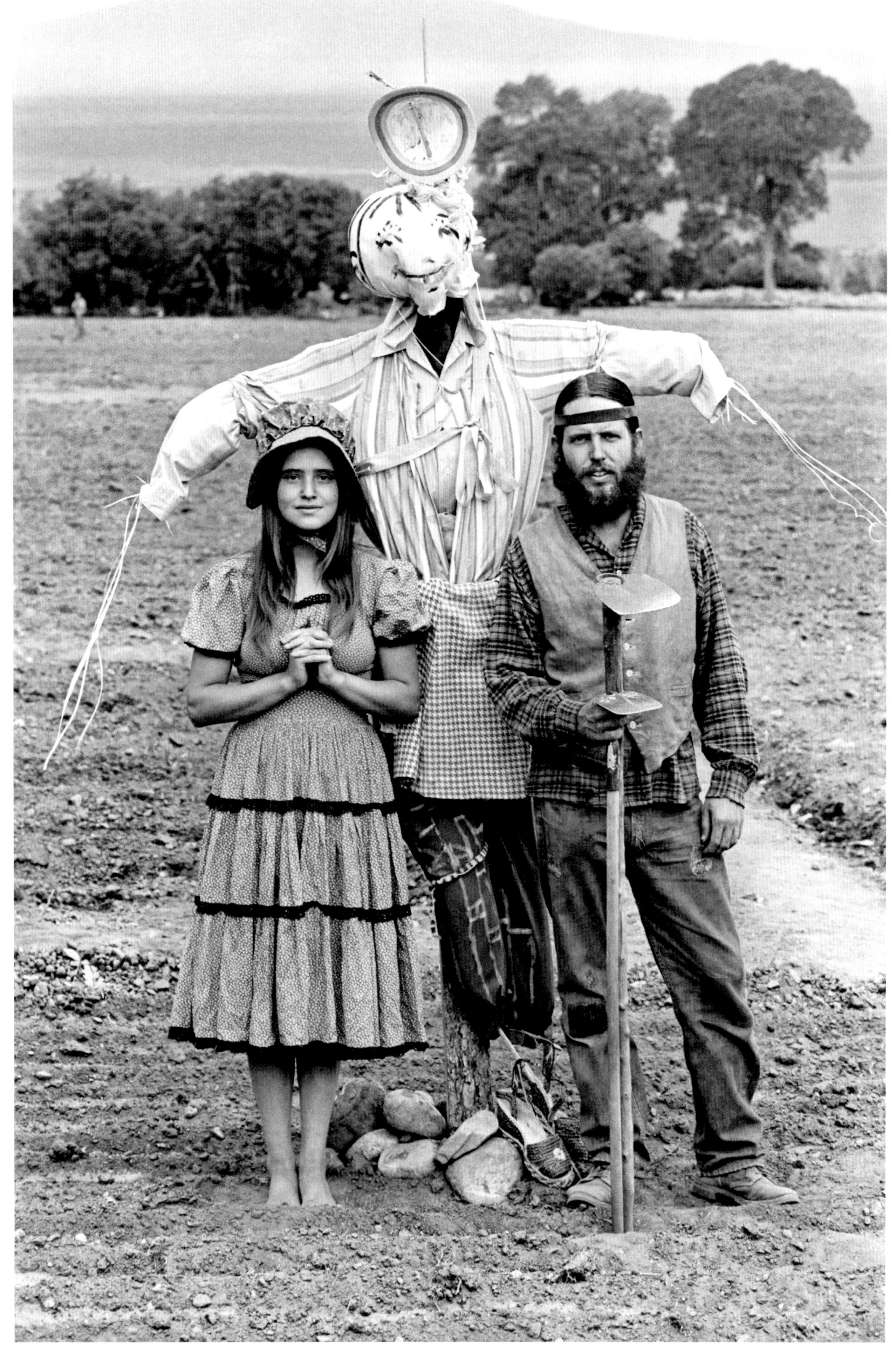

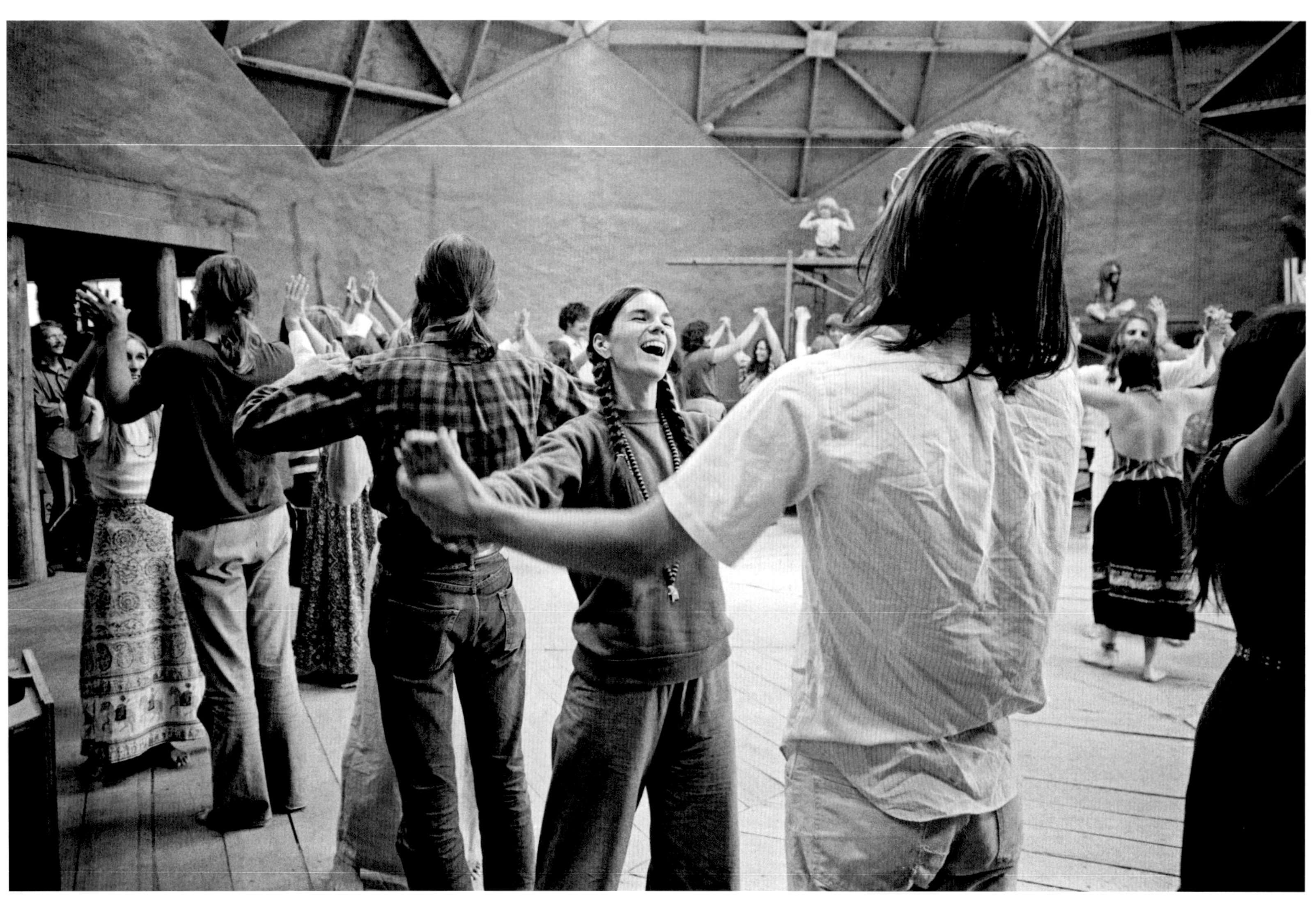

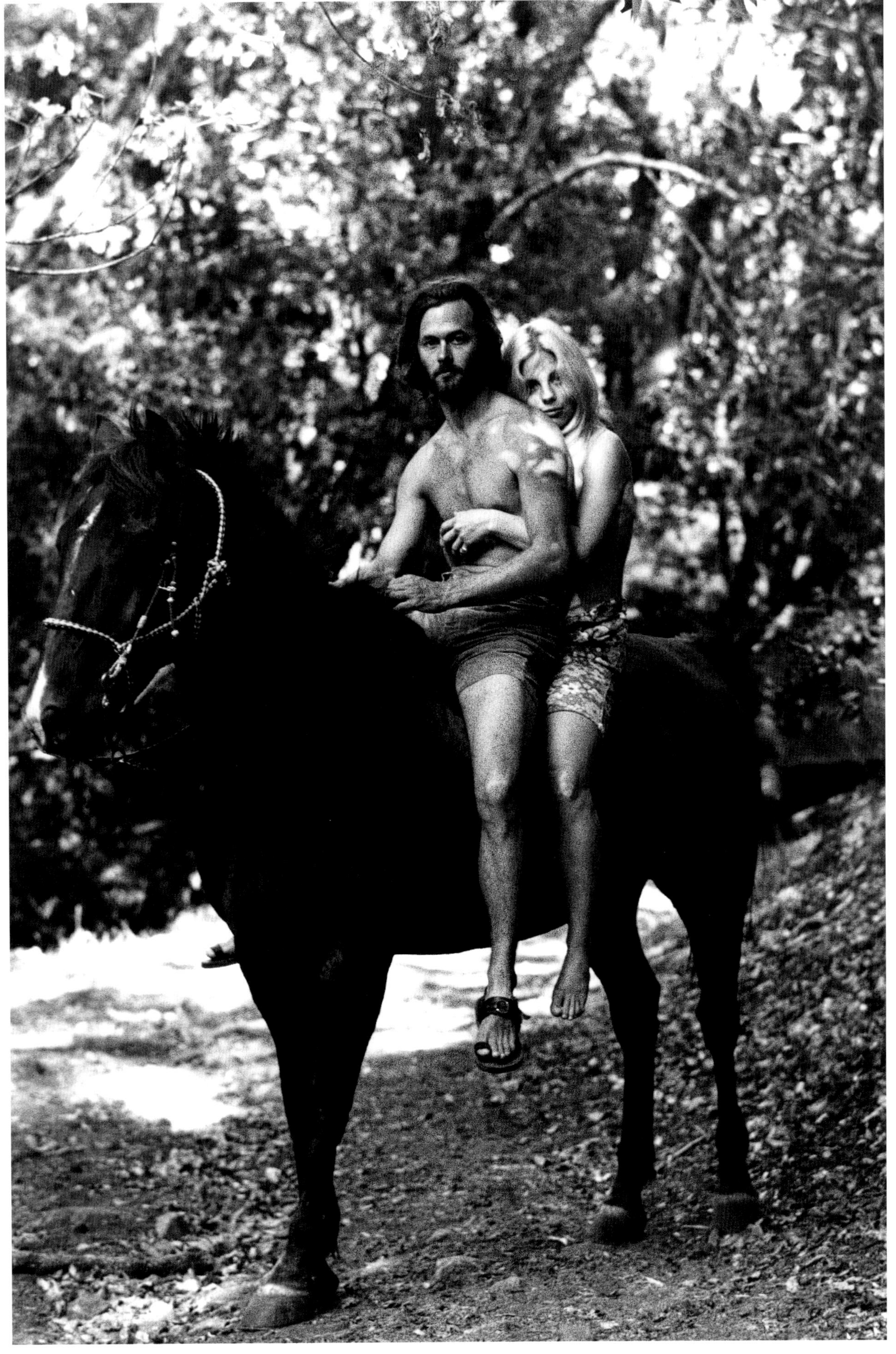

Couple. Novato, California, 1968   **133**

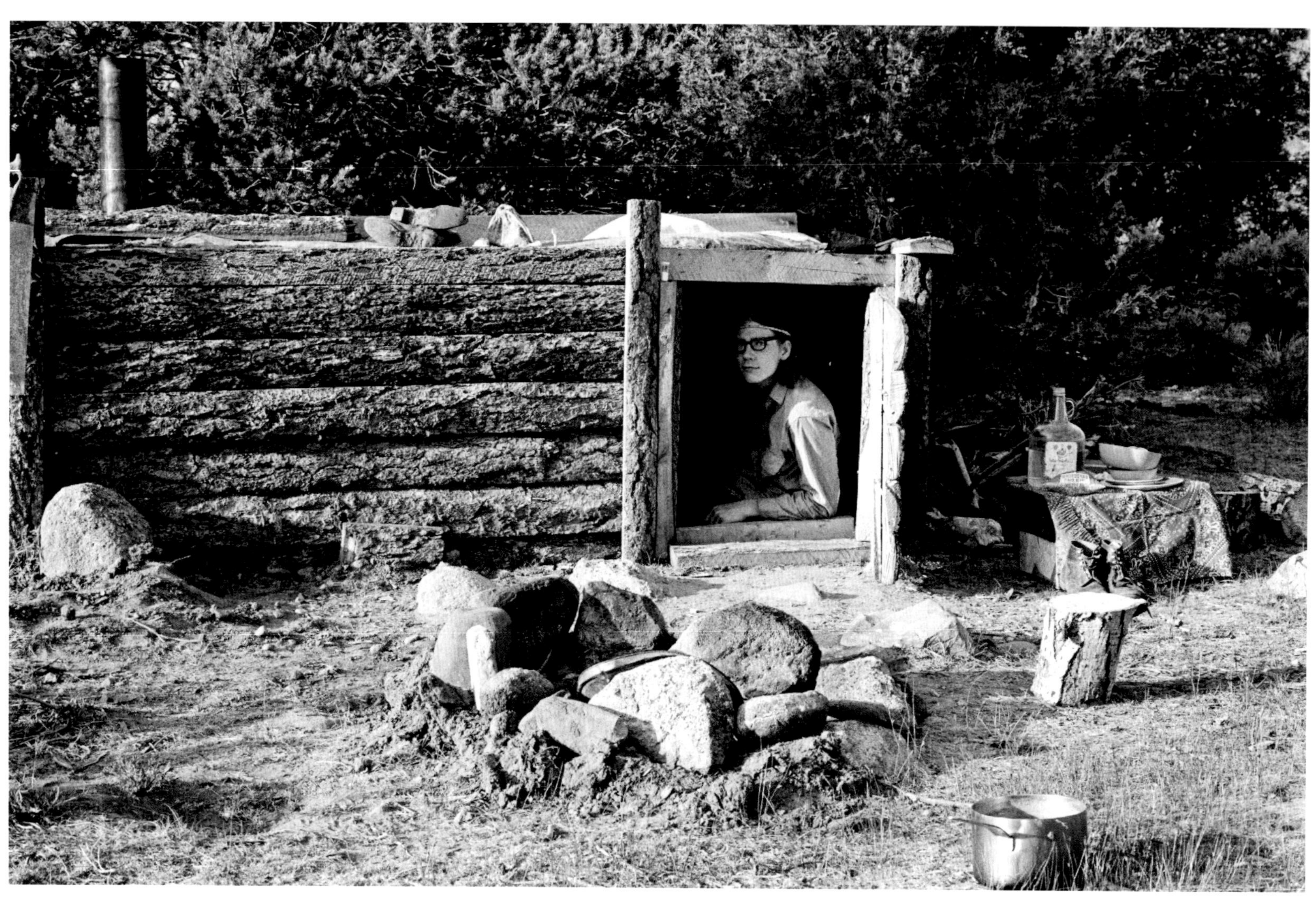

134   Lorien commune. New Mexico, 1969

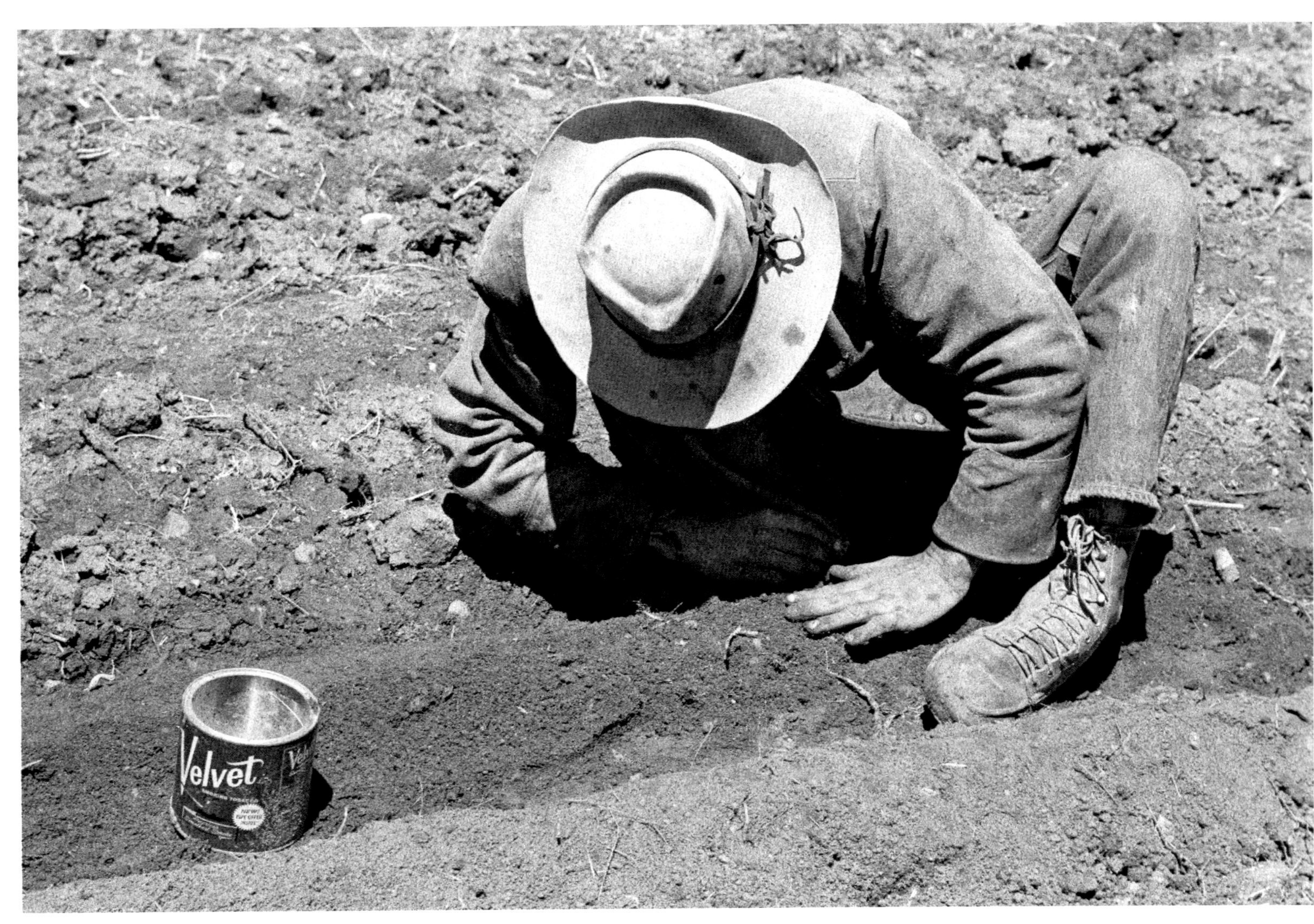

Farming at New Buffalo commune. New Mexico, 1969   **135**

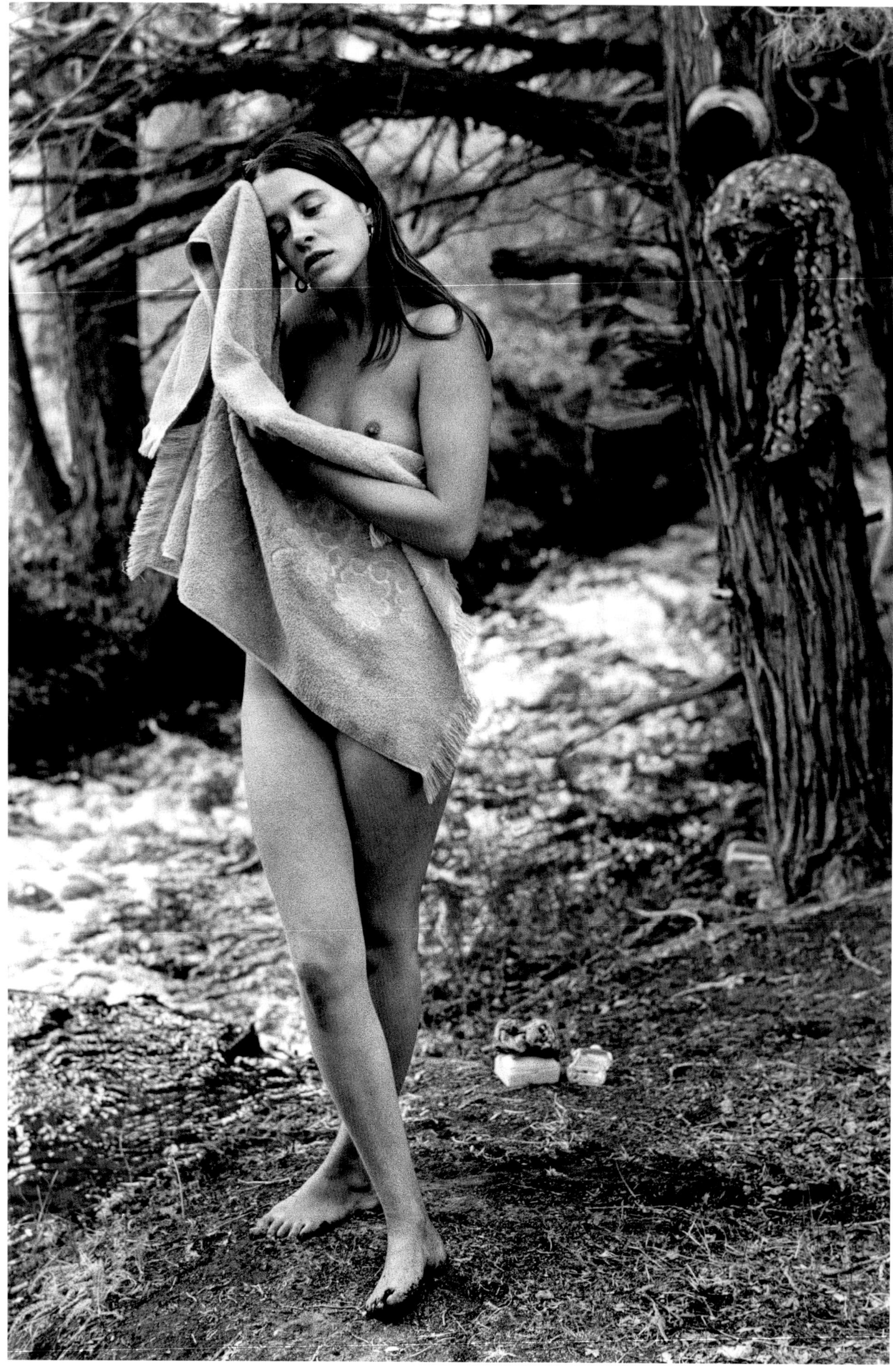

136 Morning bath. New Mexico, 1969

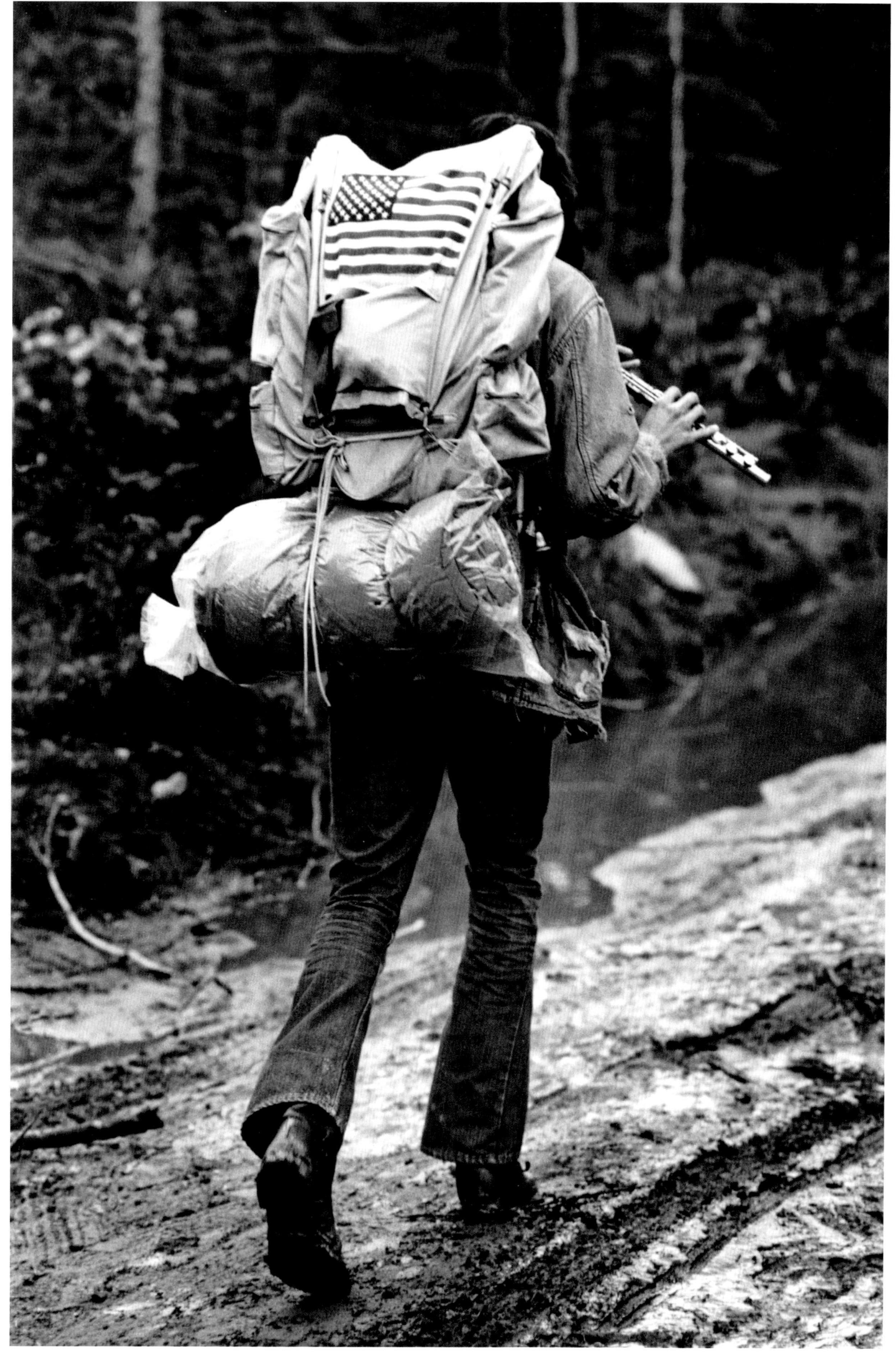

Spiritual dancing during construction at Lama. In the latter half of the sixties a generation with an energy and vision appeared on the horizon—a dramatic force that brought the American conservative scene to a halt. The young decided to take destiny into their own hands and shape a future of love and caring. Many groups formed communes throughout the nation. New Mexico, 1969

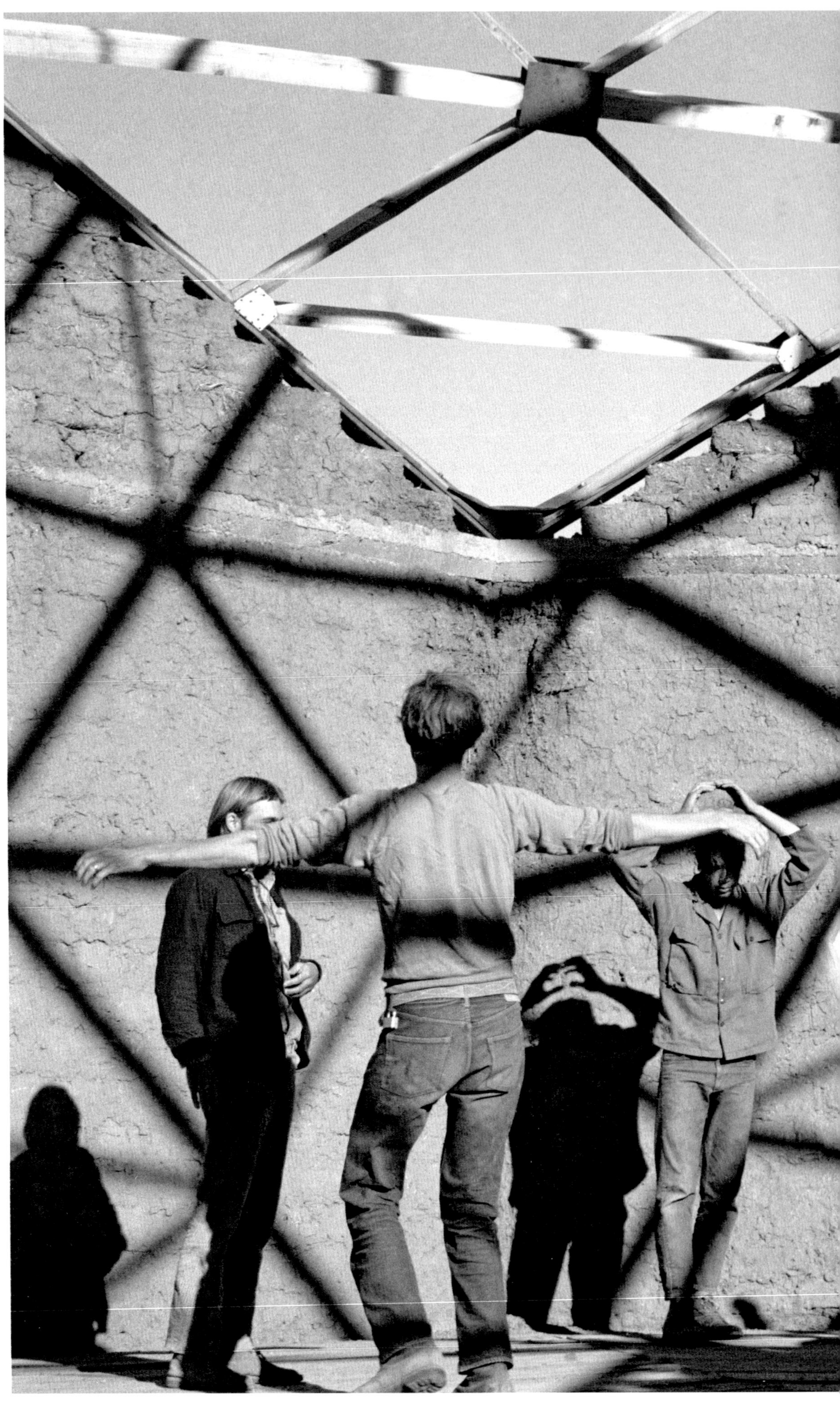

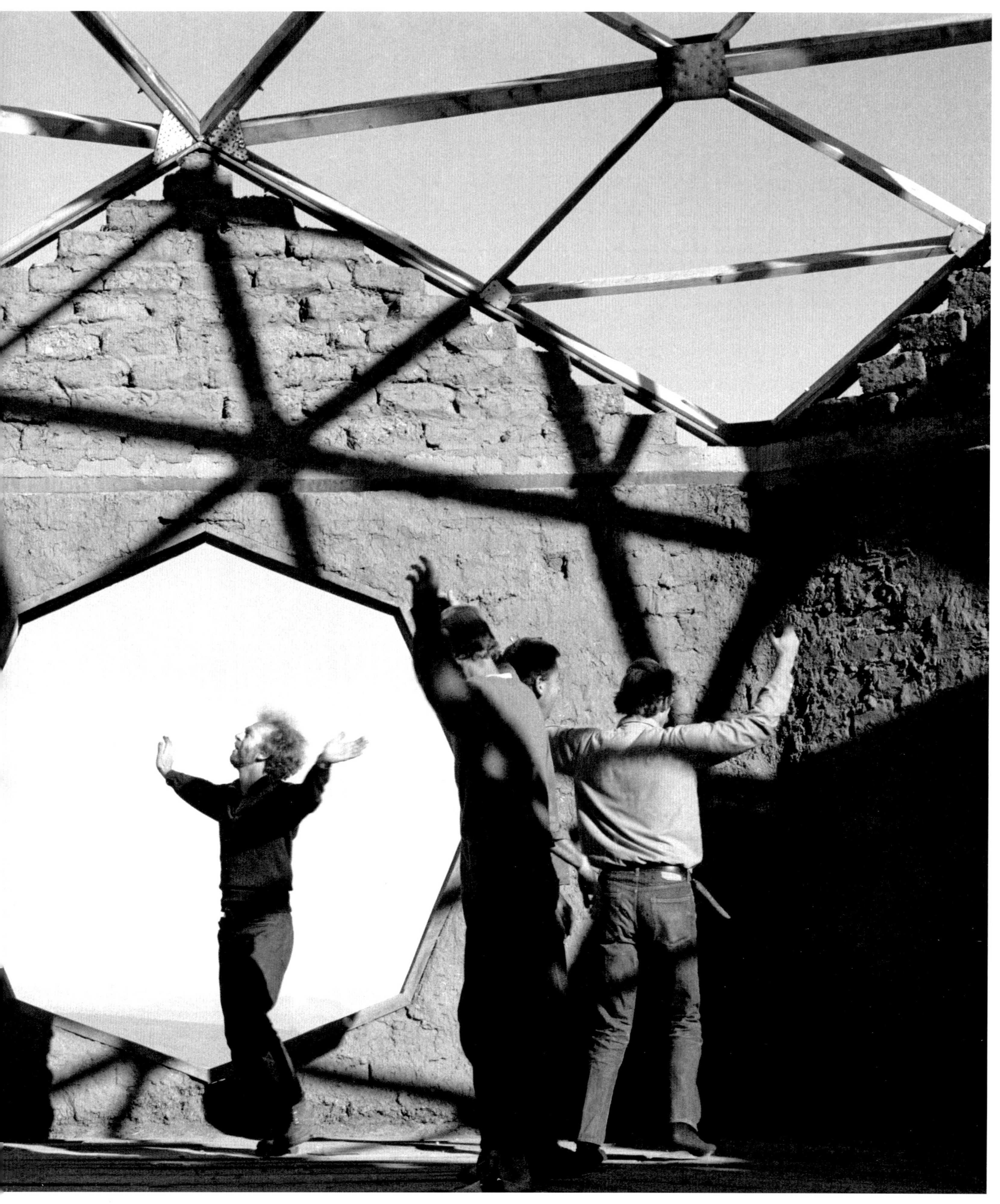

The open road for a bike rider. 1971

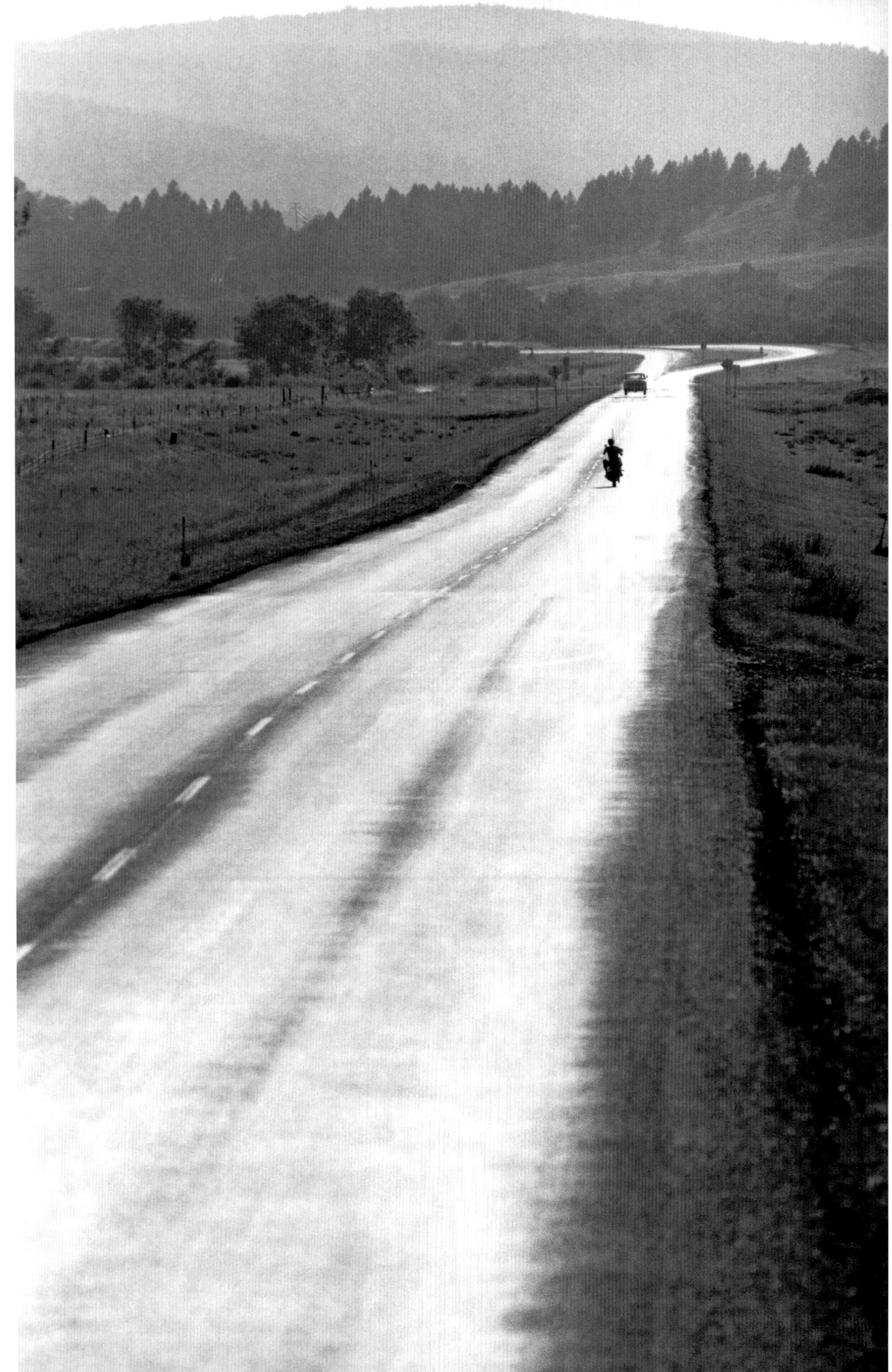

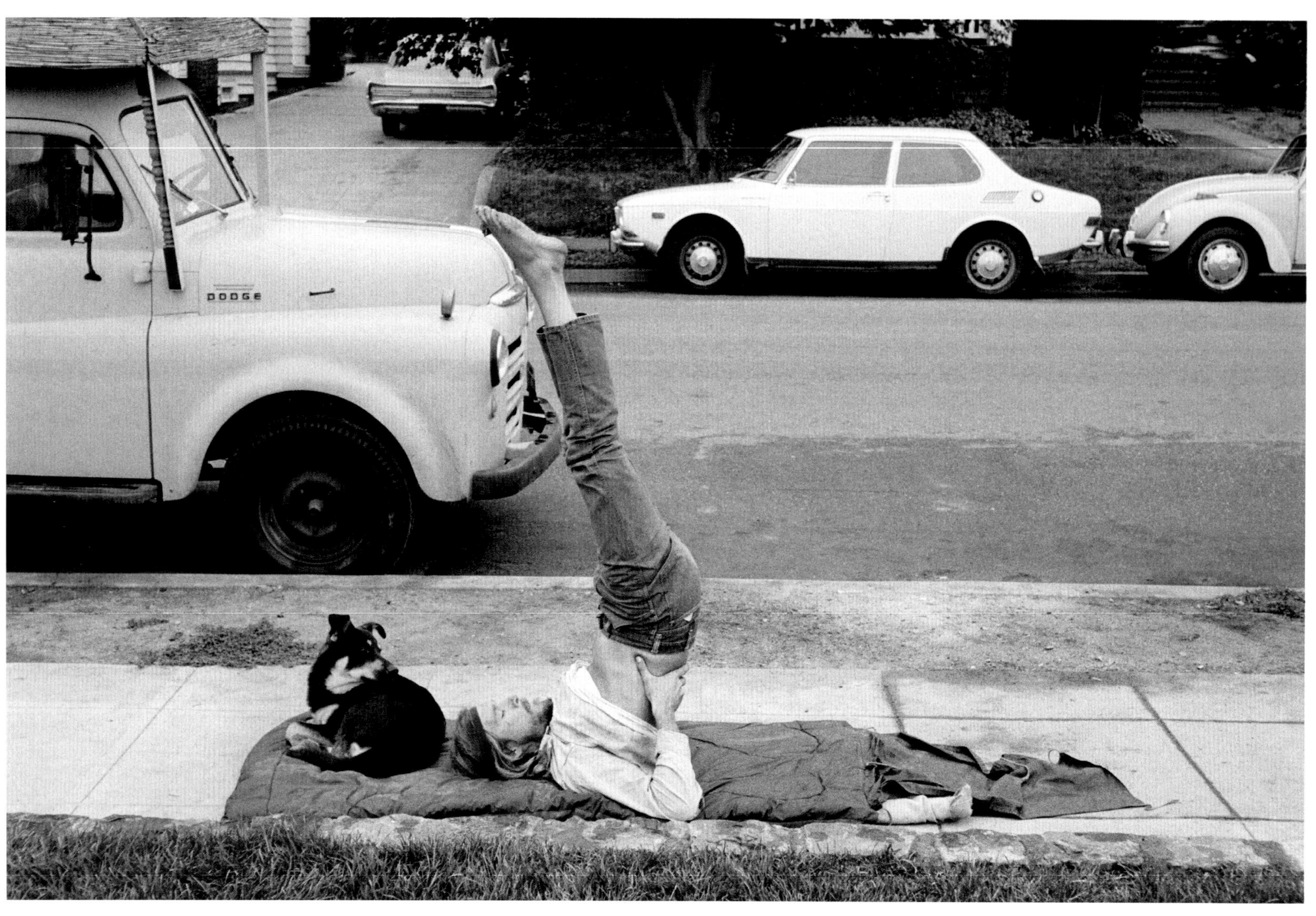

    From ROAD PEOPLE. 1971

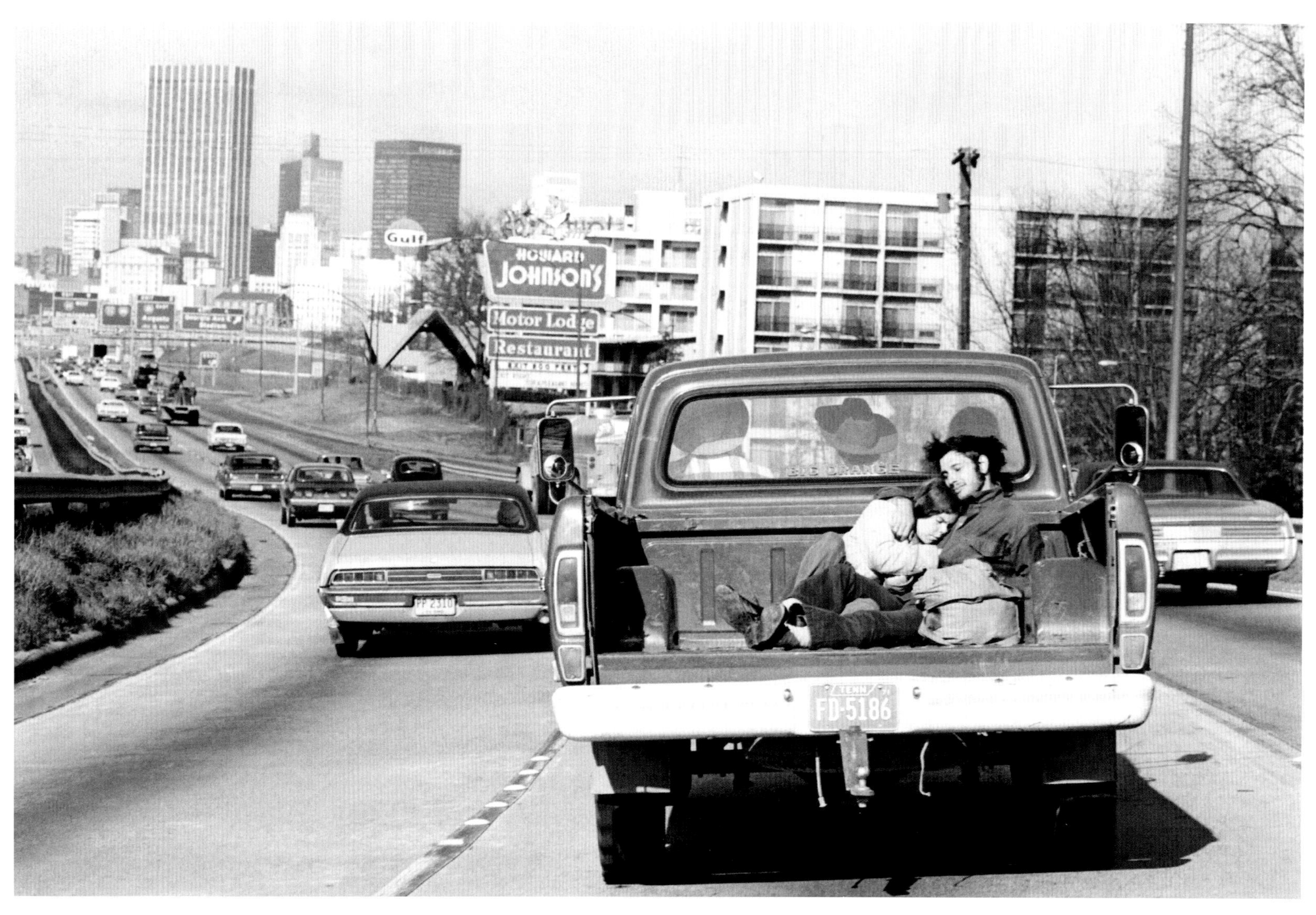

Gulf
HOWARD
JOHNSON'S
Motor Lodge
Restaurant
BIG ORANGE
TENN
FD-5186

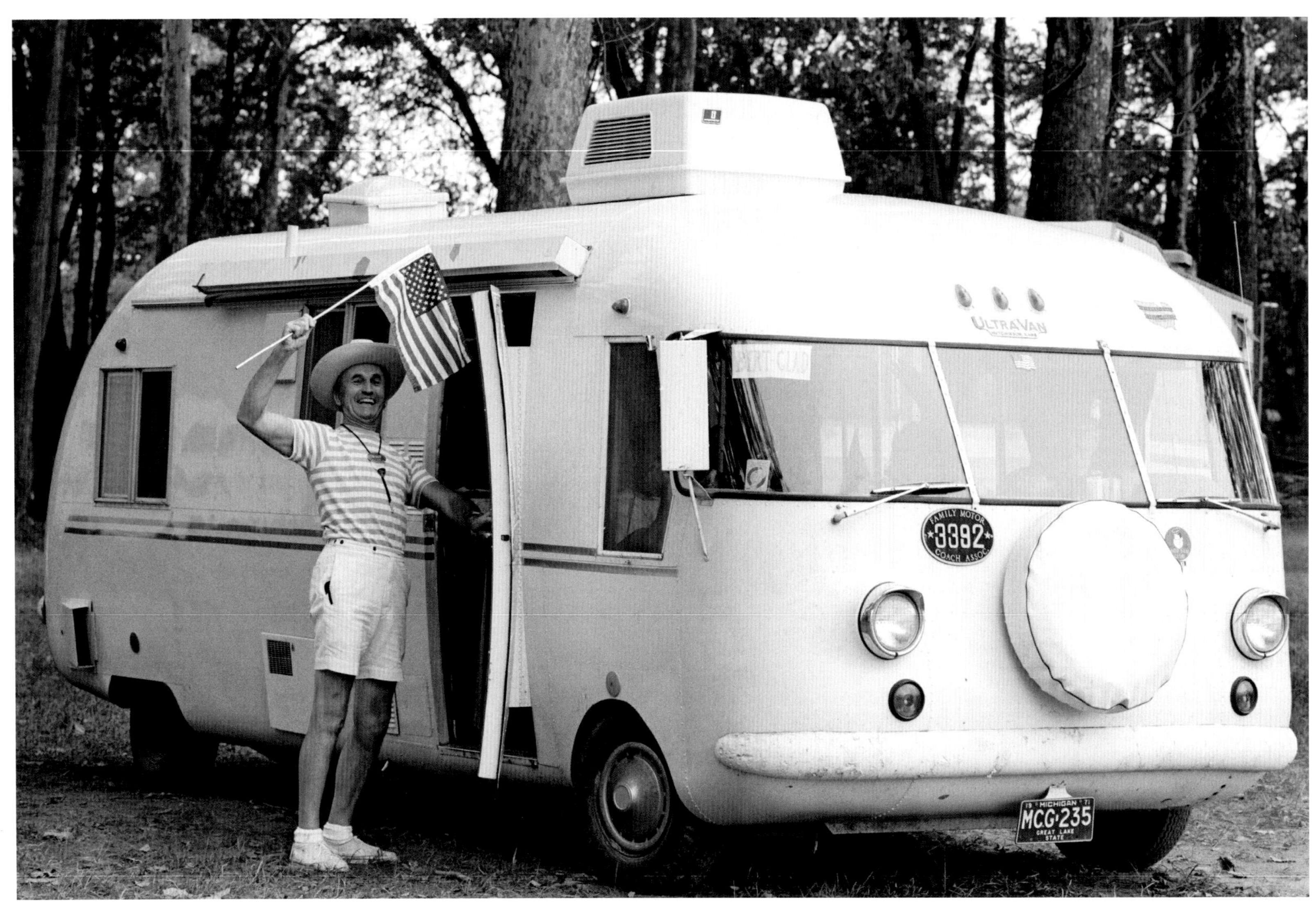

    A proud American camper with his space mobile. 1971

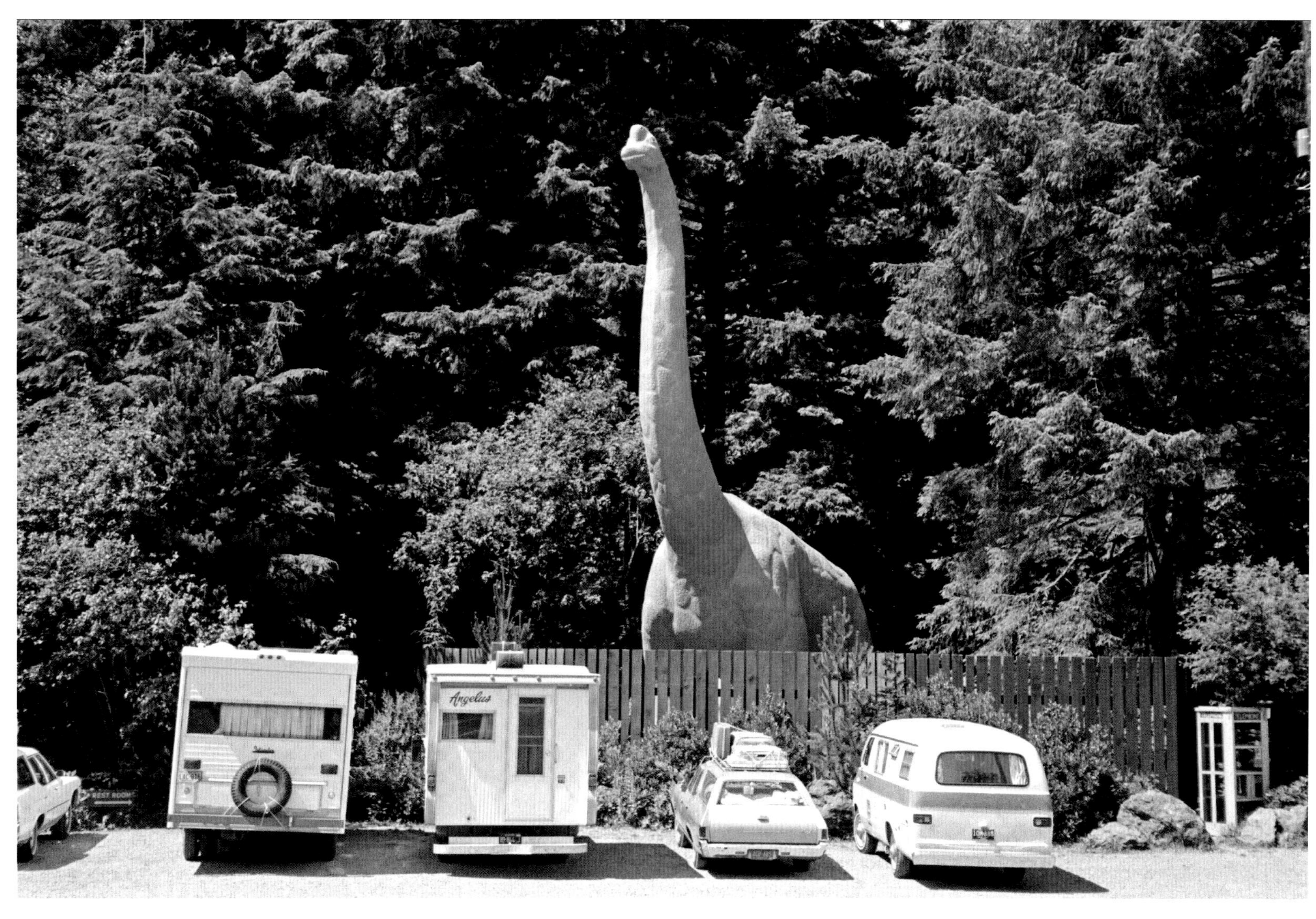

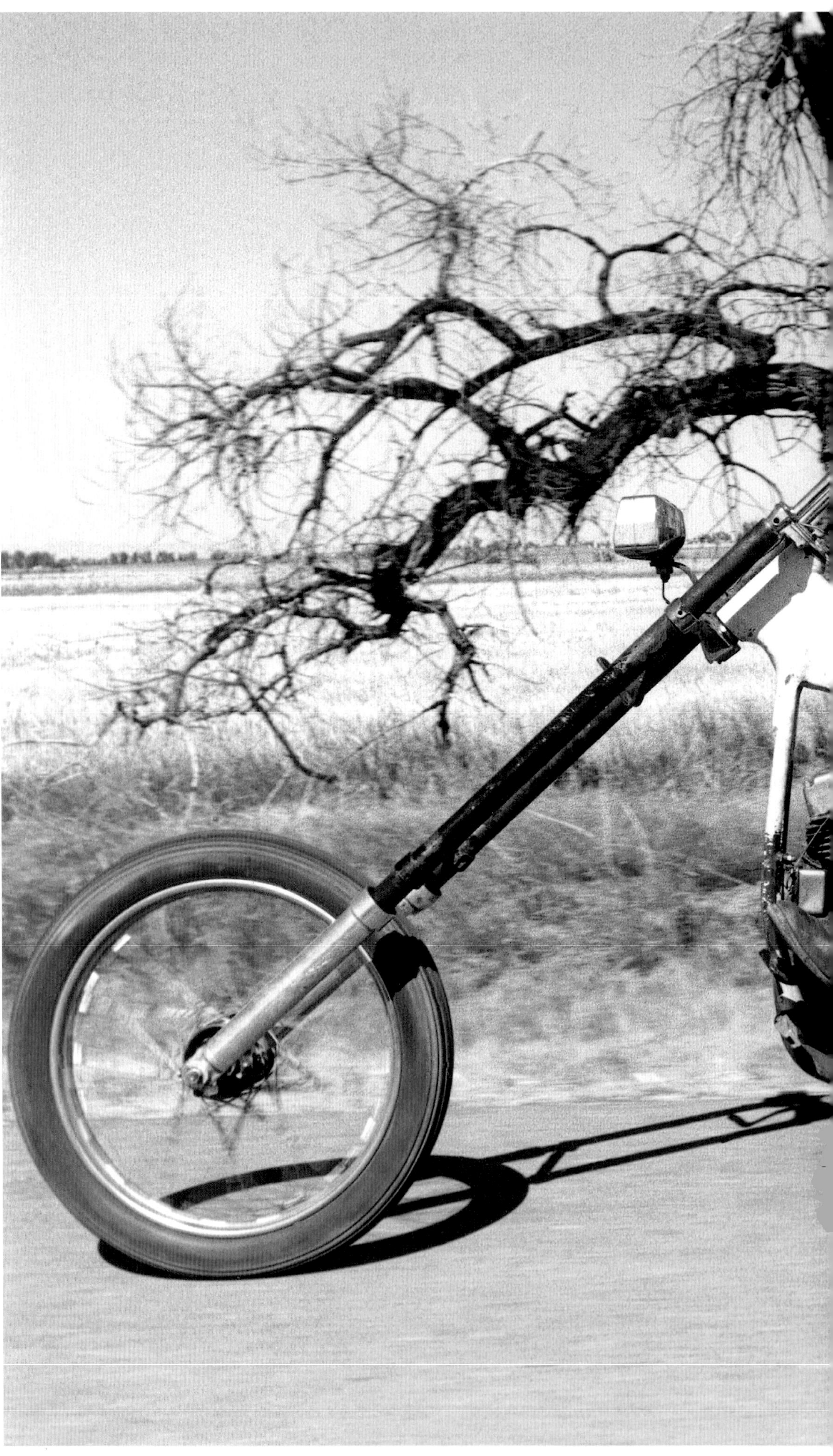

A biker in the popular "mongol" look. 1971

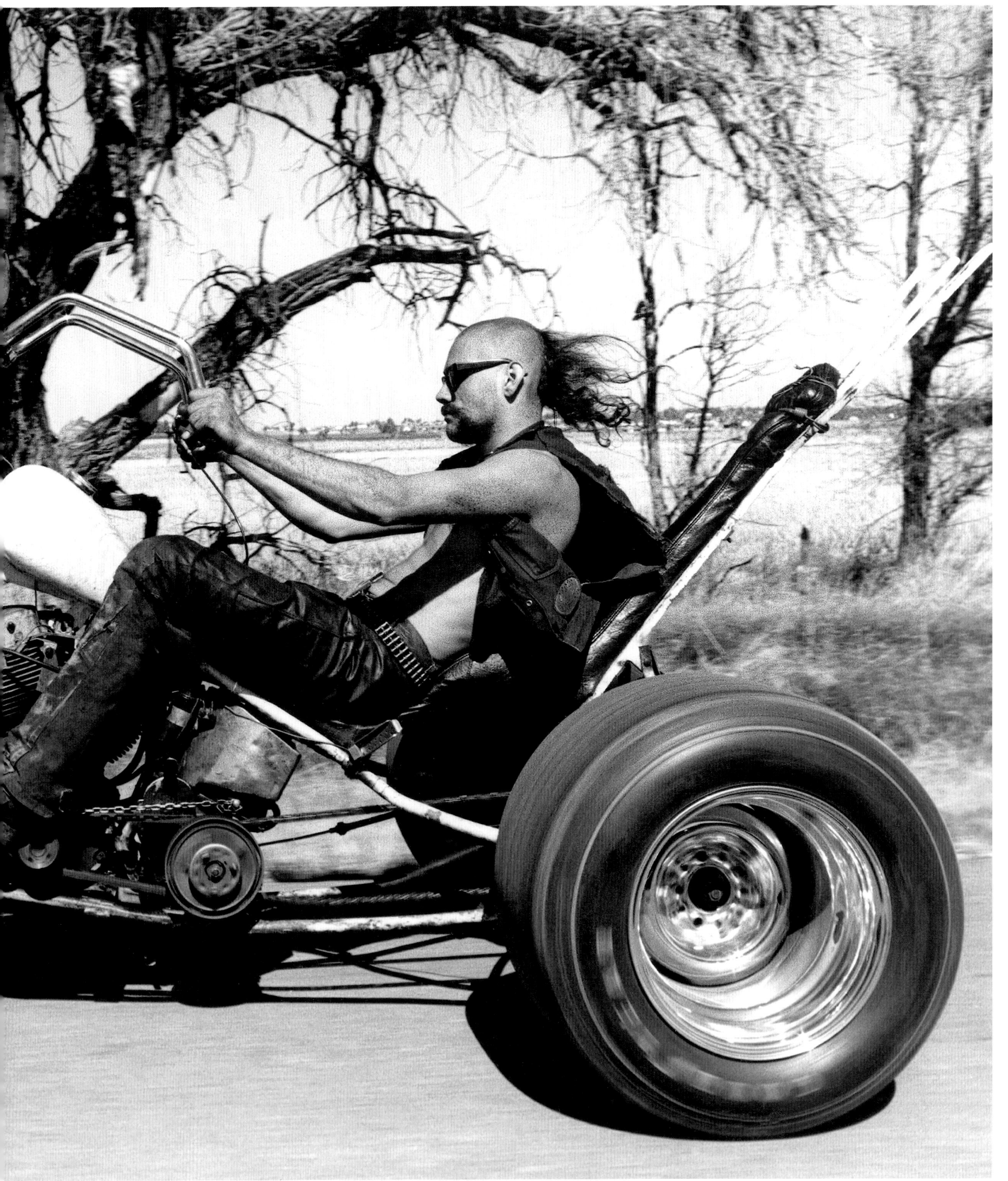

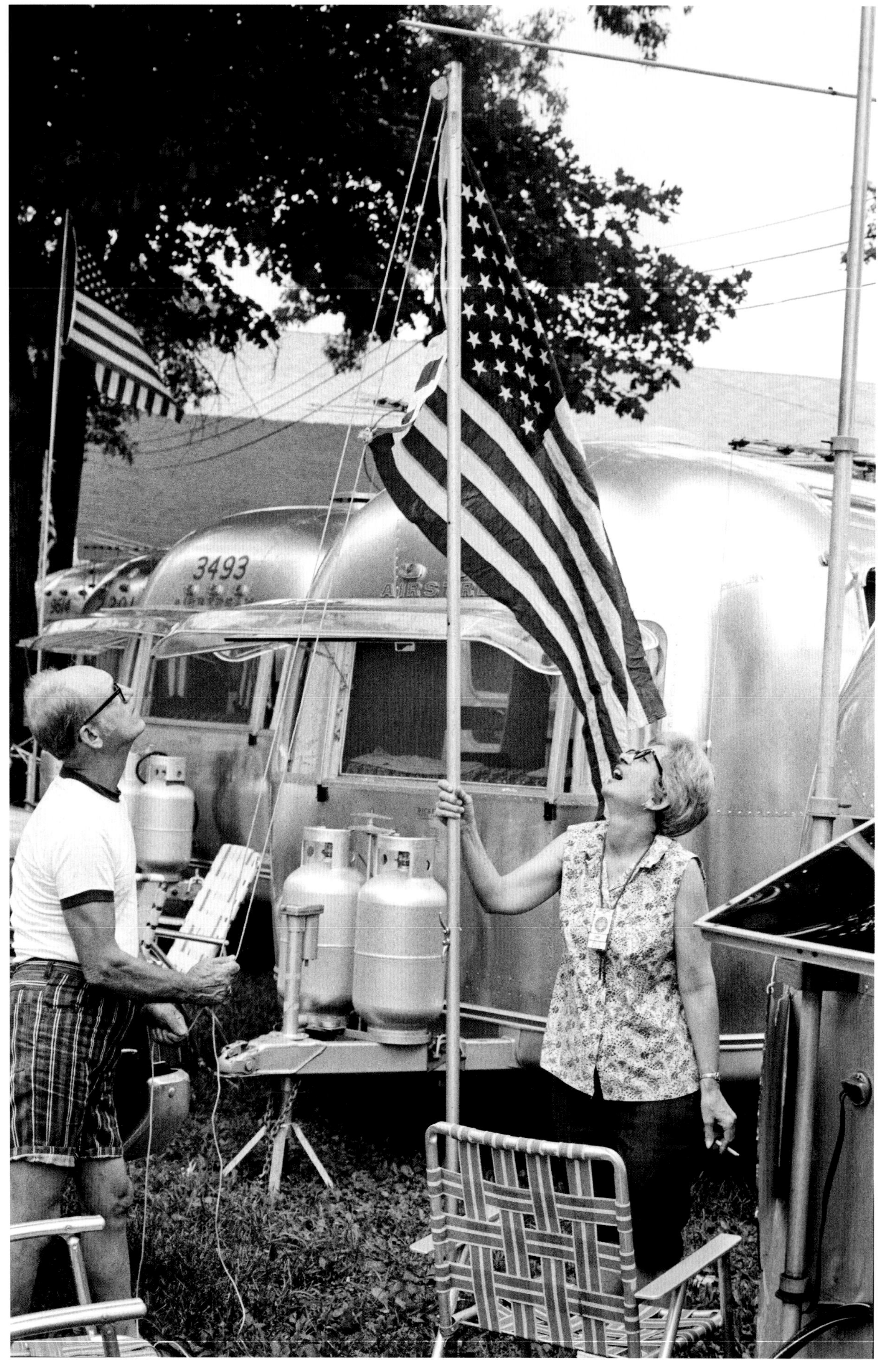

   From ROAD PEOPLE. 1971

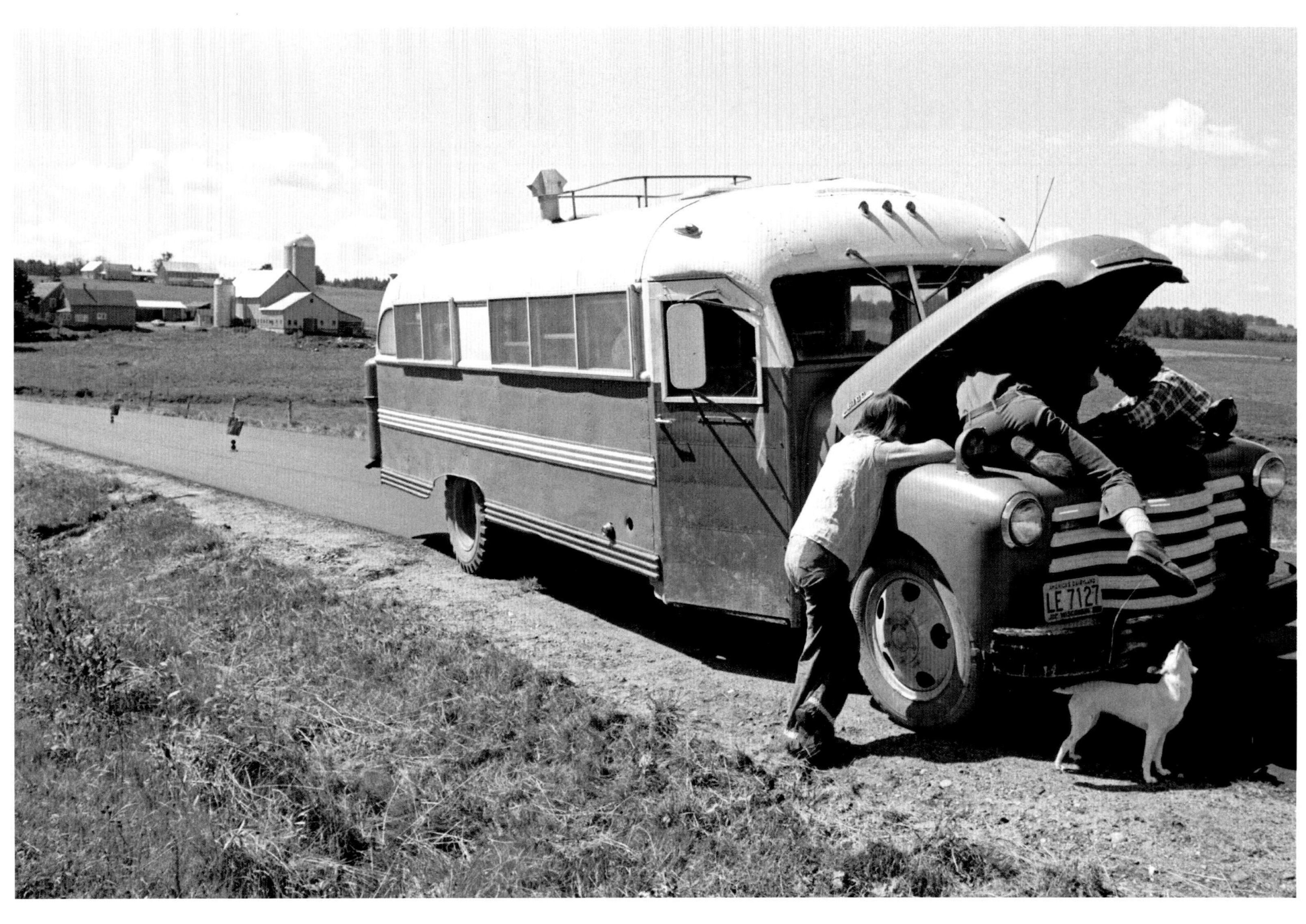

A family of three lives in an old school bus converted into a motorhome, an unintentional stop. 1971   **149**

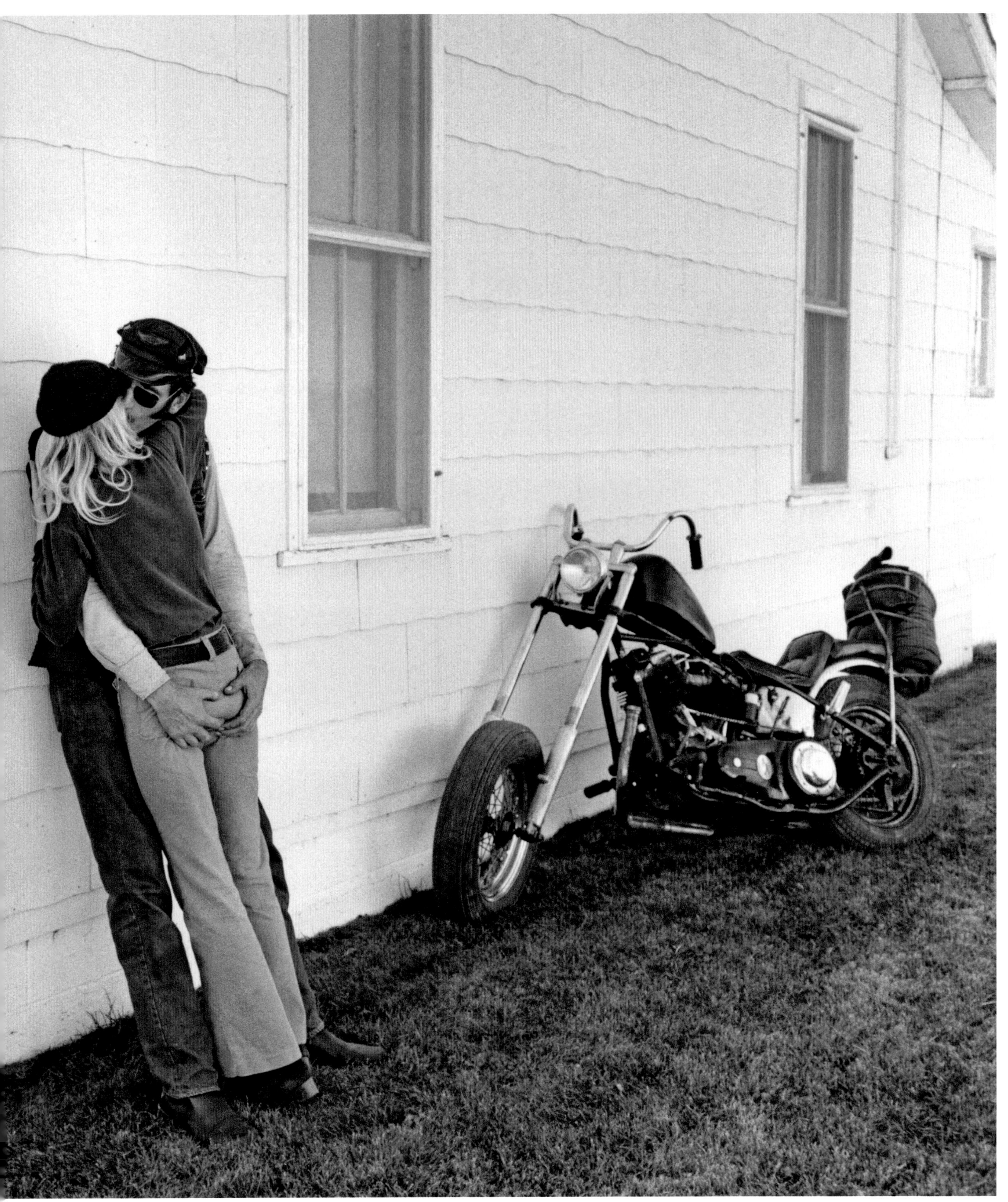

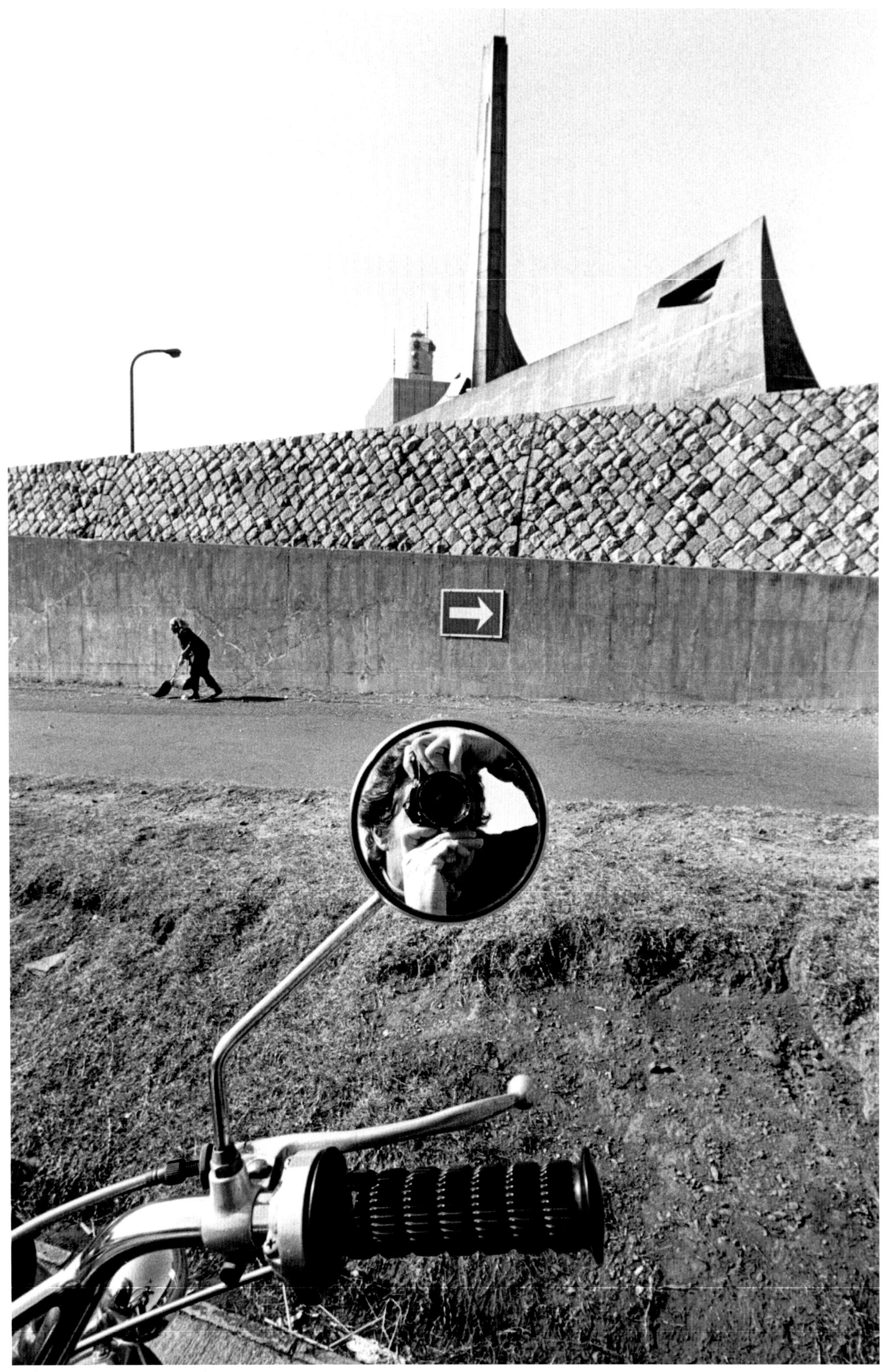

Dennis Stock
"I'll meet you tonight at noon"
Carole Naggar

Self-described as "a brassy kid from the Bronx,"[1] and by many others as a curmudgeon, Dennis Stock hated affectation in both photography and people. "Right away he launched himself into the heart of the matter, without bothering to study a tradition," says his colleague Guy Le Querrec.[2] In life, too, he could be direct to the point of harshness, and John Morris, a former director of Magnum Photos, the agency Stock joined in 1951, "jokingly called him 'Dennis the Menace' because of how pugnacious he could be in meetings."[3]

"He had little patience for those who did not agree with him," recalls his friend, gallery owner Howard Greenberg, "He had enormous confidence … he could become combative and even arrogant, which cost him relationships over time."[4]

Dennis Stock also possessed a wry sense of humor, apparent in many of his pictures but also in the comments he sent to Magnum during his reportages. While working on the set of QUO VADIS, he first remarked on the uncanny resemblance of the actor playing Nero to Groucho Marx, then added, "Several of the guests, clad principally in helmet and spears, retired eventually with head colds before day light."[5]

In a famous portrait by Andreas Feininger, THE PHOTOJOURNALIST, Dennis Stock's face is obscured by a Leica lens and a Tewe viewfinder that hide his eyes and form a mechanical mask; as in the image, Stock's hard surface concealed a deeper truth: a vulnerable, intuitive, intense, idealistic, at times tender and generous personality. Dennis Stock had tremendous charm, and possessed a rare gift to inspire. Maybe because of his difficult childhood and the early loss of his father, he was never a father to his own children; as his son Rodney Stock wistfully recalled, "He made a point of having no family life…. I have siblings that are twenty years younger, and he ignored them too."[6]

However, Stock did serve as a mentor to younger photographers and enjoyed the role. He was often generous, helping them with their portfolios and with career advice, and was also supportive of his students. "He was a seducer," his colleague Bruno Barbey remembers. "He lived with very beautiful women. He did not have an easy personality but he was very brilliant. When he spoke up during Magnum meetings it was always very well formulated."[7]

Born in Harlem Hospital in the South Bronx on July 24, 1928, to an English mother (to whom he was never close) and a Swiss father, Stock grew up during the Depression. He did not like to talk about his childhood, but on a rare occasion he confided, "In 1929, the banks failed. From then on we got by, but barely. By the mid-thirties, we had moved seven times. My dad, who had a painting and contracting business, totally failed and had to become a janitor so he could be sure we could have a roof over our heads. I was very aware of it because my mother was always very vocal and very fearful about our circumstances, how we'd get food. The sadness was, my father died when I was sixteen, from lung cancer … my mother and I had to go on from there, to do our best."[8]

Dennis had been very close to his father. At his father's side, even at the age of five, they walked from their apartment on Upper Manhattan's 138st Street down to 125th Street, then across town. At the counter of a Harlem bar they ate free hard-boiled eggs and salted herring, and his father would order a five-cent beer. Then they would go to the famous Apollo Theater where a seat cost twenty-five cents. There Dennis first listened to Louis Armstrong and other jazz greats.

As soon as he could legally do so, Dennis quit school and joined the Navy "to get away from it all. I was still wounded by the death of my father."[9] While he was based in Baltimore, the Coast Guard asked him to take pictures at a party. He only had a little box camera. They bought his pictures for a dollar each. "First of all I did not know that I had an aptitude. I was simply drawn to a way to make a living."[10] His other efforts, working in a factory and in shipping, failed.

So photography it was. For a few weeks, Dennis Stock was an apprentice to W. Eugene Smith, who made a deep impression on him with his concept of the long-term, in-depth photo essay. Smith recommended him to the Albanian photographer Gjon Mili. He remained in New York with Mili from the winter of 1947 to the end of 1951. "I worked unlimited hours, twenty-five bucks a week. He was an enormous influence in my life … he was a surrogate father … and he was a tough taskmaster. By then I was married, and I had a child."[11] After four years, he moved on to become a full-time professional.

Three thousand dollars? The first prize for a LIFE contest for young photographers looked very good to Stock. Inspired by the photographs of Lewis Hine, he went down to the docks, at first together with photographer Ernst Haas, another mentor, then alone. He started covering the arrival of the new immigrants coming from East Germany and Poland. "Part of the motivation was my own background," said Stock, "both my parents were immigrants. My father was a stowaway, and my mother was a legal immigrant."[12]

Stock's photographed immigrants still aboard ship, peering at the docks, overcome with emotion, then, later, forming a dense crowd making its way onto a New York dock like a flowing river. In another image, a lonely, dignified woman wearing a flowery dress and a hat waits near her suitcases. And in yet another image a family is depicted having their first meal in America, using as makeshift tables the wooden boxes containing their belongings and stamped with their future addresses; a soft light outlines their faces as they seem to emerge from the shadows of their past. Stock framed this poignant passage when people have left what they know but do not yet belong elsewhere. He managed to capture a panorama of raw emotions written on faces old and young after they have landed—from fear to joy, sadness and tears, to hopefulness and pride. He caught the absurdity of the moment when a couple in dark suits, hats on, expressions tense, have to pledge their "no Communist affiliation"—while having just fled a Communist country. Stock's images are both subtle and empathetic, yet not maudlin, while their strong graphic quality arrests the viewer.

More symbolically, he also seized the chance moment of seeing a baby in its mother's arms in front of a warehouse bearing on its façade the inscription "United States," making the image emblematic of the promised land for the upcoming generation. The baby looks at us gravely, its hand clutching the mother's shoulder; yet we only see the mother's back. It is as if, while the infant stares ahead, she is still looking back at a gray sea, between worlds.

With these photographs, Dennis Stock won first prize, sharing honors with Robert Frank, Elliott Erwitt, and Ruth Orkin, among others. Almost immediately, Robert Capa invited him to join the recently formed Magnum Photos agency (founded in 1947): he would never leave it. More then assignments, there he found a family of sorts, and inspiration from colleagues such as Henri Cartier-Bresson and Ernst Haas, whose color images would inspire him later in life. "I came into the ideal era," Stock said, "It was the golden age. Photo magazines like LIFE and LOOK existed. It gave photographers who wanted to be storytellers an opportunity. And of course there were master photographers by the handful, so you had inspiration."[13]

In 1954, Stock, fascinated by the film industry, was living in Hollywood and met Humphrey Bogart, who became his friend and mentor. They went sailing, and Bogart invited him to his home and introduced him to important actors, producers, and film directors. One of them was Nicholas Ray; in January 1955, he in turn invited Stock to a soirée in his bungalow on the grounds of the Chateau Marmont Hotel and introduced him to James Dean, a young actor on the rise. Stock had a long conversation with Dean and, intrigued, attended a sneak preview of Dean's film EAST OF EDEN at a Santa Monica theater. Mesmerized, Stock mentally photographed Dean's repertoire of gestures. He was deeply impressed by Dean's acting and sensed that the charismatic young man would soon join Marlon Brando and Paul Newman as a major film star of his generation.

He decided then and there to shoot a story about Dean and he received a two-day guarantee from LIFE—$150 a day. He would work for two months.

"What I was specifically trying to illustrate was the concept of 'you can't go home again,'" Stock explained. He wanted to create "a visual biography, which was unheard of … so we were making in stills a little movie."[14] Stock accompanied Dean on a journey to his hometown, Fairmount, Indiana, where he had grown up on a farm with his aunt and uncle, Ortense and Marcus Winslow; then they went to New York City before returning to Hollywood, as Dean started work on Ray's film REBEL WITHOUT A CAUSE.

In one of Stock's images, Dean, wearing glasses and a cap, sits in a deserted classroom, looking wistfully at the empty desks; in a farm pen, he playfully responds to the pig's oinking by playing a bongo drum; a famous image shows him posing with a huge white sow, his hand resting on the animal's flank. He is wearing his old work clothes: army shirt, army surplus fatigue pants, well-worn boots. In one of Stock's favorite images, Dean, in profile with his old camel cap tilted over his eyes, looks into the distance, surrounded by the farm's landscape, low stone walls, and trees bared by winter. In another, he stares at his shadowy reflection on an iced-over pond.

In the whole series James Dean seems to be an actor in his own life, the people and places around him no more than a theater set. He cuts a lonely figure, disconnected from his surroundings by an invisible line. Dean was, Stock said, "an alienated soul who bounced around—he did not realize what he had."[15]

In New York on the contrary, in cafés, at newsstands, in his fifth-floor walkup apartment on West 68th Street, filled with books and music, at the barbershop, at the dance school where he joins his friend Eartha Kitt, Dean seems at ease, and Stock's photographs form an intimate and sensitive diary. An insomniac, Dean snatched sleep when he could: in a picture taken at Jerry's Bar, on West 54th Street, across from the old Ziegfeld Theatre, his head is on the table: "At odd times and odd places he would simply pass out, for a few minutes or a few hours, then wake up and set out again," Stock recalled.[16]

Frame number nineteen on one of Stock's contact sheets is a portrait that would become world-famous. It is the third image in a sequence of Dean at Times Square. Hunched over, cigarette dangling from his mouth, hands in pockets of a Chief Petty Officer's Navy bridge coat bought at an army surplus store, Dean is shown on his way to the Actor's Studio. He appears as a somber figure seen from a distance and reflected in a puddle, walking towards the photographer in a drizzly, misty Times Square. Showing an actor from such a distance was unusual at that time: the surroundings of billboards and movie marquees take on as much importance as the person, illustrating the actor's milieu as well as his dreams.

In one of the images that Stock shot in Dean's hometown of Fairmount, at Hunt's furniture store on Main Street, an array of coffins was on display in a back room. James Dean playfully poses in a casket, dealing with fear by making fun of it. Then, at Stock's request, he stopped clowning and sat up, hands crossed, hair askew, looking startled and scared. Only seven months later, he would die at the wheel of his Porsche Spyder racecar. On his way to Salinas, where he planned to race the new car that he had bought with his earnings, Dean was killed in a head-on collision on the highway near Paso Robles. It was September 30, 1955.

"After the death of my friend Jimmy Dean," Stock wrote, "few illusions about the paradise of Hollywood remained. In the face of the reality of his austere funeral, all fantasies attached to the world of stars were greatly reduced."[17]

Maybe this explains in part why Stock's pictures of Hollywood from the early sixties rarely show actors in glamorous situations but rather in unguarded, offbeat, private moments, or during the shooting of a film, in between scenes. "I was especially interested in what transpired to the sides of the scene that was being shot," said Stock.[18]

Simone Signoret in an emotional moment, clutching the Oscar statuette that she has just received for her role in ROOM AT THE TOP; Frank Sinatra, hat askew, making a phone call during the preparations for the Presidential Inaugural Ball; John Wayne between takes on the set of THE ALAMO while a stagehand carries a fake horse: these are a few of Dennis Stock's unconventional photographs of actors.

On the set of THE MISFITS, Stock photographed a radiant Marilyn Monroe posing in her white bathrobe; she smiles, eyes closed, playfully standing on one foot. It was a sunny day, but Stock captured Monroe with a shadow falling diagonally across her face and body. A more glamorous shot of Marilyn in a lace-encrusted gown and dangling earrings was taken as she looked on during the shooting of another film, DÉSIRÉE. Attentive, she bends slightly forward in a graceful movement, apparently unaware of the photographer. In sharp contrast, a candid shot made during the filming of BUS STOP shows her in mid-scream, her hands covering her ears, as her co-actor Don Murray leans against her. The viewer is left to imagine what is happening on the set.

Director Billy Wilder went to Dennis Stock one day and told him about a movie he was planning with Audrey Hepburn, "a kid I think that you should know more about."[19] Wilder arranged for Paramount to show him a previous Hepburn film, ROMAN HOLIDAY, and Stock found Hepburn stunning. He received an assignment from ESQUIRE and followed Hepburn on the set of SABRINA, in which she was starring alongside Humphrey Bogart.

This series is especially beautiful. In one of the images, Billy Wilder points intently at something that we don't see while Hepburn looks down at her feet, like a brooding girl being scolded by a teacher. A crowd of onlookers standing on the pavement forms a fuzzy background. In another image Hepburn stands on one foot, clad in shorts and a man's jacket that make her seem more frail; a half smile plays on her lips as she looks both dreamy and mischievous. A beautiful portrait shows her sitting in a black limo, her face resting on her elbow, looking out the window. The polished body of the car reflects distorted silhouettes of the passersby. Stock isolated the star in a quiet, reflective moment, bringing us into her private world while, outside, life goes on, as if projected on the car's screen.

Dennis Stock would go on to photograph other Hollywood stars, such as Rock Hudson, Ginger Rogers, Buster Keaton, Bing Crosby, Jack Lemmon, Liz Taylor, Charlton Heston, Tony Curtis, and Maria Schell. He used the same understated style that made his photographs different from nearly everyone else's from that time.

"By 1957, the year after Chim [photographer David Seymour] died," Inge Bondi recalled, "Dennis was a full member of Magnum."[20] In 1959, a German publisher, Gert Hatje, approached the agency looking for a photographer to do a book on jazz. "I seemed like an ideal candidate because I had a passion for jazz," said Stock.[21] With an advance of $3,000, he went out for two years, following musicians all over the country while portraying a jazz scene that included the famous—Louis Armstrong, Billie Holiday, and Ella Fitzgerald—but also musicians and singers who had a reputation at the time but are now less well known, such as Clark Terry, Jonathan "Jo" Jones, and Velma Middleton.

From night to dawn and from stage to home, he followed the musicians. They were very aware of his presence and appear to have been accepting of what he was trying to do. They were generous with their time and their privacy: "They said, 'we do our job and you do your job,'" Stock recalled.[22] The resulting images range from close-up portraits to images taken at home with their families, jamming after hours, working in smoky clubs and taverns or formal recital halls, to commuting home in the predawn darkness.

Maybe because this essay connected to some of Stock's happiest childhood memories, the photographs have a quality of discovery and wonder about them. "When we were young," explained his colleague, photographer Costa Manos, "there was a kind of innocence to us. Dennis Stock did JAZZ STREET, René Burri did THE GERMANS, I did THE GREEK PORTFOLIO. Then we became more sophisticated, but maybe lost some of the poetry, because it was more thought than emotion."[23]

However, the JAZZ STREET series artfully combines a sense of sophistication with wonderment; Stock reveled in the unconventional shot: movement that gives violinist Stuff Smith's face a blurry double, as if reflecting his speed in improvisation; he etched a chiaroscuro form in which saxophonist Illinois Jacquet's silhouette, face, and instrument barely emerge from the darkness, prefiguring Roy DeCarava's dark images in the essay he began in the late fifties, THE SOUND I SAW; in a photo of John Lewis, a pianist and composer, the foreground of the picture is a blurry close-up of another musician, whose huge hand hangs over Lewis's head. Rufus Perryman, playing the piano at his local barbershop, is photographed from the back, hat screwed on, or on the stage, in a bird's-eye view.

In a shot of Louis Armstrong, the musician's face is obscured by his trumpet's mouth, while another famous image shows the musician in his dressing room: he relaxes before a set in a reclining chair, eyes closed, cigarette in hand, a wide smile on his face. His hair is tucked under a knotted white headkerchief, emphasizing his dark skin and sculptured features. Dennis remembered: "In those days, for a black man to have his picture taken with a kerchief around his head was reminiscent of slavery, but because Louis was an individual, he didn't care. As long as it had dignity."[24]

In other photographs, Earl Hine sits at the keyboard, head thrown back and in full throat. Bill Crow commutes home, his double bass on his back, among the ads of a deserted Times Square, the scene of the famous James Dean image. "So accustomed are the musicians to working by dark and sleeping by day," said Stock, "that a trumpeter, making an appointment, once said logically, 'I'll meet you tonight at noon.'"[25]

Stock's highly nonconventional book JAZZ STREET, which he designed and sequenced himself, has hardly aged. The image juxtapositions, the variation in image format, and the images' unconventional placement on the page mark the book as very modern and considerably ahead of its time. A double page, for instance, features on the left pianist Rufus Perryman seen from the back, then on the right he is turned around so we can peer at him from the side and above. In another, Billie Holliday is posed at left singing, with a fringe of light outlining her silhouette, and at right standing in the night next to her dog, a contrasting image of great loneliness. A cinematic sequence on yet another double page follows Duke Ellington in a recording session for Columbia. "Improvisation, the essence of their art, dictated the form of the book," Stock explained in the preface. Like their subjects, his pictures have great energy, intensity, and the image equivalent of perfect pitch.

"He was not a journalist," explained his colleague Bruno Barbey. "He did not cover conflicts, rather societal phenomena."[26] To Dennis Stock, festivals and fairs were such a phenomenon, and he thought that they represented some of the essence of America. In 1964 and 1965, he set out to uncover these aspects of a country little known to outsiders and tourists. He had an assignment from HOLIDAY magazine, but, as usual, his trip took him further than any magazine would have expected. In the process he became an anthropologist of sorts, one that studied the strange customs of his own country, and especially some that could not be further from the life of a Bronx-born, New York-bred photographer.

Many of these pictures display a mixture of tenderness and humor: a photograph taken in Des Moines, Iowa, before a beauty contest for cattle, shows a young woman in hair curlers sitting in the straw next to a large cow, and, like a hairdresser, carefully combing the animal's tangled tail. The cow stands muzzle to muzzle with another, and, heads locked in a symmetrical embrace, the animals seem to kiss.

A picture of an archery contestant concentrating on his shot debunks ideas about the nobility of the sport: the man's nose is tilted against the string, echoing his straw hat's tilt, and he rolls his eyes while taking aim. In an Iowa fair, a matron in curlers and a hairnet holds, with a pointed index finger, a mask of a slickly coiffed politician over her face, her own glasses pulled up over the mask. A cow at a state fair seems to gaze at a small cutout of a cow while two bespectacled women and a boy watch. At Dennis the Menace Park in Monterey, a screaming child's open mouth repeats that of a yawning (or laughing) lion statue. A line of dancers dressed as Santa Clauses, complete with white beards and pom-pom hats, lift their legs in unison. Another group of tired, disillusioned-looking Santa Clauses sit at long tables, apparently waiting to be called.

In the tradition of Henri Cartier-Bresson's 1937 London reportage on King George VI's coronation—Cartier-Bresson had concentrated on the public watching the event in Trafalgar Square rather than the coronation itself—Dennis Stock enjoyed photographing the event's reflection on onlookers' faces, and what happens at the margins rather than the event itself: a crowd in a sports arena with vertical dividers that look like a prison's bars watches an unknown parade or event. In another picture, onlookers watch a film shoot while a young boy somewhat bizarrely rests his head on a huge cigarette sticking out of a cardboard pack stamped with the word "Nicotine" and a skull.

In 1964, Stock photographed Native American festivals and powwows in Taos, New Mexico, where he would continue to work until 2000. In several pictures he captured the contrast between tradition and modernity: two dancers wearing eagle masks and wings pose in front of a parking lot's gleaming cars; a Navajo in full regalia, including fringed jacket and feathered headdress, films a Native American festival while being photographed.

In 1968, Dennis Stock assigned himself the subject of the state of California. He thought that this was where things were going to happen: "the style-maker, the leader of the pack," he said.[27] This was, and still is, a state where technological and spiritual quests intermingle. As Stock put it, "Every idea that Western man explores in his pursuit of the best of all possible worlds will be searched at the head lab—California. Technological and spiritual quests vibrate throughout the state, intermingling, often creating the ethereal. It is from this freewheeling potpourri of search that the momentary ensembles in space spring, presenting to the photographer his surrealistic image. However, to the Californians it is all so ordinary, almost mundane. The sensibility of these conditioned victims is where it is all at, right, left, up and down. Our future is being determined in the lab out West. There, a recent trip blew my mind across this state of being, as I collected images along the way to remember the transient quality of the Big Trip."[28]

There are times when Dennis Stock found a way to symbolize the new era, as in his famous image of the girl at a Venice Beach rock festival. As he was photographing the audience massed on the beach, a young girl dressed in white suddenly jumped on the stage, hair whipping in the wind, holding an arm up, and started dancing; at that split second he clicked the shutter, catching her up close from the back and creating an image that summarized the enthusiasm and spirit of a whole generation.

"Surrealism was everywhere," Stock wrote, "the juxtaposition of relative levels of reality projected chaos."[29] He found surrealism and the whimsical in unexpected juxtapositions, such as a bikini-clad woman on a beach embracing a man wearing a grinning skeleton mask; another image shows a man on the steps to the beach of Corona del Mar holding a surfboard. His whole body remains hidden, except for his arms, turning the surf into a polished white mask with the stark shadows of the stairs creating a geometric background as his shadowed hands seem like small animals with open jaws. Another picture shows, over the sands of Playa del Rey, the huge shadow of a plane floating, seeming to repeat like a ghostly double the silhouette of a bather with outstretched arms. In Berkeley, a mustachioed father in sunglasses and with a serious, stern face holds his baby like an offering, bearing a poignant sign: "Baby Needs Mother, Sincere—Permanent." An attentive greyhound, paws crossed, sits on top of a conference table, surrounded by men in business suits. In an amusement park, a gigantic dinosaur plaster model cranes its neck over a parking lot, as if curious of the RVs. With the background of a Ferris wheel, a man perched on top of a U.S. Air Force Titan II missile container washes the armament carefully with a long-stemmed mop—his domestic gestures seem incongruous.

Other times, such as during the filming of PLANET OF THE APES, Stock created the juxtapositions himself and acted like a director, bringing the actors dressed as apes into town in a limousine and posing them in locations of his choice: on a bench bearing an ad for a funeral home, on the steps where a man is reading, seemingly unaware of the actor's presence or indifferent, at the entrance to a go-go girl show. "I like the surrealism," Stock said, "It's my level of humor."[30] He was initially hoping to show people's reaction to the apes' foray into town, but quickly found out that there was none: Californians had seen it all.

In the news media of the sixties and seventies, the hippies were almost always portrayed negatively. It seemed inevitable that Dennis Stock, with his contrary mindset, would get interested in their culture; he spent the entire year of 1969 visiting alternative communities in Colorado, New Mexico, and California. These communities ranged from the hip to the political and the spiritual, from the poor transient camps—people living in converted buses or under tents—to large and self-sufficient rural communities. Each commune was different, and their members shared different passions: music, art, environmental or political concerns, sexual liberation, draft resistance, fear of the apocalypse. The war in Vietnam demanded large numbers of troops, and many in the younger generation were starting to think that they were deemed expandable. Stock also explored free high schools and clinics.

To him, the hippie way of life, their sharing of property and their decision to turn away from material values, was attractive and perhaps he recognized part of himself in their idealism. Some of the ideas of the counterculture were quintessentially American: a pioneering outlook that fit the country's heritage. Stock explained, "I was attracted by the hippie movement that was defined by two main principles: caring about others, and a taste for adventure. My pictures of hippies are about the search of a better life. I was drawn by what they were trying to achieve. The hippie instinct was countercultural, it said, 'Let's try to go back to basics.' Hippiedom, in a sense, is a return of teenage rebellion, a new, stronger rebellion. Each one of us had a period of rebellion at a certain moment of our lives."[31]

Looking at Dennis Stock's photographs of the hippies published in his book CALIFORNIA TRIP, one can sense his empathy for their vision. To him, the hippies were getting back to fundamental American values that had been obscured by the prevalence of capitalism. His images possess a tender, almost innocent, emotional quality. However, he did not idealize the hippies; some of his photographs, for instance, explore the difficult aspects of subsistence farming. "If you look at the range of photographs, there's pain in a lot of instances, because not every youngster was successful at survival. Some of them lived very meager existences," he explained.[32]

A picture of a couple in old-fashioned outfits standing in a field in front of a straw scarecrow, the man holding a hoe, is an optimistic and resolute reinterpretation of Grant Wood's 1930 painting AMERICAN GOTHIC, where a dour couple stands in front of their house and field. In a joyful image, a group of men performs a spiritual dance under the dome at the Lama Foundation Commune in New Mexico, the shadows from the iron and glass structure striping their bodies with erratic markings. Quieter images depict family life on communes: a bearded man from the Messiah's World Commune roughhouses with children at the Golden Gate Park; a man, his wife, and their baby share a bath in a wooden cabin while sunshine falls through the window upon them. Stock shows the easy relationship of the hippies with their bodies: in Novato, California, a bare-chested couple rides a black horse;[33] in another image, a young naked beauty steps out of her outdoors morning bath, wiping herself with a towel. These images carry a sense of nostalgia and lost innocence, perhaps the feeling that this was only a moment in time and that the hippie movement would not survive.

Enduringly attracted to subcultures, Stock went on to photograph itinerants, bikers, road people, hikers, travelers, and motorhome owners along the country's interstate highways. To him, they were another symbol of independence and of the restlessness of American society. "In 1971 I went out to explore their lifestyles on the open road. Like most photographers, I am an itinerant by preference, so it was a natural attraction. At a bikers' meet in Colorado, I met the Sons of Silence, and I asked to stay with them. They trusted and accepted me, even though I only ever rode a bike once in my life—as it happens riding pillion with James Dean. They made me an honorary member."[34]

In a more romantic image from that period, a hiker, seen from the back, walks on the side of a snowy road, an American flag affixed to his bulging backpack. He is playing the flute. Two hikers who hitched a ride are resting in a truck bed. One of Stock's best images depicts a biker seen from a distance on the unraveling ribbon of a country road, an image symbolic of independence and movement: "For me, the Sons of Silence piece is an example of how I like to work as a photographer; my inclination for affirmative images, humor and beauty; being on the road, outside and away from the city."

"The photo essay," Dennis Stock wrote, "is essentially like a composer's variations on a theme. You are always pushing the envelope more, asking 'Is there one more thing I can say?'"[35]

Following in the steps of W. Eugene Smith, Ernst Haas, and Henri Cartier-Bresson, his strength was the eloquent, in-depth photo essay, on themes most often self-assigned at his own expense, and pursued for months, even years.

Later on in his life, weary of the world's problems, Stock would work almost exclusively in color and shift from human subjects to silent and beautiful ones, landscape and flowers, but he still remained true to the essay form. His wife, author Susan Richards, with Stock the last five years of his life, remembers: "He said he had done exactly what he wanted to do, and loved every minute of it."[36]

As he said, "Photography is a marvelous way of saying, 'I've been here.' It is better than a headstone."[37]

July 2014, New York

1   My heartfelt thanks go to Bruno Barbey, Inge Bondi, Jimmy Fox, Howard Greenberg, Guy Le Querrec, Constantine "Costa" Manos, John Morris, Matt Murphy, and Rodney Stock for their contributions to this text, either in interviews or in locating sources. Special thanks are due to Susan Richards for making available to the author excerpts of texts by Dennis Stock, and to Jonathan Fox for his superb editing.
2   Guy Le Querrec, phone interview with the author, Paris, May 19, 2014.
3   John Morris, interview with the author, Paris, May 20, 2014.
4   Howard Greenberg, interview with the author, New York, May 13, 2014.
5   Dennis Stock archive, Magnum New York.
6   Rodney Stock, phone interview with the author, New York, June 11, 2014.
7   Bruno Barbey, interview with the author, Paris, May 19, 2014.
8   Quoted from Hana Sawka, BEYOND ICONIC: PHOTOGRAPHER DENNIS STOCK, DVD, 75 min. (New York, 2011).
9   Ibid.
10 Ibid.
11 Ibid.
12 Quoted from David Snider, THE ARTICULATE IMAGE, video, 40 min., The Photography Channel (2013).
13 Quoted from Sawka, BEYOND ICONIC.
14 Ibid.
15 Ibid.
16 Dennis Stock, Preface to JAMES DEAN REVISITED (San Francisco, 1987).
17 Dennis Stock, distribution text (distro) for JAMES DEAN REVISITED, Dennis Stock archive, Magnum New York, 1987.
18 Inge Bondi, interview with the author, Princeton, New Jersey, June 6, 2014.
19 Dennis Stock archive, Magnum New York, 1953.
20 Inge Bondi, interview, June 6, 2014.
21 Dennis Stock, text communicated by Susan Richards (exact source unknown).
22 Ibid.
23 Constantine "Costa" Manos, phone interview with the author, New York, June 12, 2014.
24 Dennis Stock, JAZZ STREET (Garden City, N.Y., 1960).
25 Ibid.
26 Bruno Barbey, interview with the author, Paris, May 19, 2014.
27 Dennis Stock, text communicated by Susan Richards (exact source unknown).
28 Dennis Stock, Preface to CALIFORNIA TRIP (New York, 1970).
29 Ibid.
30 Dennis Stock archive, Magnum New York.
31 Dennis Stock, text communicated by Susan Richards (exact source unknown).
32 Ibid.
33 This image in fact features on the cover of CALIFORNIA TRIP, a body of work dating from roughly the same time as THE ALTERNATIVE: COMMUNAL LIFE IN NEW AMERICA, but that also in many respects deals with alternative lifestyles.
34 Ibid.
35 Ibid.
36 Susan Richards, phone interview with the author, New York, June 17, 2014.
37 Quoted from Sawka, BEYOND ICONIC.

This book is published on the occasion of the exhibition DENNIS STOCK: TIME IS ON YOUR SIDE at the Suermondt-Ludwig-Museum, Aachen, October 30, 2014 – February 25, 2015. The exhibition was created in collaboration with the Howard Greenberg Gallery, New York. Special thanks to Howard Greenberg and Karen Marks from the Howard Greenberg Gallery, New York; Lorenza Bravetta, Hamish Crooks, Andréa Holzherr, and Nikandré Koukoulioti from Magnum Photos; Sylvia Böhmer from the Suermondt-Ludwig-Museum, Aachen; as well as Anton Corbijn, Stephen Hoffman, Jeffrey Klotz, Carole Naggar, Susan Richards, Robert Steinke, and Jonathan Weiss.

Front Cover: James Dean, returned to the town where he spent his youth and visited his old school, Fairmount High School. Fairmount, Indiana, 1955 (detail). See page 28.

Prestel Verlag, Munich
A member of Verlagsgruppe Random House GmbH

Prestel Verlag
Neumarkter Strasse 28
81673 Munich
Tel. +49 (0)89 4136-0
Fax +49 (0)89 4136-2335

Prestel Publishing Ltd.
14-17 Wells Street
London W1T 3PD
Tel. +44 (0)20 7323-5004
Fax +44 (0)20 7323-0271

Prestel Publishing
900 Broadway, Suite 603
New York, NY 10003
Tel. +1 (212) 995-2720
Fax +1 (212) 995-2733

www.prestel.com

Library of Congress Control Number: 2014951450
British Library Cataloguing-in-Publication Data: a catalogue record for this book is available from the British Library; Deutsche Nationalbibliothek holds a record of this publication in the Deutsche Nationalbibliografie; detailed bibliographical data can be found under: http://www.dnb.de.

Prestel books are available worldwide. Please contact your nearest bookseller or one of the above addresses for information concerning your local distributor.

Editorial direction: Curt Holtz with Dorothea Bethke
Copyediting: Jonathan Fox, Barcelona
Design and layout: Benjamin Wolbergs, Berlin
Production: Friederike Schirge
Origination: Longo AG, Bolzano
Printing and binding: Longo AG, Bolzano

Printed in Italy

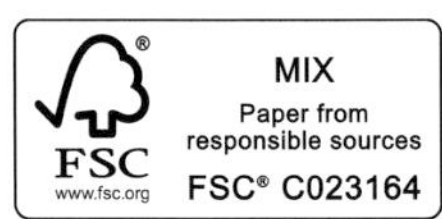

Verlagsgruppe Random House FSC® N001967
The FSC®-certified paper Condat matt Périgord has been supplied by Papier Union, Germany

ISBN 978-3-7913-4951-0